DIDACHE

DAILY BIBLE REFLECTIONS FOR CATHOLICS

SHEPHERD'S
VOICE
PUBLICATIONS, INC.

DIDACHE

DAILY BIBLE REFLECTIONS FOR CATHOLICS

DIDACHE (dee-da-ke), the Greek word for teaching, is a Catholic daily Bible reflection guide published annually. It wishes to encourage the use of Sacred Scriptures among Catholics. It also wishes to reach the entire Christian people.

Reprinting or reproducing any part of this devotional must be done with written permission from the publishers.

EDITORIAL STAFF

Editor in chief: RISSA SINGSON KAWPENG

Copyeditors:
TESS V. ATIENZA   MARJORIE ANN DUTERTE
DINA MARIE PECAÑA   KRIZELLE TALLADEN
MAYMAY R. SALVOSA

Layout Artist: REY DE GUZMAN
Editorial and
Asst. Layout Artist: ANGIE B. ESPUERTA
Cover Design: PIO MALLARI

SHEPHERD'S VOICE PUBLICATIONS, INC.
60 Chicago St., Cubao, Quezon City 1109 Philippines
P.O. Box 1331 Quezon City Central Post Office 1153 Quezon City
Tel.: (632) 725-9999/Fax: (632) 727-5615 or 726-9918
E-mail: sales@shepherdsvoice.com.ph
subscription@shepherdsvoice.com.ph

SHEPHERD'S
V O I C E
PUBLICATIONS, INC.

CAST YOUR VISIONS

When I was young — which was not so long ago — I wrote my dreams in my journal. You already know this story, about how I filled pages upon pages of paper with great visions of my future: build a home for the poorest of the poor, publish a monthly magazine that proclaims the Word of God, have a daily radio program, have a weekly TV show that proclaims God's love.

All of these dreams seemed so daunting years ago. But all of them have come true today. We have Anawim, our ministry for the abandoned elderly; *Kerygma,* the country's leading inspirational magazine; *Gabay sa Radyo,* a daily radio program aired on Radio Veritas; and we have *Kerygma TV* airing on many TV channels and even online.

What started out as visions became words on paper that have now become reality. The secret?

Passion. Purpose. Pain. Perseverance. People.

Your passion is the spark that jumpstarts your vision.

Purpose is the force that boosts your movement.

Pain is the power that propels you forward.

Perseverance is the fuel that keeps you going.

People are the ones who will push you when you think you can go no further.

Let *Didache,* this small book you're holding now, inspire you to follow your purpose and pursue it with perseverance — through ordinary people's stories.

My friends, this year, cast your visions onto God. And with faith, hope and love, work your way towards their fulfillment.

May your dreams come true,

Bo Sanchez

P.S. Get your daily dose of spiritual nourishment through our weekly TV shows. I preach God's Word on IBC 13 every Sunday at 8 a.m., and on ANC every Sunday at 7:30 a.m. You may also watch a live streaming of The Feast, the Light of Jesus Family's weekly prayer gathering, via **www.kerygma.tv**. For other details, call (02) 725-9999.

Numbers 6:22-27
Psalm 67:2-3, 5, 6, 8
Galatians 4:4-7
Luke 2:16-21

Solemnity of the Blessed Virgin Mary,
Mother of God

CLIMB YOUR MOUNTAINS THIS YEAR

Let his face shine upon you. – Numbers 6:25

One day, I did something absolutely nuts. I went to the mountains of Sagada and went rock climbing.

My definition of rock climbing is being insane enough to suspend yourself 100 feet above the air with your fingernails hanging onto tiny cracks and indentions on the rock that ants can't even crawl on — and you wonder why you even paid to do this lunacy.

But when I was up there, I felt no fear. None whatsoever. I wish I could say, "Because of Jesus." But actually, I felt no fear because I had this thick rope tied around my torso. I knew that whatever happens, that rope would keep me safe.

Friends, today is the first day of the year. We don't know what lies ahead. But one thing I know for sure — God wants you to climb your mountain.

He wants you to keep on growing, to be wiser, to be more loving, to be better, and to be even more blessed.

Let His face shine upon you today and every day — and face the world, confident that God is your rope. Hold on tight to Him; He'll never let go of you. *Bo Sanchez (bosanchez@kerygmafamily.com)*

Reflection: What dream does God want you to aim for this year?

Vanquish my fears, Lord, as I face the coming year. Let Your face shine upon me.

Mary, Mother of God, pray for us.

1 John 2:22-28
Psalm 98:1, 2-3, 3-4
John 1:19-28

Memorial of Sts. Basil the Great and
Gregory Nazianzen, bishops and
doctors of the Church

BE GOD'S COMPASS

"I am the voice of one crying out in the desert, 'Make straight the way of the Lord.'" – John 1:23

Praise God for priests, preachers, parents and selfless people who pastor and lead us closer to God. They serve as our compass, guiding us whenever we lose our way. But our goal doesn't end just by perfectly navigating through life. We are also called to become another voice of God, another compass to others.

Friends, God is not asking you for much. You don't need to lead an entire community with thousands of attendees to echo His voice and answer His call. You just need to open your heart to Him and share His love to others in your own simple way. Through your day-to-day actions, you can be His voice and His compass to those who've lost their way.

Worried? Don't be. Just follow Him. He will equip you. He will lead you so you can lead others closer to Him.

The path that leads to God is narrow and rough. It's a road less traveled. That's why we cannot journey alone. We need each other. Be each other's compass and point people to Jesus!

Monching Bueno (ramon_bueno@yahoo.com)

Reflection: Can people see and feel God through your actions? Be His compass!

Lord God, lead me as I lead people closer to you. I may not have much to offer, but I surrender everything to You. Multiply the goodness in me as I share it to others. Amen.

Sts. Basil the Great and Gregory Nazianzen, bishops and doctors of the Church, pray for us.

JANUARY 3
TUESDAY

1 John 2:29-3:6
Psalm 98:1, 3-4, 5-6
John 1:29-34

CAPTAIN'S CHILD

*See what love the Father has bestowed on us
that we may be called the children of God.
Yet so we are. – 1 John 3:1*

My dad became a pilot for two
Asian airlines in his career. Whenever
we would travel with him on his flights,
the crew would of course find out that we were his children. We
would be immediately upgraded to first class, space permitting.
But even if we stayed in economy, we would still get first-class
treatment from the flight attendants.

I always cherished the feeling of flying with my dad. Aside
from the security of knowing I'm in the hands of the best pilot
in the world, I'm not just one of the faceless, nameless hundreds
of passengers on board. I'm the child of the man on the helm.

You, too, are the child of the Man on the Helm. He doesn't
fly a B747 that will bring you safely to your destination. He
is the one Who commands the morning and shows the dawn
its place (Job 38:11), and Who speaks and it becomes reality
(Genesis 1:3). When you know who your Father is, come hell
or high water, you can remain at peace and secure. *Rissa Singson
Kawpeng (justbreatherissa@gmail.com)*

Reflection: "If one of us in life, having so much trust in man and in
ourselves, we end up losing the name, losing this dignity, there is still a
chance to say this word that is more than magic, it is more, it is strong:
'Father.' He always waits for us to open a door that we do not see and
says to us: 'Son.'" (Pope Francis)

*I have set the Lord always before me; because he is at my right hand,
I shall not be shaken. (Psalm 16:8)*

Most Holy Name of Jesus, pray for us.

JUST ASK
"What are you looking for?" – John 1:38

1 John 3:7-10
Psalm 98:1, 7-8, 9
John 1:35-42

You have been following Jesus. Attending prayer meetings. Finding ways to serve Him. Reading your Bible every day. Attending First Friday Masses.

But today He is asking you, "What are you looking for?" (John 1:38).

Peace? Prosperity? Passionate work?

Tell Him. Ask Him your craziest questions. Talk to Him today about what's been bothering you. Don't be afraid. It's Jesus. Look into His eyes and you will see that He's crazy about you. Listen to Him.

"Come, and you will see" (John 1:39).

After listening, go! Do as He tells you. Let Him bring you where He wants to. And stay with Him. Even if it means the "whole day," which may translate to giving up an old unhealthy belief or habit, a job, a relationship. Don't think of it as sacrifice. See it for what it is — a divine privilege. The transformation of your life — from mediocrity to magnificence!

Just ask Him. *Marc Lopez (lamblightschool@yahoo.com)*

Reflection: Have you felt disappointed by God before? Today, He wants you to know, He has always been listening. This time, He wants you to listen, to come with Him, so you can see.

Jesus, I have a question…

St. Elizabeth Ann Seton, religious, pray for us.

JANUARY 5
THURSDAY

1 John 3:11-21
Psalm 100:1-2, 3, 4, 5
John 1:43-51

EQUAL ISN'T EQUAL

*If someone who has worldly means sees a
brother in need and refuses him compassion,
how can the love of God remain in him?*
– 1 John 3:17

I've heard many stories of how children of wealthy families would quarrel among themselves when splitting the inheritance. Successful entrepreneurs eventually closed shop and let go of decades of hard work because their kids couldn't compromise or refused to sustain operations together. After one of my favorite restaurants shut its doors for the same reason, I asked my dad, "Why can't they just divide the assets equally between themselves?" He shook his head and said, "There's no such thing as equal. What is equal for one will never be equal for the other when greed and pride are involved."

I was confused. "So being equal isn't the solution?" I probed. My dad then gave me one of the best pieces of advice that I have carried with me in the years I've spent working with my two brothers, both of whom I love and highly respect. "It's never worth sacrificing harmony within your family for money. But you need to be willing to sacrifice your own personal interests to protect that of your siblings. Kindness starts at home. If one chooses to give way and give more, then we can build and sustain great things — not just great businesses but great families — which matter more." *Eleanore Teo (elyo.lee@gmail.com)*

Reflection: How do you encourage harmony in your family?

Father, teach me to be selfless especially to members of my family.

1 John 5:5-13
Psalm 147:12-13, 14-15,
19-20
Mark 1:7-11
(or Luke 3:23-38)

WELCOME HOME

"You are my beloved Son; with you I am well pleased." – Mark 1:11

He belonged to Iglesia ni Cristo. She was a Born Again Christian. After getting married, they stopped going to either of their churches. But it was her mother's dying wish for them to attend any church, as long as they go together. They decided to "shop around" for a church.

First stop: The Feast, our weekly prayer meeting. There they felt joy at being welcomed and not judged that they had been unchurched for a long time. The next Sunday, they tried another church. But unknown to each other, they were both longing for what they had found the week before. On the third Sunday, he suggested they go back to The Feast instead. From attendees, they became dedicated servants of the Couples Ministry.

He was chosen to bring the cross around during the veneration at Feast Alabang's Holy Week Recollection. When Arun Gogna, our district builder, shared that this brother had been newly baptized into the Catholic faith just three weeks before, I understood the joy he exuded as he carried the cross with quiet pride. I could imagine God looking down at him with great pleasure. A son of God had found his way home. *Lella M. Santiago (lellams88@gmail.com)*

Reflection: How can you give pleasure to the One who created you?

Lord, You are my joy and my salvation. You are my one true pleasure.

1 John 5:14-21
Psalm 149:1-2, 3-4,
5, 6, 9
John 2:1-11

DREAM YOUR WAY TO SUCCESS

"…the water that had become wine…"
– John 2:9

I was in high school then and I wanted to attend a rock concert. We were poor but thank God for friends who provided me with clothes for the night and chipped in for my concert ticket.

As I was about to leave, *Nanay* stopped me. "Who will get the *kaning-baboy* (pig feed) from the neighbor?" So I went to get a pail loaded with leftover food. Then the unthinkable happened. I tripped along a wet alley and was covered with pig feed!

I wept as I headed to the bathtub, I mean the bat-tab *(batya't tabo,* or pail and dipper). As I washed myself, I looked up to heaven dreaming, "On my 10th wedding anniversary, I'll bring my wife and my kids to Disneyland." (Talk about daring faith! Not only was I poor, I couldn't get any girl to answer me.)

But God made my wish come true. On my 10th wedding anniversary, I brought my family to Disneyland and had a blast! The Lord turned my water into wine — my dream into my destiny.

It's your turn now. Surrender your dream to Him and He will crown your efforts with success. *Obet Cabrillas (obetcab@yahoo.com)*

Reflection: "I can't believe that God put us on this earth to be ordinary." (Lou Holtz)

Lord, get me out of the prison of the ordinary. Enable me to live out Your design as an extraordinary person by doing that little "extra."

St. Raymond of Peñafort, priest, pray for us.

Isaiah 60:1-6
Psalm 72:1-2, 7-8, 10-11, 12-13
Ephesians 3:2-3, 5-6
Matthew 2:1-12

Solemnity of the Epiphany of the Lord

ABOUT FACE

They departed for their country by another way. – Matthew 2:12

Robert lost his job and sought ways and means to get through life. He unknowingly got involved in a syndicate and began to deliver drugs. Eventually, he became a drug user. His relationship with his wife was in shambles. They were forced to pay off huge debts that arose from other debts. They lived in fear because of threats from the syndicate. His life went down the drain.

But his wife didn't give up. She kept praying on bended knees and never stopped looking up to heaven.

They had a heart-to-heart talk. Robert heeded the call to change his life and move forward. They worked day in and day out and lived simply so they could pay their debts. They attended prayer meetings and sought a friend priest for spiritual guidance.

When we find ourselves in times of trouble, let us not go to "little kings" that this world offers. Rather, let's seek the star that will lead us to Jesus. And when we find and accept Him, let's leave behind our old sinful ways and tread the right path to victory. *Sol Saura (sol_saura@yahoo.com)*

Reflection: Are you sinning endlessly? Are you feeling helpless and hopeless? Are you living in fear? Are you always irritable and angry? Fix your eyes on Jesus.

Lord, in times of adversity, grant us the grace to gaze on You and stay faithful and true, trusting that You are always with us.

St. Angela of Foligno, pray for us.

Isaiah 42:1-4, 6-7
Psalm 29:1-2, 3-4, 3,
9-10
Acts 10:34-38
Matthew 3:13-17

Feast of the Baptism of the Lord

WIN OR LOSE

"In truth, I see that God shows no partiality."
– Acts 10:34

"We won the UAAP game because God was on our side!" someone said.

Really? What made God decide? Or did the team that simply prepared and played better that day win the game? And for the team that lost, was there not something to gain from that as well? In that sense, was God not also on their side by allowing them to learn valuable lessons in defeat that would be beneficial in the future?

I believe what we need to pray for is the grace to prepare for whatever comes our way. We can't explain every occurrence and it's difficult to judge in whose favor God decides, because the truth is we don't always get what we want.

That's why my favorite line from my alma mater is, "Win or lose, it's the school we choose." That is to say, it doesn't matter if things don't go our way this time — we still know what our identity is.

I think it should be the same with our faith. "Lord, whether I get what I want or not, I choose You because You know best." Therefore, God is on everyone's side. *George Gabriel (george.svp@gmail.com)*

Refection: Are you praying for something? Trust that God has the best answer for you.

I choose You, Lord, not just what I'm praying for.

REFINER'S FIRE

"… perfect through suffering…"
– Hebrews 2:10

Hebrews 2:5-12
Psalm 8:2, 5, 6-7, 8-9
Mark 1:21-28

Fire is the best way to purify gold. When all the impurities have melted, what is left is 24-karat pure gold, the highest valuable grade.

Thirteen years ago, soon after we got married, Matthew was misdiagnosed by the doctor. We were in and out of the hospital. We spent hundreds of thousands of pesos (provided mostly through help of family and friends). Aside from that, there was also the psychological and emotional stress that it brought us.

This suffering crushed us. It burst the bubble of the many dreams we had before we got married. But now in hindsight, I see that the Lord allowed this misfortune for a greater purpose. He wanted to purify us, humble us, and mold us more into His likeness.

This furnace of suffering is part of life's journey. Because of what we went through, God has changed us into better persons. I pray that when my time comes to face my God, He will see not me but the face of Jesus who has granted me the grace and strength to endure till the end. *Marisa Aguas (jojangaguas@yahoo.com)*

Reflection: Are you going through trials right now? Believe in the goodness of the Lord and ask Him for the grace to endure. Thank Him for this opportunity to become more like Him.

Heavenly Father, I may not understand the purpose of what I am going through in my life right now. Help me find my strength in You. In Jesus' name, I pray. Amen.

St. Gregory of Nyssa, pray for us.

Hebrews 2:14-18
Psalm 105:1-2, 3-4,
6-7, 8-9
Mark 1:29-39

EMPATHY

Because he himself was tested through what he suffered, he is able to help those who are being tested. – Hebrews 2:18

She called me in the midst of a busy workday. I answered, "Hello! What's up?" At the other end of the line, I heard my friend sobbing. As I listened, I felt her anxiety, desperation and fear. I remained silent and just let her cry. A few minutes after, she said, "I was asked to give a speech during our company's event and I have no idea about what I'm going to say. What will my officemates think of me? My boss might be disappointed…" She was having a panic attack. I knew how she felt because I have the same attacks, too – sudden fear, heart palpitation, difficulty in breathing. My friend and I "survive" by sharing our episodes with and praying for each other.

Do you sometimes feel that no one understands your suffering? Jesus does — He is empathy personified. Like us, He became man and "was tested through what He suffered." Jesus knows our affliction; He feels our pain. Believe Him when He tells you, "Come to me, all you who labor and are burdened, and I will give you rest" (Matthew 11:28). *Dina Pecaña (dina.p@shepherdsvoice.com.ph)*

Reflection: "Could a greater miracle take place than for us to look through each other's eyes for an instant?" (Henry David Thoreau)

Jesus, as we go through our own pain, let it deepen our capacity to feel for others. Enlarge our souls, expand our minds, and soften our hearts towards all who suffer. Amen.

Hebrews 3:7-14
Psalm 95:6-7, 8-9, 10-11
Mark 1:40-45

SHOW, NOT TELL

"See that you tell no one anything, but go, show yourself… that will be proof for them." – Mark 1:44

Why do you think Jesus instructed the leper not to tell anyone of the healing that He did? After all, it was good news, right?

But the leper was ecstatic about being healed of his leprosy and did what anybody in his place would have done: He announced the good news to everyone! The news spread far and wide, and people from everywhere followed Jesus to ask for healing, too. Did they follow Jesus because of the change they saw in the leper? No.

Jesus' instruction to the leper was to show himself to the priest and give the prescribed offering for his cleansing. If the leper did that, his healing would have been complete because the priest would have reinstated him in the religious community. He would have been healed physically, spiritually and even socially. And God would be more glorified because people would see, not merely hear, the change that happened to him.

As a lector-commentator, I'm able to proclaim the Word of God on the ambo to many people. To glorify Him more, I strive to live out the Word in my life because what people see and experience with me will be remembered more than what they merely hear me proclaim. *Bella Estrella (blestrella@gmail.com)*

Reflection: Let our actions speak of His glory even without saying many words.

Father, help me to glorify You through my every deed.

St. Marguerite Bourgeoys, virgin, pray for us.

Hebrews 4:1-5, 11
Psalm 78:3, 4, 6-7, 8
Mark 2:1-12

WHO ARE YOU IN THE BIBLE STORY?

Many gathered together... – Mark 2:2

"Run, run, run!" That was something my football coach always shouted to me when I used to play in the team. I was a midfielder, which meant that I had to constantly run towards the opponent's goal and then run back again to defend our goal. But sometimes I'd be lazy to run back and defend, giving our opponent an opening to score.

In today's Gospel story, there were also a number of characters that played different roles: Jesus, the crowd, the paralytic man, his friends, and the scribes.

Years ago, I failed my team by not running back to defend our goal. I invite you to think about your life today. Are you a scribe who judges people? Are you the paralyzed man who has a lot of problems? Are you the friend who gives hope to others? Or are you like Jesus who makes miracles in this world?

I exhort you to be more than what you are today. Be like Jesus or the friend of the paralytic man. *JPaul Hernandez (jpaulmh@yahoo.com)*

Reflection: How ready are you to truly change your life for the better?

Father, I thank You for the opportunity to be a new person. Thank You for not judging me. I pray for the strength to sincerely transform my life. Amen.

St. Hilary, bishop and doctor of the Church, pray for us.

Hebrews 4:12-16
Psalm 19:8, 9, 10, 15
Mark 2:13-17

SCUM SCAN

"Why does he eat with tax collectors and sinners?" – Mark 2:16

Jesus seems to have a scanning app that's unparalleled in its technology. It sees beyond the visible. It transcends what's obvious. It scans a corrupt customs official and then invites him, "Follow Me." He scans a scum crowd at a glance and then quickly decides to party with them. Obviously, the scanning report yielded something of goodness and beauty that's beyond our operating system's "optical recognition capability."

In her book *Who Calls Me Beautiful?*, Regina Franklin shares that Miss Sweden 1951 was 5'7" and 151 pounds but Miss Sweden 1983 was two inches taller at 5'9" and 45 pounds lighter at 106 pounds. Regina wonders how it is that if today's standards were used on Miss Sweden 1951, she would be judged fat, ugly and the pageant's biggest joke. Conversely, if today's Miss Sweden joined the pageant's 1951 version, she would be rushed to the emergency room for anorexia, needing the Social Welfare Department's six-week feeding program.

My friend, only God's standards matter. The ultimate Judge smiles at you. His scanning report today declares you beautiful, forgiven and worthy of a glorious destiny. *Jon Escoto* (faithatworkjon@gmail.com)

Reflection: You may have sinned. You may be hurt or even feeling weak. But let the truth of God's love heal you today.

Lord, I know You accept me. Thank You for loving me.

St. Felix of Nola, pray for us.

JANUARY 15
SUNDAY

Isaiah 9:1-6
Psalm 98:1, 2-3, 3-4, 5-6
Ephesians 1:3-6, 15-18
Matthew 18:1-5, 10

Feast of the Sto. Niño

A CHILD'S PRAYER

"Amen, I say to you, unless you turn and become like children, you will not enter the kingdom of heaven." – Matthew 18:3

I received a lot of greetings during my last birthday. It came in different forms such as phone calls, birthday cards, texts, e-mails, social media and other creative ways. I was overwhelmed by all the greetings. I never realized that the best greeting was yet to come.

It was already mid-evening when I received a text message. I was resting in my room and was ready to call it a day. The message came from my 11-year-old godson, Nicky. He used his mother's phone to send his birthday greeting for me. I replied with, "Thanks. Please pray for me."

I assumed that it was the end of our chat. Suddenly, I got a call from his mother. She said Nicky wanted to talk to me. Then I heard my godson say, "Lord Jesus, I pray for *Ninong* Alvin. May you bless him always and keep him healthy. Guide him all the time. Amen. Happy birthday again, *Ninong!* Bye!"

That was the best birthday greeting I received that day! It was a simple and sincere prayer, yet it made my day extra special. May we all pray like this child whose prayer was simple yet full of love. *Alvin Fabella (alvinfabella@yahoo.com)*

Reflection: Find time to pray for the concerns of others before you pray for your personal needs.

Lord, embrace the person in need of Your love and assurance right now. Amen.

JANUARY 16
MONDAY

Hebrews 5:1-9
Psalm 110:1, 2, 3, 4
Mark 2:18-22

CHANGE IS GOOD

"Rather, new wine is poured into fresh wineskins." – Mark 2:22

Getting married meant I needed to adjust my schedule. I couldn't work overtime whenever I chose. Some habits I had at home had to change too because I was no longer living by myself.

Then we had our first child. Again, schedule changes had to be made. We couldn't just pack up and leave like we did when it was just the two of us. We couldn't go out on a date and watch a movie whenever we wanted. We couldn't stay up late. We had to change.

And I believe that's what Jesus means in today's Gospel.

"No one pours new wine into old wineskins." We can't just settle for what we're used to or how we always do things. There's a need for change.

When Jesus comes into our lives, we must change, too. We cannot come to Christ and keep living the same life of sin.

He wants to fill our lives with His love.

But if we live the same life as before, we'll be like old wineskins bursting from the fullness of the new wine.

We need to change to let Jesus do His work in us.

And for sure, it's gonna be better. *Paolo Galia (pgalia@gmail.com)*

Reflection: What things in your life are not compatible with Jesus? What changes do you need to create to accommodate Him?

Dear Lord, change me today. Change me to be a better person for myself, for others and for You.

JANUARY 17
TUESDAY

Hebrews 6:10-20
Psalm 111:1-2, 4-5, 9, 10
Mark 2:23-28

GOD KNOWS

We earnestly desire each of you to demonstrate the same eagerness for the fulfillment of hope until the end.
– Hebrews 6:11

It was the start of the New Year. I was in Baguio with key leaders of Shepherd's Voice Publications and Shepherd's Voice Radio and TV Foundation to plan and brainstorm for a newer, bigger, better ministry — one that will combine all their strengths to reach out to more people as possible. We had visions of hope, of progress, of change.

But my heart was plagued with dark clouds. I was afraid. I was anxious. And frankly, I was tired of serving, giving, loving. I knew in my heart that I wouldn't ever stop following Jesus and serving His people, but during that time, I felt as if the entire world was on the cusp of change while I stood at the edge of the same cliff — unchanging, unmoving.

But God spoke to me in prayer. I was telling Him about my uncertainties about the present and fears about the future, but He interrupted me with just three words: "Karren, I know."

An unexplainable sense of peace suddenly came over me. He is the Alpha and Omega. He knows what was, what is, what will be. My past, my present and my future are in capable hands. There is no room for doubt. No room for fear.

God knows. God sees. And God delivers. *Karren Renz Seña (karren.s@shepherdsvoice.com.ph)*

Reflection: Anxious about your future? God's already there.

Dear Father, may I have the grace to always put my trust in You. Amen.

St. Anthony, abbot, pray for us.

Hebrews 7:1-3, 15-17
Psalm 110:1, 2, 3, 4
Mark 3:1-6

ONCE A PRIEST, ALWAYS A PRIEST

…he remains a priest forever…
– Hebrews 7:3

Amos was a man who, from the age of seven, dreamt of becoming a priest. He lived and breathed parish activities. He volunteered in church, would wipe the altar clean, and do errands for the parish priest.

By God's grace, he did become a man of the cloth. But that didn't make him instantly holy. For many years, he fell into all sorts of temptations. There was a coworker who fell in love with him and pestered him daily. He succumbed to her wiles. Then a friend introduced him to poker — and he soon got into gambling. Neighbors invited him to drink, and he did — till the wee hours of the morning. After an hour of sleep, he would preside at the morning Mass reeking of liquor.

Many years passed. After a long struggle and a "knock" on his head from God, he came to his senses. He turned his back on the woman, the poker cards and alcohol, and he declared to himself, "I am a Son of God. I am a priest forever."

Today he is the official parish priest of a town in Mindanao.

Chelle Crisanto (ellehcmaria@gmail.com)

Reflection: Do you stand firm in your promise to love Jesus?

Help me, Jesus, to be strong and firm in my love for You. Your love for me will be my sword and shield against the enemy.

JANUARY 19
THURSDAY

Hebrews 7:25-8:6
Psalm 40:7-8, 8-9,
10, 17
Mark 3:7-12

CLEAN AGAIN

And whenever unclean spirits saw him they would fall down before him and shout, "You are the Son of God." – Mark 3:11

Did you read that? Even unclean spirits fall down before Jesus and shout, "You are the Son of God!"

I know of many "unclean people" — drug users, alcoholics, gamblers, adulterers, corrupt politicians, thieves, swindlers, cheaters, liars, gossipers, etc. Yet, they too have fallen down before Jesus and have believed.

Two things to note here: First, it's very possible to believe and profess your faith yet continue with your unclean practices. (The classic band Yano referred to these kinds of people as *"Banal na Aso, Santong Kabayo,"* or hypocrites for short.) Second, you have hope if you are this kind of a person.

I know because I, too, am unclean. I, too, at times, am one of those hypocrites. Yet, unclean as I am, I will not stop believing in God and proclaiming Him!

Because by God's pure mercy, especially through the sacrament of reconciliation, I am made clean again. Forgiven, I continue to live, to love, and to serve Him by His grace.

Profess your faith. Act out your faith. And by His mercy this New Year, be clean again. *Alvin Barcelona (apb_ayo@yahoo.com)*

Reflection: Do you know of "unclean people" who continue to profess their faith? Be careful not to judge them. You may be one of them.

Lord, help me to genuinely proclaim my faith in my day-to-day life. But if I fall, let me run to Your mercy and love that I may be clean again.

St. Fillan, pray for us.

JANUARY 20
FRIDAY

Hebrews 8:6-13
Psalm 85:8, 10, 11-12,
13-14
Mark 3:13-19

MERCIFUL LIKE GOD

*"For I will forgive their evil doing and
remember their sins no more."*
– Hebrews 8:12

Children often get into fights with playmates or siblings over the most trivial matters. It was no different for me. I had two older brothers who always teased me till I cried. I remember that whenever they'd hurt or offend me, I'd have a hard time forgiving them. I'd refuse to talk to them for days. On the rare times that the offender would ask for forgiveness, I'd reply, "OK, I forgive you." But deep in my heart, I'd say, "I forgive you but I won't forget this. I'll get back some other time." (Note that this happened when we were still kids and I love them dearly now that we're adults.)

I'm happy that God is not like me at all. I can't imagine what life would be if He didn't forgive our wrongdoings. Worse, imagine if He kept a list of the sins we committed during our lifetime. A ream of bond paper might not be enough for that list.

Be like our God. Forgive those who have hurt you and remember not their transgressions. *Reng Morelos (norinamorelos@gmail.com)*

Reflection: "To be a Christian means to forgive the inexcusable because God has forgiven the inexcusable in you." (C.S. Lewis)

Lord, let me be more like You that I may forgive those who have wronged me and forget all the hurts they have inflicted on me.

Sts. Fabian and Sebastian, martyr, pray for us.

Hebrews 9:2-3, 11-14
Psalm 47:2-3, 6-7, 8-9
Mark 3:20-21

MODERN-DAY FRANCISES

"He is out of his mind." – Mark 3:21

Chinese real estate and hotel tycoon Yu Panglin grew up in poverty and endured so much hardship before he became a millionaire. Fearing that his wealth might corrupt his two sons, he donated most of his remaining millions to charity. He knew, as he experienced, that they didn't need that much wealth to live happy lives.

Russian businessman Yevgeny Pushenko felt empty even as his garment business was booming. One night, he shocked his friends by handing them the keys to his factory. They learned why the next day. He wanted to be a monk and was set to go on a pilgrimage to Jerusalem.

These two men's lives may not equal those of the saints that we know. But in their own ways, they followed the tiny whispers in their hearts that told them that no amount of worldly wealth can satisfy their longing to be happy and fulfilled in life. They didn't mind that people told them, "He is out of his mind!"

I, too, made a crazy decision. I jumped from the bed to the floor, so to speak, but leaving everything behind to work for the Lord's ministry remains the best decision I ever made in my life. *Tess V. Atienza (theresa.a@shepherdsvoice.com.ph)*

Reflection: Have you made a crazy decision in your life that prompted people to say you are out of your mind?

Dearest Lord, grant me courage to follow Your stirrings in my heart.

St. Agnes, martyr, pray for us.

Isaiah 8:23-9:3
Psalm 27:1, 4, 13-14
1 Corinthians 1:10-13, 17
Matthew 4:12-23

SURVIVING THE DARK

"The people who sit in darkness have seen a great light..." – Matthew 4:16

Have you ever experienced praying your deepest, hardest and most desperate prayers but you felt God wasn't listening?

I have. I was kidnapped in the hinterlands of Mindanao. The abductors tied me and pointed guns at me.

At almost every waking moment, I prayed. I asked God to save me. I asked for signs. Signs in the wind, the weather, the movements of the leaves on the trees, anything that would make me feel and see that He was with me. I saw and felt no sign.

I sat in darkness feeling all alone. I recalled how God had been good to me. The memories of His goodness and His promises in the Bible were my light. I embraced my fate and held on to my faith that all things will work for the good of those who love and serve the Lord. If it was my time, I simply surrendered.

After six days that seemed like six years, I was rescued. It was a miracle. There was no bloodshed, no firefight. And I saw the light again. Even in darkness, I should not fear because His promises endure forever. *Carlo Lorenzo (carloflorenzo@yahoo.com)*

Reflection: Are you praying desperately for something but you feel that God is silent? How can you keep your faith strong in this situation?

Holy Spirit, grant me the gift of strong faith.

St. Vincent, deacon and martyr, pray for us.

Hebrews 9:15, 24-28
Psalm 98:1, 2-3, 3-4,
5-6
Mark 3:22-30

THE RIGHT CONNECTIONS

"He is possessed by Beelzebul," and "By the prince of demons he drives out demons."
– Mark 3:22

I didn't realize the events in the days and weeks that passed were too much for me. Stress upon stress had piled up. At a late-morning meeting, my nose bled, which I hastily dismissed as caused by the summer heat. But it recurred on our way home. My wife told me my blood pressure was super elevated so they rushed me to the hospital late in the evening. The doctors administered medicine three times to bring down my blood pressure, but it all proved ineffective. When my cardiologist arrived, he gave me sleeping pills that knocked me out the whole day. My blood pressure normalized.

In these episodes, the Spirit revealed that I had been working too much that I overlooked my relationship with God and my wife. I allowed the spirit of busyness to overcome me. I had overcommitted to ministry work but realized I was "underconnected." I had to reconnect to God and to my wife to stabilize my health. I'm thankful that I have the right connections to see me through life. *Rolly España (rollyespana53@gmail.com)*

Reflection: "Discipline yourselves; keep alert. Like a roaring lion your adversary the devil prowls around looking for someone to devour." (1 Peter 5:8-9)

Lord, make me steadfast in my faith so when the devil and tests come, I will have the grace to resist.

St. Marianne Cope, pray for us.

JANUARY 24
TUESDAY

Hebrews 10:1-10
Psalm 40:2, 4, 7-8,
10, 11
Mark 3:31-35

THE FRIENDSHIP ADVANTAGE

"Whoever does the will of God is my brother and sister and mother."
– Mark 3:35

I flashed a triumphant smile.

It was my birthday celebration and I invited a few friends to come over. To make the preparation extra-special, I challenged the best cook in the world — our father — to a cooking competition. Whoever receives a majority vote from my guests wins.

Lo and behold, I won by a landslide. One of my sisters asked me, "How did it happen? Did you bribe them?"

I laughed. "Of course not. They're my close friends! I know them well, including the food that they like. So that's what I cooked."

When we are in a personal relationship with someone, it's not too hard to figure out what pleases them.

It's the same with God. Jesus reminds us that we cannot call Him our brother or friend if we don't carry out His will. And it's only by being in a relationship with God that we can discern — and hopefully follow — His will for our lives. How can we completely obey someone we're not connected with?

Obedience underscores the confidence that we have in our relationship with Christ. *Maymay R. Salvosa (christiane.salvosa@gmail.com)*

Reflection: On a scale of 1 to 10, how would you rate your personal relationship with Jesus nowadays? Why?

Help me to know Your will for my life, Jesus. And grant me the grace to carry it out.

St. Francis de Sales, bishop and doctor of the Church, pray for us.

Acts 22:3-16
(or Acts 9:1-22)
Psalm 117:1, 2
Mark 16:15-18

Feast of the Conversion of St. Paul,
Apostle

PROCLAIM!

"Go into the whole world and proclaim the Gospel to every creature." – Mark 16:15

This verse is a tall order.

Many times, I shrink at the thought of this "call" to go and proclaim the Gospel. I usually think that proclaiming means preaching or sharing the Word of God.

How do I tell people about the Gospel? Do I organize a ministry? Do I give a talk? These questions would run in my mind. But I realized lately that a better way of "proclaiming" is "doing the Word," not just speaking about it. I realized that the Lord wants me to "preach" in action and not in word.

One day, my daughter confided to me her wish for her birthday: a free dental service to benefit the poor. We gathered dentists and friends to join our family for this unique celebration.

On her birth month, we went to this remote rural village together with a dental team and performed our mission. It was a mission of love.

The rural folks tell me, "Thank you, Bro. Danny. We are so lucky to get these services for free."

I believe this is love in action — the very way I sense the Lord is telling me to "go and proclaim" the Gospel. *Danny Tariman (dtariman.loj@gmail.com)*

Reflection: You do not have to say it to proclaim it. Share the Gospel through your actions.

Father, grant me the grace I need to proclaim the gospel of love.

2 Timothy 1:1-8
(or Titus 1:1-5)
Psalm 96:1-2, 2-3, 7-8, 10
Mark 4:21-25
(or Luke 10:1-9)

Memorial of Sts. Timothy and Titus,
bishops

LIVING IN THE SPIRIT

For God did not give us a spirit of cowardice but rather of power and love and self-control. – 2 Timothy 1:7

This is my birth month, and last year, I became a senior citizen. Aging gracefully has its perks. I proudly brandish my senior citizen's card and enjoy its many benefits. I can use express lanes at the mall or bank, avail of 20 percent discount on food, medicine and other items, and even watch movies for free on certain days in my city. And every time I pull it out, I say, "Yes, I don't look it but I'm a senior citizen." (Ahem.)

We like to joke that we are "dual" citizens when we reach our sixties because we're Filipinos and senior citizens at the same time. But let me remind you that we are, in fact, not just dual, but triple citizens. As citizens of God's Kingdom, we enjoy benefits that are out of this world.

The Holy Spirit gives us the power to act and look like heavenly citizens. We may not be card-bearing members but we enjoy the benefits of God's mercy and favor. We experience Him in personal ways that never cease to amaze us.

I pray we glorify God in whatever way we can as a "triple" citizen. *Grace Princesa (grprincesa@yahoo.com)*

Reflection: A life lived in the Spirit is a shining example of God's presence in the world.

Lord, fill us always with your Spirit of power, love and self-control as pilgrims in this world. Amen.

JANUARY 27
FRIDAY

Hebrews 10:32-39
Psalm 37:3-4, 5-6,
23-24, 39-40
Mark 4:26-34

SOWING THE SEEDS

"To what shall we compare the kingdom of God…? It is like a mustard seed..."
– Mark 4:30-31

I have a confession to make. As the editor-in-chief and main writer of *Mustard,* the children's magazine published by Kerygma Books, I sometimes find my work burdensome. There are occasions when I lack inspiration to write or am frustrated when I need to look for contributors for some of our sections.

During such times, God reminds me of the deeper purpose behind my work: to sow seeds of faith in the hearts of *Mustard's* young readers (and maybe even the adults who read it). My mission — *our* mission — is to build the Kingdom of God here on earth as a foretaste of what we will experience in heaven.

So, dear friend, I invite you today: Let's say "yes" to this mission of sowing seeds. When we do, God will surely equip and bless us. *Tina Santiago Rodriguez (trulyrichandblessed@gmail.com)*

Reflection: "Let us not grow tired of doing good, for in due time we shall reap our harvest, if we do not give up." (Galatians 6:9)

Here I am, Lord. Help me to do what You want me to do.

St. Angela Merici, virgin, pray for us.

Hebrews 11:1-2, 8-19
Luke 1:69, 70-72,
73-75
Mark 4:35-41

Memorial of St. Thomas Aquinas,
priest and Doctor of the Church

A LIGHT IN THE DARK

A violent squall came up and waves were breaking over the boat, so that it was already filling up. – Mark 4:37

"There is such terrible darkness within me, as if everything was dead." Extreme spiritual dryness. Loneliness that led to the brink of despair. Mother Teresa of Calcutta felt the absence of God from the time she founded her congregation until her death, except for a brief five-week period. She wrote to her confessors about her dark nights, and 10 years after her death, these were published in the book, *Mother Teresa: Come Be My Light.*

Through the wise counsel of a Jesuit priest, Mother Teresa somehow found a ray of light. "For the first time in 11 years — I have come to love the darkness…. I felt a deep joy — that Jesus can't go anymore through the agony — but that He wants to go through it in me." Despite the darkness that plagued her soul, she never wavered in her ministry work and in her faith, realizing that her suffering was a "mysterious link" that united her to the heart of Jesus.

Dark storm clouds may loom over our life's horizon. Waves of adversity may sweep over us. But like the disciples in today's Gospel, we only need to call on Jesus and He will calm our fears.

Judith Concepcion (svp_jmc@yahoo.com)

Reflection: "When the storms of life hit you, you don't waver, you don't fall over, you don't give up, you don't quit. Why? Because you're rooted in the truth of the Word of God!" (Charles F. Stanley)

Help me, Lord, to ride out my storms in life and hold on to You.

St. Thomas Aquinas, priest and Doctor of the Church, pray for us.

Zephaniah 2:3; 3:12-13
Psalm 146:6-7, 8-9,
9-10
1 Corinthians 1:26-31
Matthew 5:1-12

THE BE-ATTITUDES
"Blessed… Rejoice and be glad…"
– Matthew 5:11, 12

"You have the gift of intercession."

These were words spoken to me during a session on Charismatic Gifts of the Holy Spirit. Seldom mentioned as a "gift" and more often called a "ministry," I relegated intercession to simply "praying for others." Little did I know that this gift possessed so much opportunity to be a blessing. The fact that the intercessor "stands in the gap" between God and His people struck me as significant since I'm a leader of a Feast, our weekly prayer meeting. I am truly blessed!

However, what was spoken to me next proved to be more important than being blessed. "You need the fruit of joy." In a span of a few months, my joy for service waned due to the demands of reorganizing my two Feasts. I lost the victory in being a Christian.

Friend, believe it or not, you are blessed more than you realize. But do not let the "gift" rob you of the "fruit." All that we "have" or "do" should not contradict what we are called to "be." As the Lord teaches us the Beatitudes, let our *attitude* lead us not only to *be* blessed, but to also *be* a blessing. Rejoice!

Jonathan Yogawin (jyogawin@gmail.com)

Reflection: Do you have the joy of the Lord? What area of your life needs to bear this fruit?

Lord Jesus, let me walk and not just talk of Your Beatitudes. Amen.

Servant of God Brother Juniper, pray for us.

Hebrews 11:32-40
Psalm 31:20, 21, 22, 23, 24
Mark 5:1-20

WHO DO YOU REALLY SERVE?

"Go home to your family and announce to them all that the Lord… has done for you." – Mark 5:19

The priest arrived at the house of his friend who was helping him bring relief goods to a calamity area where many had died. His friend was barking orders to her exhausted helpers, hurrying them to load the goods into the vehicles. Her cook seemed dazed and inattentive to all the frenzy around her. Finally, the cook approached her employer and asked if she could be excused from the relief mission because she just learned that her mother in the province had died. The woman responded that she didn't care who died and that this mission was more important than any of their present concerns. The priest was aghast in disbelief.

Before you go out and evangelize other people — even if it means speaking before thousands of people — look around you first and see if all that God is asking of you is to minister to one who lives under your own roof. Nobody may see you or hear you. Nobody may be there to applaud you. Nobody may be there to pat your back and shake your hand for your inspiring service. But one day, God will be there to say, "Well done, good and faithful servant. Come and enter My Father's house." *Ronna Singson Ledesma (ronna_ledesma@yahoo.com.ph)*

Reflection: Do you seek the applause of man or the approval of God?

Father, for the times I did not serve my nearest neighbor, please forgive me.

CHANCE TO CHANGE

In your struggle against sin you have not yet resisted to the point of shedding blood.
– Hebrews 12:4

Hebrews 12:1-4
Psalm 22:26-27, 28, 30, 31-32
Mark 5:21-43

Benjie has girlfriends left and right. This seemed to be a normal way to have relationships sans consideration or guilt for the women he cheats on. Then he met Ana, a decent and kindhearted woman. He did everything to win her heart. When he finally did, he promised to remain faithful to her.

Ana accepted him for his past, believing everybody deserves a second chance. She took good care of him, gave his life a new direction, and more importantly, guided him back to the Catholic faith. He started to hear Mass, make the sign of the cross, and pray the rosary. Soon, he was no longer temperamental and became a responsible and loving son.

But the devil doesn't rest. Because Benjie was not vigilant, he succumbed to temptation a few months later and returned to his old ways. He cheated on Ana and lost her.

God sends us angels to rescue us from sin. But it's up to us if we want to accept this grace and resist our sinful desires.

Marie Franco (mariefranco_pie@yahoo.com)

Reflection: Who are your angels who keep you from doing wrong? Do you acknowledge their presence or drive them away?

Father God, I am weak. Send me yoke mates to keep me from being a sinner. Have mercy on me.

St. John Bosco, priest, pray for us.

FEBRUARY 1
WEDNESDAY

Hebrews 12:4-7, 11-15
Psalm 103:1-2, 13-14,
17-18
Mark 6:1-6

RISE FROM AGONY
Make straight paths for your feet…
– Hebrews 12:13

I met a single woman who complained, "Bo, my boyfriend and I have been a couple for seven years now. But I don't see him making plans for us. Whenever I bring up the topic, he avoids it. What should I do?"

I asked a very delicate question. "Do you go to bed with him?" She looked down and nodded.

I said, "There's your answer. He already has what he wants. Why will he hurry marrying you if he already enjoys the benefits of marrying you?"

So I told her to tell her boyfriend, "Bro. Bo says that from now on, my entire body is off-limits to you until you bring me to the altar." Once you cut supply, his demand for you will grow. If he really loves you, he'll realize that he needs to hurry up.

I don't care if you've made many mistakes in the past. Virginity is essentially spiritual, not physical. Consecrate your body and soul to God. Claim secondary virginity. And promise that you won't give your body except to a guy who is man enough to marry you.

Rise from your suffering. Rise from your agony. Rise from your slavery. *Bo Sanchez (bosanchez@kerygmafamily.com)*

Reflection: What area of your life do you need to straighten out so you can please God more?

Dearest Lord, grant me courage to follow Your ways, no matter how much I've sinned in the past. Amen.

St. Ansgar, bishop, pray for us.

FEBRUARY 2
THURSDAY

Malachi 3:1-4
Psalm 24:7, 8, 9, 10
Hebrews 2:14-18
Luke 2:22-40

Solemnity of the Presentation
of the Child Jesus

THE GOD OF SILENCE

And the Holy Spirit was upon him.
– Luke 2:25

Waiting. Confusion. Unknowing. Nobody likes these feelings. I was thrust into this whirlwind of darkness last year. For months, I was discerning between two life options that could change my direction forever. They were both good, so the choice wasn't easy.

During those moments, my prayer was that God would give me an assurance of my choice. But there was none. He was silent and still. And I felt I was so alone.

Then as I was driving home one night, I heard a familiar song on the radio. It spoke to me. "The smile on your face lets me know that you need me, there's a truth in your eyes saying you'll never leave me. The touch of your hand says you'll catch me wherever I fall. You say it best when you say nothing at all." My eyes welled up as I sang this as my love song to God.

Sometimes, it's when God is silent that He calls for more trust. He wants us to have faith that He is in control. He wants us to hold on because He will give the best to us.

And like Simeon, the answer came in God's perfect time.

Migs Ramirez (migsramirez.seminars@gmail.com)

Reflection: Have you been waiting for an answer? Enjoy the embrace of God while you wait.

Mama Mary, you had moments of confusion but you kept everything in your heart. May I, too, treasure my moments of unknowing, so that my trust in Jesus increases. Amen.

St. Joan de Lestonnac, pray for us.

Hebrews 13:1-8
Psalm 27:1, 3, 5, 8-9
Mark 6:14-29

ENOUGH!

*Let your life be free from love of money but
be content with what you have…*
– Hebrews 13:5

"Don't buy a luxury item unless you can afford 10 of them," said Rose Fres Fausto during her talk at the Truly Rich Club Wealth Summit. It was a steep advice especially for a generation where materialism is a feel-good drug.

I see it all around. A household helper who wants to buy a cell phone that costs more than twice her monthly salary. A kid who blows all his savings on a pricey toy. A social-climbing professional who buys a Rolex watch using borrowed money.

Today, the Lord is reminding us to relearn the meaning of the word "enough." He teaches us to acquire the elusive virtue of contentment. And it starts by being grateful for what we have instead of yearning for what we don't have.

Slay the insatiable monster of greed. Isolate your needs from your wants. Be grateful for what you have. And learn to say, "Enough!" *Rissa Singson Kawpeng (justbreatherissa@gmail.com)*

Reflection: "The worship of the ancient golden calf has returned in a new and ruthless guise in the idolatry of money and the dictatorship of an impersonal economy lacking a truly human purpose…. Man is reduced to one of his needs alone: consumption." (Pope Francis)

Jesus, You are enough for me!

FEBRUARY 4
SATURDAY

Hebrews 13:15-17,
20-21
Psalm 23:1-3, 3-4, 5, 6
Mark 6:30-34

DON'T POSTPONE LOVE

His heart was moved with pity for them…
– Mark 6:34

My father is a busy man. Aside from his meetings, project site visits in his construction business, he also actively serves in the ministry. He plays the keyboard for our parish and prayer community. He gives talks once in a while. With Mom, he heads the couples' ministry of our community, and many more. Rest time is almost a luxury for him.

But whenever my mom or any of his five children needs attention and help, he gets up from his bed without hesitation and takes care of our concern. He needs his rest but he won't.

In today's Gospel, Jesus and His disciples were probably tired doing ministry work. Thank God they found a good place to rest and recharge. But even before they were fully rested, Jesus saw the crowd and His heart was moved with pity for them. Jesus had all the right to say, "Come back in a few hours, we're still resting." But He didn't. Why? Because He knows that you can't postpone love.

Maybe you're busy like Jesus and my dad. Go and rest. But when God moves your heart with compassion, get up and move.

Don't postpone love. *Velden Lim (veldenlim@gmail.com)*

Reflection: Are you postponing anything in your life? Obey God now. Delayed obedience is still disobedience.

Lord, when I'm tired of loving, grant me the grace to carry on.

St. Joseph of Leonissa, pray for us.

FEBRUARY 5
SUNDAY

Isaiah 58:7-10
Psalm 112:4-5, 6-7, 8-9
1 Corinthians 2:1-5
Matthew 5:13-16

KEEP IT LIT

"Then light shall rise for you in the darkness…" – Isaiah 58:10

"Brownout!" my friend shouted the moment the lights went off. I was in an out-of-town getaway with friends at a lake town in Batangas. Pitch black darkness was all around us with only the stars lighting up the sky, the waters, and our way. They suddenly shone brightly and beautifully!

This reminded me of how much we are surrounded by darkness — the refugee crisis, war-torn Middle East, ISIS terrorism, sex trafficking, corruption, poverty, just to name a few. Sometimes the darkness can be so overwhelming that the light of our goodness seems insignificant.

Friend, God calls us to shine our light, no matter how seemingly small or simple, to dispel the darkness around us. In fact, we are called to be light in the darkest of places so that we may light the way of others who are walking in darkness. So don't turn off your light. Keep it lit. Keep it on. Darkness exists because some have turned off their light.

Remember, light shines brightest in the dark. So keep shining because there's always someone who needs a flashlight in the dark. *Mike Viñas (mikemichaelfcv@yahoo.com, @mikevinas)*

Reflection: "Darkness cannot drive out darkness; only light can do that. Hate cannot drive out hate; only love can do that." (Martin Luther King, Jr.)

Jesus, You are the light of the world. May I reflect Your light through my love.

St. Agatha, virgin and martyr, pray for us.

THE POWER OF TOUCH

... and as many as touched it were healed.
– Mark 6:56

Genesis 1:1-19
Psalm 104:1-2, 5-6, 10,
12, 24, 35
Mark 6:53-56

In 1966, I became an exchange student under the American Field Service International Scholarship program. I stayed with an American family and studied in a senior high school in Minneapolis, Minnesota. I was only 16 years old, the first in my family to ever set foot in the United States, so it was kind of big deal for us.

When I came back home a year later, some relatives and friends rubbed my arms or touched my dress, saying in jest, "Oooh, let me have a feel of America!"

But the hullabaloo naturally died down after a few days as we all just went on living the daily grind.

It's not like when the people touched the edge of the cloak of Jesus as we read in today's Gospel.

No matter how light or fleeting that touch was, it was enough to heal because of the faith of the people.

Despite all that Jesus had done and continues to do for us, we still need to touch, to feel God from time to time, to be assured of His presence. Blessed are those who do not see, or hear, or touch Him, yet still believe and trust our faithful God.

Chay Santiago (cusantiago@gmail.com)

Reflection: When did you last touch God, or when did He last touch you?

Lord, let me feel You today.

Genesis 1:20-2:4
Psalm 8:4-5, 6-7, 8-9
Mark 7:1-13

GOD'S ENABLING POWER!

"You disregard God's commandment but cling to human tradition." – Mark 7:8

We live in a world that operates on this principle: Act or be acted upon. If we don't do anything, we'll be drowned by destructive worldly beliefs. But blessed be God, the authority of His Word stands despite human tradition. "(God's) grace is sufficient for you, for power is perfected in weakness...That is why, for Christ's sake, I delight in weaknesses... For when I am weak, then I am strong" (2 Corinthians 12:9-10).

God's grace is always sufficient. It overflows into gratitude to God and unto the service of mankind. It is God's enabling power!

'Twas His grace that transformed my criminal mind that said, "The world owes me a great deal," into a missionary mind that declares, "I owe a great deal of service to the world."

Never let evil triumph. Instead, let good triumph over evil.

Choose the good. Choose God! *Obet Cabrillas (obetcab@yahoo.com)*

Reflection: "The only thing necessary for the triumph of evil is for good men to do nothing." (Edmund Burke)

Lord, I pray the prayer of surrender: I can't but You can. Take over.

St. Colette, pray for us.

FEBRUARY 8
WEDNESDAY

Genesis 2:4-9, 15-17
Psalm 104:1-2, 27-28,
29-30
Mark 7:14-23

HOPE

Nothing that enters one from outside can defile that person; but the things that come out from within are what defile. – Mark 7:15

Josephine Bakhita is the patron saint of Sudan. She was born in 1869 to a happy African family. Things changed when she was kidnapped in 1876, sold as a slave and tortured throughout her captivity. By God's grace, she was taken to Venice and was given to a kind Italian family. She became a Canossian sister in 1893 after being declared a free person.

When asked what she would do if she were to meet her captors and torturers again, she replied, "I would kneel and kiss their hands, for if that did not happen, I would not be a Christian today."

In Mark 7:15, Jesus said, "The things which come out of a man are what defile him." Life may deal with us cruelly and make us suffer. But what defines us is not what life throws at us. Instead, it is how we respond to it. St. Josephine's trauma was so great that she forgot her own name as a child. But none of the suffering deterred her from being kind, forgiving and loving. May we learn to be as Christian as St. Josephine Bakhita. *Rod Velez (rod.velez@gmail.com)*

Reflection: How can your suffering be redemptive?

When we retrace the steps of Calvary, we realize that You suffered more than any of us. Teach us to never lose hope, dear Lord.

St. Josephine Bakhita, pray for us.

FEBRUARY 9
THURSDAY

Genesis 2:18-25
Psalm 128:1-2, 3, 4-5
Mark 7:24-30

GOD WILL SEE YOU THROUGH

Soon a woman whose daughter had an unclean spirit heard about him. She came and fell at his feet. – Mark 7:25

Have you ever been in a hopeless situation where you've done everything and yet nothing seems to go right?

I remember a time when our business experienced a big hump. In June 2014, we started losing clients one by one until we had none. I was at the point of giving up ministry work to go back to full-time corporate life. As I was praying to God on my knees one night, I felt a strong reassurance and peace in my heart that God would see us through. Then in April 2015, with almost nothing left in our bank account, a new client came. The following month, another client came. The clients kept coming even without us looking for them. Today, we are back in business and it continues to flourish.

When you are at a loss, when you no longer know what to do, that's the perfect time to witness the hand of God at work. Surrender everything to Him and trust in His great plan for you. Know that God will always see you through, even in your most difficult times. *Joel N. Saludares (joelsaludares@yahoo.com)*

Reflection: What trials are you experiencing today? Can you come to God in total surrender, trusting and believing that He will see you through?

Lord, I surrender to You my worries. I surrender to You my trials. May Your peace reign in my heart today.

FEBRUARY 10
FRIDAY

RETREAT!
"Be opened!" – Mark 7:34

Genesis 3:1-8
Psalm 32:1-2, 5, 6, 7
Mark 7:31-37

The year 2015 was definitely the most challenging year of my life. I had been pushed too far and I ended the year with a tired heart.

But God has His ways of coming to my rescue just when I'm at my lowest point. I didn't want to end my year with questions and prayers left unanswered.

So I spent my year-end holiday in deep moments of silence and allowed God to speak to me. It was only during my time of reflection that I realized that I spent the whole year busy with too many things on my plate that I had forgotten to pause. I wanted to accomplish so many things my way that I neglected to slow down and listen to His directions. I felt like the deaf man in today's Gospel. I also realized that I only needed to open my heart and give God space for prayer and solitude.

If you're tired and things are weighing you down, retreat. When you're running on empty, gas up. Spend time in prayer and be open to His message and leading. Believe me, He will speak to you and it will give you the peace that you need in your heart. And just like the deaf man, you will be healed. *Ruby Albino (r_jean07@yahoo.com)*

Reflection: "Be still and know that I am God." (Psalm 46:10)

Father, help me appreciate the pause. Help me ignore the momentary distractions so I can open myself to Your directions.

FEBRUARY 11
SATURDAY

Genesis 3:9-24
Psalm 90:2, 3-4, 5-6, 12-13
Mark 8:1-10

LEFT OVER

They ate and were satisfied. They picked up the fragments left over – seven baskets.
– Mark 8:8

My mom, aunt and I just had a hearty lunch when my aunt requested the waitress, "Miss, could you wrap the *pla-pla* (St. Peter's fish) for me?" Only the head and bones were left but those are the parts of the fish she enjoys the most. Aunt Vy is known to be frugal and believes nothing should go to waste.

In today's Gospel, Jesus miraculously fed 4,000 people with seven loaves and a few fish, and they ate and were satisfied. And the disciples even collected seven baskets of leftover food.

Lesson 1: When God provides for our needs, He gives us more than what we ask for so we can share His blessings with others. Maybe the disciples gave extra food to the people to take home or gave to the needy they met along the way.

Lesson 2: Whatever little we offer to God, He multiplies. For Him, everything has a purpose. In His divine scheme of things, nothing and no one goes to waste: Mary, the innocent teenage girl, became the virgin mother of Jesus; Peter, the impulsive fisherman, became the first pope; St. Therese of Lisieux, a sickly young Carmelite who never left the convent, became patroness of missions. *Dina Pecaña (dina.p@shepherdsvoice.com.ph)*

Reflection: Give to Jesus whatever little you have and see what great things He can do in and through you.

Father, whatever little I have, I offer to You. Use me to bring Your great love and mercy to others. Amen.

FEBRUARY 12
SUNDAY

Sirach 15:15-20
Psalm 119:1-2, 4-5,
17-18, 33-34
1 Corinthians 2:6-10
Matthew 5:17-37

CHOOSE TO BE BRAVE

If you choose you can keep the
commandments. – Sirach 15:15

The Catholic Bishops Conference of the Philippines gave the theme "Choose to Be Brave" when it declared 2014 as the Year of the Laity. Courage or fortitude is one of the gifts of the Holy Spirit.

Since I was young, I have been courageous enough to speak against wrongdoing around me. I fought with a male playmate when he cheated during our game. When co-servants constantly aired their complaints to me about the bad treatment they'd get from their leader, I elevated the matter to the higher-ups after talking with the concerned leader. My friendship with her cooled off but many people were pleased at the result of the process.

Even in raising our kids, it took courage to discipline them even when it hurt to see them cry. But I chose the harder path and today, I'm a proud and happy mom because my children have grown up to be good and loving individuals. *Bella Estrella (blestrella@gmail.com)*

Reflection: Do you do things for your own comfort? Choose the path that leads to good, even if it may be difficult.

Father, help me to always stand up for what is right and just, to achieve the needed good in the end.

FEBRUARY 13
MONDAY

Genesis 4:1-15, 25
Psalm 50:1, 8, 16-17, 20-21
Mark 8:11-13

PROJECT 77

"Why does this generation seek a sign?"
– Mark 8:12

There were no other instructions given by His Excellency, Archbishop Angel N. Lagdameo, Bukas Loob Sa Diyos (BLD) global spiritual director, except to get the job done. We were to complete the project in time for the next Inter-District Conference, a twice-yearly gathering of BLD global leaders.

My hubby, Raul, and I, serving as global Servant Leaders for Management, were unfazed, albeit clueless where to get the funding. We launched Project 77, determined to increase the capacity of our BLD Covenant House from 44 to 77 rooms. We conducted the bidding process as though the money for the project that would cost almost P10 million was already sitting in the bank for our disposal. In truth, we had nothing. But amazingly, money came in with clockwork precision. Never did the funding fell short of disbursements.

The 2015 BLD Inter-District Conference opened as scheduled and the delegates arrived from places far and wide. Thirty-three additional rooms were completed just in time. The BLD Covenant House had 77 rooms ready for occupany and we didn't need any sign. "Unless the Lord build the house, they labor in vain who work" (Psalm 127:1). *Mari Sison-Garcia (mari_sison_garcia@yahoo.com)*

Reflection: Do you demand for a sign before accepting God's assignment?

Lord, I pray for the gift of faith, that I may learn to trust You more.

St. Giles Mary of St. Joseph, pray for us.

Genesis 6:5-8; 7:1-5, 10
Psalm 29:1, 2, 3-4, 3,
9-10
Mark 8:14-21

STOP, LOOK, LISTEN

"Do you have eyes and not see, ears and not hear?" – Mark 8:18

There are times when we find it hard to recognize God's presence in our lives or God's voice speaking to us through our circumstances.

I also have those moments, even though I have been striving to follow the Lord closely for decades. When my eyes can't see past my pain and tears, when I stubbornly stick to my plans or insist on what I want, when I am in a hurry, when I don't like what I experience, when I don't spend enough time in prayer and meditation… These are the times when I can relate with Jesus' disciples who ask Him the wrong questions.

I also hear these same words from Jesus, "Do you have eyes and not see, ears and not hear?" The good news is that He patiently waits and does everything to get our attention. He also doesn't give up in teaching us what we need to learn.

Will you choose to stop, look and listen to Him today? *Teresa Gumap-as Dumadag (teresa@fulllifecube.com)*

Reflection: When did you last examine your life and connect with God?

Lord Jesus, grant me the grace to make time for You. Open my eyes and my ears so I can recognize You and learn from You.

Sts. Cyril and Methodius, bishops, pray for us.

FEBRUARY 15
WEDNESDAY

Genesis 8:6-13, 20-22
Psalm 116:12-13, 14-15,
18-19
Mark 8:22-26

THE UNLIKELY SAINT
"Do you see anything?" – Mark 8:23

Dino and I were near the restaurant's door when a boy walked up to us, strings of *sampaguita* in his hand, asking if we could buy him a two-piece chicken meal for dinner. I ignored him and thought he was demanding.

At the counter, I ordered the usual. Dino asked for a two-piece chicken meal to go. "Aren't you hungry?" I asked, expecting him to eat right there. "I'm full," he said, even if I knew he wasn't. But I let him be.

Several chews later, we were at our feet. Outside, Dino looked for the poor boy. The latter appeared, and the takeaway food met his hands.

I was ashamed of myself. Here was a colleague who was practically a clown at work, not affiliated with any Charismatic community, and an "unlikely" person to do something charitable. There I was, saying grace before meals but failing to see those who can't utter the same prayer. I was blind to that boy in need.

Opportunities to be Jesus to others may have passed us simply because we chose to look away. We chose to ignore. May the Lord open our eyes to see the suffering around us and share the love of Christ. *Osy Erica (osy.erica@gmail.com)*

Reflection: Do you see the "small" people walking past you? Or do you only see yourself and your needs?

Lord, restore my sight so I can see everything distinctly — the poor, the weak and the lonely. Make me Your helping hand to them. Amen.

St. Claude la Colombiere, pray for us.

FEBRUARY 16
THURSDAY

Genesis 9:1-13
Psalm 102:16-18, 19-21,
29, 22-23
Mark 8:27-33

THINKING DIFFERENTLY

At this he turned around and, looking at his disciples, rebuked Peter and said, "Get behind me, Satan. You are thinking not as God does, but as human beings do." – Mark 8:33

Despite the fact that the doctors told us that we can never conceive a child the natural way, I was staring at the ultrasound monitor, amazed at the heartbeat of our child. But after eight blissful weeks, the heartbeat stopped.

Have you ever lost the very gift that was given to you?

Just when we thought that everything was finally falling into place, all was suddenly lost.

No warning. No explanation. No consolation.

But believe me when I tell you that God has always something better in store for you.

It may not feel like it at the moment.

It may not even make sense at the moment.

But He is there, working without tire, to make things better.

Because He is always thinking of you.

We lost that pregnancy but today we have a three-year-old son who is the apple of our lives. *Orange Garcia (orange.garcia@outlook.com)*

Reflection: Trust God and just keep at it.

Lord, may I never give in to doubt but always remain faithful and hopeful in You. Amen.

FEBRUARY 17
FRIDAY

Genesis 11:1-9
Psalm 33:10-11, 12-13,
14-15
Mark 8:34-9:1

BEAUTIFUL WORDS

Then the Lord said: "If now, while they are one people, all speaking the same language... – Genesis 11:6

Imagine a world that speaks one language: the language of love. My imagination runs wild sometimes. In the mornings, after speaking to God, I'd open my Facebook account and see only positive, uplifting and inspiring posts. I'd open my Instagram account and see only beautiful pictures. I'd open Twitter and see only entertaining, motivational and empowering tweets.

I know that it's a far, far cry from the wretched things we see on the Internet nowadays, but I believe that we can do it. We start with ourselves. In Philippians 4:8, St. Paul reminds us to think only of praiseworthy things. I hold on to that verse every time I am tempted to say or post something nasty. I even started a small movement called "Project: Beautiful Words," where we challenge each other to post only uplifting things. As of this writing, we are around 150 to 200 members in the group. If you're friends with us, then you have 150 less complaints or negative posts in your news feeds.

One day, we'll make it. One world. One language. The language of love. *Karren Renz Seña (karren.s@shepherdsvoice.com.ph)*

Reflection: Are you mindful of the words that you say and the things that you post online? Say only beautiful things.

Lord, let the words of my mouth and the meditations of my heart be pleasing to You always. Amen.

GOD'S PROMISES

*Faith is the realization of what is hoped for
and evidence of things not seen.*
– Hebrews 11:1

Hebrews 11:1-7
Psalm 145:2-3, 4-5,
10-11
Mark 9:2-13

The Bible contains more than 3,500 promises of God to His people.

God promised that if we search for Him, we will find Him (Deuteronomy 4:29).

He promised that His love will never fail (1 Chronicles 16:34).

God promised blessings for all who will delight themselves in His Word (Psalm 1:1-3).

He promised that all things will work out for good for those who love Him (Romans 8:28).

And the list goes on and on. For every circumstance, God has an answer. There is nothing to fear when troubles or trials come our way. Because God is with us. He will never leave us nor forsake us. That's His promise!

It may take a while for promises to come true in your life. But whatever you are going through right now, know that "whatever God promises, He does; He speaks and it is done" (Number 23:19). *Lala Dela Cruz (bella.delacruz@gmail.com)*

Reflection: Be excited because God is able to do exceedingly and abundantly above all that we can ask or think!

Lord, I hold on to Your promises. Help me to wait patiently for their fulfillment.

CHRISTIANS

"For if you love those who love you, what recompense will you have?"
– Matthew 5:46

Leviticus 19:1-2, 17-18
Psalm 103:1-2, 3-4, 8,
10, 12-13
1 Corinthians 3:16-23
Matthew 5:38-48

This is one of my favorite Bible passages. To me, it's a vital test to see if you are indeed a Christian.

That's why Pope Francis insists on loving the "unlovable" — those who cannot love you back, who are different from you, who caused you pain, or even persecuted you. Only then can you say that you love — that you are a Christian. Because that's what Christ did! He died for sinners — for the unlovable.

That's why I deliberately pray for "my enemies" every day. No, I don't pray that they be struck by lightning or that their houses burn. I pray that they may forgive me for the wrongs and the pain I've inflicted on them that caused me to become their "enemy." And when I get the chance and the courage to meet them and say sorry, I do so as I too continue to forgive and love those who have wronged me.

It's not easy. But by God's grace, it's possible, especially if you call yourself a Christian. *Alvin Barcelona (apb_ayo@yahoo.com)*

Reflection: Think of someone who is most unlovable to you — a poor, dirty beggar or someone who has hurt you. Do something to love that person today… and be a Christian!

Dear Lord, I pray for (name that person) who has hurt me or who is so difficult to love. By Your grace, I forgive and will show love to him/her today. Amen.

FEBRUARY 20
MONDAY

Sirach 1:1-8
Psalm 93:1, 1-2, 5
Mark 9:14-29

WAGES OF FAITH

"Everything is possible to one who has faith." – Mark 9:23

My husband and I were at our wits' end. Bills were piling up and money was not in the horizon. How do we cope during lean times when his business was not doing well? All we could do was to pray for God's provision. And pray we did — morning, noon and night — for the Lord to provide.

One day, I fixed a drawer that we hadn't touched for ages. While going through the papers to dispose of, I chanced upon an envelope. In it, I discovered a wad of bills that amounted to P40,000 — the wages of faith with interest!

We couldn't recall keeping the money in the drawer. But we were sure that it was in God's perfect time that He allowed us to discover it.

If we trust God and believe that He works for our good, He will see us through the peaks and valleys of our life. *Rissa Espinosa (rissa_d_espinosa@yahoo.com)*

Reflection: Do you believe that everything is possible with God?

Lord, may I never forget that You are in control of my life.

Blessed Jacinta and Francisco Marto, pray for us.

THE LONGEST TRIP OF MY LIFE

… undisturbed in time of adversity.
– Sirach 2:2

Sirach 2:1-11
Psalm 37:3-4, 18-19,
27-28, 39-40
Mark 9:30-37

January 6, 2016. It was the last day of a company activity in Baguio City. With some officemates, I opted to stay for one more day before returning to Manila so we could rest.

Then the messages from my sisters in Manila came one after the other. They found my father sitting on his bathtub, and they thought he had slipped while taking a bath. They rushed him to a hospital.

"Should I take the earliest trip tonight?" I asked my sisters. Some said no because it'd be dangerous for me to travel alone at night. But when the ultrasound confirmed that my father's abdominal aortic aneurysm ruptured, I knew I had to take the midnight trip. I knew we would lose him soon.

Throughout the bus ride, I held on to my rosary and prayed nonstop. Emotions we had when we lost our mother 13 years ago resurfaced. I didn't want to go through all that pain again. But in my heart, God told me not to worry. We will overcome and He is with us in our grief, our pain, our loss, and until the day when we finally make sense of his death.

I thank God and Mama Mary for giving me a calm spirit to face our loss the next day. *Tess V. Atienza (theresa.a@shepherdsvoice.com.ph)*

Reflection: How do you face adversity?

Thank You, Jesus and Mama Mary, for accompanying me during my darkest moments.

St. Peter Damian, bishop and Doctor of the Church, pray for us.

FEBRUARY 22
WEDNESDAY

1 Peter 5:1-4
Psalm 23:1-3, 4, 5, 6
Matthew 16:13-19

Feast of the Chair of St. Peter, Apostle

LEAD BY EXAMPLE

Do not lord it over those assigned to you,
but be examples to the flock.
– 1 Peter 5:3

I was in a reunion with my high school friends. It had been years since we last met!

Over dinner, we exchanged stories to catch up with each other's lives. I shared to them that by the grace of God, I had finally finished medical school, passed the board exams, and started my medical practice.

As we were chatting, I generously poured ice-cold soda into glasses for myself and for the rest of the group. Then my classmate said, "Wait, Doc Didoy, isn't that bad for our health?"

Oops.

That day, I learned and relearned valuable lessons that I took to heart.

I can only preach what I practice.

There's a world of difference between what you know and what you do.

Action speaks louder than words. So be examples to your flock. *Didoy Lubaton (wholenessinyou@gmail.com)*

Reflection: "The authority by which the Christian leader leads is not power but love, not force but example, not coercion but reasoned persuasion." (John Stott)

Jesus, help us to live out what we profess and believe.

Sirach 5:1-10
Psalm 1:1-2, 3, 4, 6
Mark 9:41-50

SALT SHAKERS

"Salt is good, but if salt becomes insipid, with what will you restore its flavor? Keep salt in yourselves and you will have peace with one another." – Mark 9:50

Their married life had become stale and they needed something to add spice to their relationship. At my birthday bash, the wife won the overnight stay in Baguio that we raffled off. That was when the Spirit prodded me to use this as an occasion to reconcile this couple.

But it was not easy. The husband thought that the raffle was rigged and the trip was a setup. Then there were all the difficulties of scheduling. But my husband and I were determined that we had to be with them during the trip and adjusted to their schedules.

The Spirit started to work on them during the long trip to Baguio when they were by themselves. Their hardened hearts began to soften. During our counseling sessions with them, they committed to a number of resolutions to improve their married life. They chose to extend their stay and bought for themselves a new pair of rings to signify their marriage renewal. When we met them three weeks later, a rainbow appeared to them as if the Spirit was reaffirming their marriage covenant. The Spirit used my husband and me to be salt shakers. *Donna España (donna.espana@yahoo.com)*

Reflection: We are the light and salt of the earth if we let the Spirit use us.

Lord, allow me to be salt to others wherever You would lead me.

St. Polycarp, bishop and martyr, pray for us.

IT IS DONE

Therefore what God has joined together, no human being must separate. – Mark 10:9

Sirach 6:5-17
Psalm 119:12, 16, 18, 27, 34, 35
Mark 10:1-12

"You tore the veil. You made a way when You said that it is done…"

Tears fell from my eyes as I sang. I messed up big time and I was frustrated with myself. I just confessed the day before but I failed again. My guilt tormented me as the cause of other people's hurts and offenses.

Then I remembered the story behind the song. When Jesus died, the veil in the temple — which physically separated God from the people — was torn into two. It marked the forgiveness of sins and the opening of the gates of heaven. I found solace in the truth contained in the lyrics. The voice of my confessor rang in my head, "Don't be frustrated with yourself, dear. God will never give up on you."

Gratitude overwhelmed me. When Jesus spread His arms on the cross, He already welcomed me home. It is done. No sin is bigger than His love and nothing that I do can separate me from Him. As I continued singing, I asked for the grace to remain in God — without the veil, without the shame. *Maymay R. Salvosa (christiane.salvosa@gmail.com)*

Reflection: "For He rescued us from the domain of darkness, and transferred us to the Kingdom of His beloved Son, in whom we have redemption, the forgiveness of sins." (Colossians 1:13-14)

Dearest Father, grant me the grace to live every second according to Your ways. Amen.

Blessed Luke Belludi, pray for us.

CHILDREN ARE AMAZING!

"Let the little children come to me."
– Mark 10:14

Sirach 17:1-15
Psalm 103:13-14, 15-16, 17-18
Mark 10:13-16

My nephew, Zack, was three when he saw the crucifix in our house. He said, "That's the cross. That's where Jesus died to save us from our sins." I was amazed. I couldn't fathom how he learned this awesome truth.

Raygie, my friend Mariz's nephew, lived with us when he was four. We taught him to pray when he wakes up, before he sleeps, and before and after meals. One Sunday morning, while we were waiting for a cab to go to The Feast, he prayed aloud, "Lord, please give us a cab so we will not be late for The Feast." Another time, he prayed, "Lord, please don't let it rain. We don't have an umbrella."

Cosette, my friend Hershey's three-year-old daughter, would remind her mom every Monday, "Mom, are we going to worship God today at The Feast?"

Children are amazing! Sometimes, we get irritated when they make a lot of noise or when they misbehave. But we miss out a lot when we do not take time to observe and listen to them. So the next chance you get, learn from a child. *Meann Tee (meanntytee@yahoo.com)*

Reflection: Do you welcome little children as Jesus would? Do you listen to God's voice speaking through them?

Father, thank You for little children in our midst. They are Your gifts to us. Help us to listen to the wisdom You speak through them. Amen.

FEBRUARY 26
SUNDAY

Isaiah 49:14-15
Psalm 62:2-3, 6-7, 8-9
1 Corinthians 4:1-5
Matthew 6:24-34

TRUE RICHES

"No one can serve two masters..."
– Matthew 6:24

There's a story of a businessman who drove himself hard to become a billionaire. On the way to his goal, he isolated himself from his family and business partners.

On Christmas day, he closed a contract that finally got him that billionaire status. However, he was all by himself and didn't have anyone to share the news, let alone wish him a merry Christmas. He realized then how empty he felt and how low he had sunk. Jesus' words ring true when He said, "What profit is there for one to gain the whole world yet lose or forfeit himself?"

Years ago, after prayer and discernment, I accepted a position that paid less than my job then. But the latter required me to travel frequently and I was feeling the toll on my body and my family. The Lord blessed that decision because my family is now closer than ever. Health-wise, I feel great. I have time to serve in our parish and community. Our material needs are provided for, and then some. God made it clear to me that there is more to life than pursuing a higher paycheck.

What drives you? *Erwin Roceles (erwin_roceles@yahoo.com)*

Reflection: "There is absolutely nothing that can replace money in the things that money does, but regarding the rest of the things in the world, money is absolutely useless." (Jim Stovall)

Lord, thank You for making me realize what truly matters in life — the love of family, building lasting relationships, serving You, and knowing that You are enough for me.

St. Maria Bertilla Boscardin, pray for us.

NEW YEAR MIRACLE

To the penitent God provides a way back,
he encourages those who are losing hope…
– Sirach 17:19

Sirach 17:19-24
Psalm 32:1-2, 5, 6, 7
Mark 10:17-27

Homeless. Not a good way to end the year. But that's what we were going to be if we couldn't find accommodation fast on that last day of December. We were on a tour in Queenstown, the most popular place in New Zealand for New Year's eve, so all the hotels we called were fully booked. The one that still had a room available charged an arm and a leg so that was out of the question.

Sleeping in the car was our next best option. But in one of the touristy places, I happened to see a Filipina-looking lady. "Pinay?" I asked. And that started our conversation.

It turned out she worked there. When I mentioned in passing how difficult it was to find accommodation in the city, she asked how many we were. I answered, "Four." She said, "Why don't you stay at my place for the night? I live alone."

That evening, we didn't just enjoy the New Year's eve celebration with all the tourists. We also had a Pinoy *salu-salo* with a *kababayan*.

It turned out to be a wonderful start of the year for us — a miraculous one even. *Joy Sosoban-Roa (jsosoban@gmail.com)*

Reflection: When my knees are weak and I am near crumbling down in despair, the Lord is there to lift me up. How great is our God! How mighty to save!

Lord, You are our refuge and our strength, an ever-present help in distress (Psalm 46:2).

St. Gabriel of Our Lady of Sorrows, pray for us.

Sirach 35:1-12
Psalm 50:5-6, 7-8, 14, 23
Mark 10:28-31

COLLECTION BASKET

"We have given up everything and followed you." – Mark 10:28

It was December 4, 1988. I had just surrendered my life to the Lord and I received what was called a baptism or renewal in the Holy Spirit. It was a life-changing experience!

I was deep in sin… and now He saved me.

My life was a rudder-less boat but He gave me direction.

I felt hopeless but my future was now full of hope.

I felt so high that I wanted to give God my all.

Then the collection basket came. I must admit I did resist the urge to give the highest bill in my wallet. In hindsight, it should have been an easy thing to do. After all, God just changed my life! But hey, I did it and I felt Him smile.

Our giving to God comes one collection basket at a time, one call to generosity at a time, one circumstance at a time… so that one day, we can truly say by His grace: "I've given You all of me!" *Ariel Driz (adriz77@yahoo.com)*

Reflection: When was your last "collection basket"?

Lord Jesus, grant me the grace to give back to You at every moment so I may truly give You all of me!

Blessed Daniel Brottier, pray for us.

MARCH 1
ASH WEDNESDAY

Joel 2:12-18
Psalm 51:3-4, 5-6, 12-13, 14, 17
2 Corinthians 5:20-6:2
Matthew 6:1-6, 16-18

TAKE A RETREAT

"But when you pray, go to your inner room…" – Matthew 6:6

My friend Roger drives like a mad man. Every time I ride with him, my prayer life is enhanced. Deepened. Invigorated. Heaven feels so near.

One fateful day, I was riding with him again. We were blazing through a highway like a cruise missile. Roger looked at me and said, "Bo, I have good news and bad news for you."

"What's the good news?" I asked between my Hail Marys.

"We're efficiently moving at an average speed of 140 kilometers per hour."

Involuntary spasms shot through my body. "Are you trying to tell me that we'll be arriving at our destination in no time?"

"That's the bad news. We're lost. I have no idea where we are."

"Stop this car NOW!" I screamed. We were swiftly driving towards the opposite direction!

The same thing happens to us. We get busy, do a million things, move fast, get efficient. But efficiently going where? This Lent, stop for a while and see if you're heading in the right direction. Have a retreat with Your Maker. *Bo Sanchez (bosanchez@ kerygmafamily.com)*

Reflection: Are you headed towards the fulfillment of your deepest aspirations?

Dearest Lord, guide me to where I will find my deepest joy — the joy that only You can give. Amen.

St. David of Wales, bishop, pray for us.

Deuteronomy 30:15-20
Psalm 1:1-2, 3, 4, 6
Luke 9:22-25

WHAT'S YOUR CHOICE?

"I have set before you life and death, the blessing and the curse."
– Deuteronomy 30:19

In the choices we make, there are always two options: life or death, blessing or curse.

When we live life the way God wants us to live, we choose a blessed life. Unfortunately, when we live a life of sin, we choose a cursed life. I once thought I was living life to the fullest with my twisted and worldly standards. At first it was great, but little did I know I was slowly dying from within. I lost everything: my job, my family, my purpose and even the will to live. Thankfully, God rescued me by sending people who opened my eyes to His love.

There are some things in life that are worse than death. In fact, some people who hit rock bottom would gladly welcome death as a form of escape. But that shouldn't be the case. Jesus didn't suffer and die just so we can live a miserable life. He rose from the dead so we can find strength to rise up from our sins.

So what's your pick: death or everlasting life? Curses or unlimited blessings? Sin or a loving relationship with God? Choose wisely. Choose Jesus! *Monching Bueno (ramon_bueno@yahoo.com)*

Reflection: How do you live your life? It's never too late. Choose Jesus!

Father God, thank You for always picking me up every time I fall. Grant me the grace to live my life to the full, in accordance with Your will. Amen.

St. Agnes of Bohemia, pray for us.

MARCH 3
FRIDAY

Isaiah 58:1-9
Psalm 51:3-4, 5-6, 18-19
Matthew 9:14-15

THE FAST THAT MATTERS

This, rather, is the fasting that I wish: releasing those bound unjustly, untying the thongs of the yoke; setting free the oppressed, breaking every yoke.
– Isaiah 58:6

It's been a while since I fasted from food during Lent. Yes, I abstain from meat and fast on the Fridays of Lent, but for the entire season, I deprive myself of other things. Like last Lent, I fasted from anger.

I think I should have just fasted from dessert. (Eeek.)

Or from chocolates. (Double eeek.)

Or breathing. (Gasp.)

Because all that was much easier than depriving myself of getting angry.

I realized that anger was my default emotion to almost anything. Especially when it came to my kids.

They take forever to get up in the morning. *I'm angry.* They don't do their homework. *I'm angry.* They're noisy. *I'm angry.*

I admit I failed on my fast almost every day. But after 40 days, I think I can safely say I'm not so angry anymore.

It's also a fast I intend to keep not just during the season of Lent but every day of every year. *Rissa Singson Kawpeng (justbreatherissa@gmail.com)*

Reflection: "Anger is never without a reason, but seldom with a good one." (Benjamin Franklin)

Holy Spirit, help me to bear fruit in patience, kindness and love.

St. Katharine Drexel, pray for us.

MARCH 4
SATURDAY

Isaiah 58:9-14
Psalm 86:1-2, 3-4, 5-6
Luke 5:27-32

'FOLLOW ME'

Jesus saw a tax collector named Levi sitting at the customs post. He said to him, "Follow me." – Luke 5:27

The next 40 days is a wonderful time to accept Jesus' invitation: "Follow Me" (Luke 5:27). If you're like me, you might be tempted to "buy" His love through acts of piety. Or you may feel burdened by fasting, almsgiving and praying longer. It's all a matter of attitude. You can follow Him as a servant who feels forced or coerced to be pious. Or you can choose to follow Him as a friend and enjoy every second of the journey!

Fast, so that when you feel hunger or desire, you will be reminded to focus on Him, no longer on His gifts or provision. Instead, focus on His face and His loving gaze.

Whatever money you save by fasting from a tall cup of coffee, give as alms. Give it lovingly and joyfully. Maybe God wants you to surprise your laundrywoman with a pack of goodies for her kids!

Pray a little longer. Pray more often. Don't just recite your prayers — revel in them! Sincerely lift up every word of prayer and enjoy the fact that God is listening, delighting in the time you take to be with Him.

Finally, the most pious act you can do is this: Let Jesus love you! *Marc Lopez (lamblightschool@yahoo.com)*

Reflection: Jesus says, "Follow Me." What's your response?

Jesus, thank You for inviting me. Here I am! Lead the way.

St. Casimir, pray for us.

MARCH 5
SUNDAY

Genesis 2:7-9; 3:1-7
Psalm 51:3-4, 5-6, 12-13, 17
Romans 5:12-19
(or Romans 5:12, 17-19)
Matthew 4:1-11

First Sunday of Lent

YAYA'S WISDOM

"One does not live by bread alone, but by every word that comes forth from the mouth of God." – Matthew 4:4

Our *yaya* (nanny) has been a part of our family for years. She helped us raise both our kids since they were newborns. I'm grateful to her for many things, but above all, I'm thankful that she never took advantage of our trust in giving her free rein around our home.

One night, we were watching a news report about a family that had been burglarized by their own househelper. *Yaya* was frowning at the TV. "You know, Ma'am," she said in Tagalog, "these people are the reason why it's so hard for other decent, hardworking helpers to find jobs, especially when they don't have anyone to refer them. If they went to Mass more often, they would know that if they treat their employers right, they will have free meals and shelter every day. They do it because they think they need money when they actually lack God in their lives."

I found that her words were insightful and relevant both to the rich and poor. Sometimes the best way to satisfy our hunger and temptation to do evil thing is to feed off of the Word of God and let Him guide our actions. *Eleanore Teo (elyo.lee@gmail.com)*

Reflection: Prayer is a powerful remedy to resist temptation.

Lord, as the wealth of the world is laid in front of me, speak to me as I close my eyes and tell me what is rightfully mine.

St. John Joseph of the Cross, pray for us.

MARCH 6
MONDAY

Leviticus 19:1-2, 11-18
Psalm 19:8, 9, 10, 15
Matthew 25:31-46

"You shall not go about spreading slander among your kin… Take no revenge and cherish no grudge… You shall love your neighbor as yourself." – Leviticus 19:16,18

I have a confession to make. I'm a certified nutcase for this phenomenal love team the country was gaga over a year ago. Well, not to the extent of joining a fans club or following them to location shoots or collecting all the magazines with their faces on them. I just stalk them on social media.

It's appalling to see how bashers and haters are so filled with envy that they'd do anything to try and bring this love team down. They pose as fake fans to spread rumors and incite negative comments. Loyal fans call them negatrons. Clearly, they are minions of the dark side.

I find it admirable how the love team and the enlightened members of the fandom deal with these negative people. They take no revenge and just encourage each other to spread good vibes. This is what makes the love team and their "nation" truly phenomenal. And this is how God wants us to love others, negatrons or otherwise. *Lella M. Santiago (lellams88@gmail.com)*

Reflection: You have a choice in dealing with negative people. You can either spread good vibes or make yourself miserable like them.

Help me to follow Your code of conduct, Lord, and not give in to the negativity around me.

MARCH 7
TUESDAY

Isaiah 55:10-11
Psalm 34:4-5, 6-7, 16-17,
18-19
Matthew 6:7-15

LIKE FATHER, LIKE SON!

"This is how you are to pray: Our Father who art in heaven hallowed be thy name, thy Kingdom come…" – Matthew 6:9-10

I used to have the mindset that all rich people are uncaring while poor people are good and saintly. I believed that when people become rich, they become evil. And that heaven awaits the poor, while hell awaits the rich.

I thought this way because I had a deep hatred for the rich. English-speaking people reminded me that I was poor in English. I hated being with tall people because it emphasized my small stature all the more. I hated mingling with the well-off because they reminded me of how miserable I was.

Then I encountered a quote from St. Cyprian explaining the Our Father. He said, "When we call God 'our Father' we ought to behave as sons of God."

Change began. I still have a long way to go, but as I surrender to His grace, Jesus restores me step by step from an unlovely sinner into the likeness and image of God! *Obet Cabrillas (obetcab@yahoo.com)*

Reflection: The Our Father is the Ultimate Restoration Power because it presents the nature of God as: Father, Holy, King, Almighty, Provider, Forgiver, Preserver and Deliverer!

Lord, let me maximize Your grace when I pray the Our Father. Let me pray as a trusting child and never as a conceited Pharisee. Amen.

MARCH 8
WEDNESDAY

Jonah 3:1-10
Psalm 51:3-4, 12-13,
18-19
Luke 11:29-32

ABOUT FACE

*"Man and beast shall be covered with
sackcloth and call loudly to God; every man
shall turn from their evil way..."*
– Jonah 3:8

Jenny lived a simple life when she was younger. But many times she felt out of place. To feel a sense of belongingness, she tried to level up with her friends' whims and caprices. She went with them on various gimmicks and travels, and bought clothes and accessories here and there. She got buried in debt for using five credit cards. She lived a life of lies to cover up her financial difficulties. She became irritable and was always angry. Her relationship with her parents and siblings got strained. Her performance at work deteriorated.

She came to her senses when she hit rock bottom. She called out to God for help. She talked to a counselor. She asked for forgiveness from her family, and their compassion and love lifted her from the dark pit of her life. Jenny immersed herself in prayer gatherings where she met friends who accepted, supported and loved her.

She turned away from sin and believed in the Gospel. *Sol Saura (sol_saura@yahoo.com)*

Reflection: In this season of Lent, let us seek the face of God in our lives, in our country, in our relationships, in our service, in the people who need us.

Father, I have sinned. I have turned my back and walked away. I depended on my strength and lived life my own way. Forgive me. (From the song "Father, I Have Sinned")

St. John of God, religious, pray for us.

FINDING *LOLO*

"Ask and it will be given to you; seek and you will find; knock and the door will be opened to you." – Matthew 7:7

One day, I received a private message from Diko (not his real name) who lives in Manila. He asked for help because his 79-year-old grandfather has been missing in Cagayan de Oro for two days.

Lolo got separated from his chaperone at the Agora CDO bus terminal while on their way back to Ozamis coming from Davao. Their relatives sought the help of authorities, yet they got no favorable feedback. We asked the assistance of the different media companies to publicize the matter, and everyone cooperated to find *Lolo*.

In the morning of the third day, we still didn't receive any news. We kept praying for a miracle. In the afternoon, I received another message from Diko. *"Lolo* is finally home!" he said. *Lolo* walked from CDO all the way to Ozamis covering 160 kilometers. He had no money in his pocket; he was exhausted and hungry. But *Lolo* survived! Truly, God is a God of miracles!

Friend, when nothing good seems to be happening in your life, remember: God is working behind the scenes! *Aben Garlan (mail@abengarlan.com)*

Reflection: Do you have unanswered prayers? Keep asking, keep seeking, and keep knocking. Then be prepared to see the miracles unfold before your eyes.

Father in heaven, increase my faith in You.

MARCH 10
FRIDAY

Ezekiel 18:21-28
Psalm 130:1-2, 3-4, 5-7, 7-8
Matthew 5:20-26

ADMIT YOUR MISTAKES

Settle with your opponent quickly while on the way to court. – Matthew 5:25

My friend Val found out that the cashier had been stealing from their pharmacy. When shown the evidence, the cashier cried and admitted her wrongdoing. Wanting to be just and merciful, Val gave the cashier a chance to settle everything discreetly. He only wanted her to realize her wrongdoing and return the money she took.

In their next meeting, the cashier suddenly claimed innocence and even filed a complaint to force Val to drop the charges. End result: The cashier is now facing criminal charges and imminent imprisonment because she didn't want to own up to her misdeed. If only she had the humility to admit her mistake, she wouldn't be facing jail time.

How many times have we denied that we have sinned? We make excuses like, "It's just a white lie," "Nobody knows about it anyway," or "Everybody does it." Our reasoning doesn't make any wrongdoing right. Before long, we're prisoners to our sins.

When you fall, admit and confess your sin. Do not let sin keep you in bondage. You do not want to face a sentence of "afterlife" imprisonment. *Jun Asis (mabuting.balita@gmail.com)*

Reflection: Admitting mistakes may be hard. But not admitting them may have bitter consequences in the end.

Lord, grant me the grace to admit my mistakes and make reparation for my sins. Amen.

Deuteronomy 26:16-19
Psalm 119:1-2, 4-5, 7-8
Matthew 5:43-48

DIFFICULT TO LOVE?

"For if you love those who love you, what recompense will you have?" – Matthew 5:46

When I was a new employee in Shepherd's Voice, I was eager to make friends. I went to the Accounting Department and approached one of the girls I had met earlier. I asked if she would like to attend our community's prayer meeting sometime. She gave me a stern look and, with a raised eyebrow, replied, "No, thanks," then turned away. I complained to God, "I thought this was a Catholic company and that good people work here." And I felt Him ask, "So what are you going to do about it?"

I took the Lord's challenge. I went on greeting people, particularly that crabby girl from Accounting. Most of them were pleasant and greeted me back, save for one. Imagine my surprise when this girl went to me one day and said, "I'm sorry I was rude to you. I know you're just trying to be friendly." Since then, she and I have become good friends. We would go to Mass, have dinner and just talk over cups of coffee and dessert. When I was depressed, she never asked me why. She just called me every day to ask how I was and said, "We can get through this together." I am honored to have her trust, as she has mine.

Is there a difficult person you'd love to hate? Maybe Jesus is telling you: "That's the one I want you to love. After all, I love you, sins and all." *Dina Pecaña (dina.p@shepherdsvoice.com.ph)*

Reflection: "Love difficult people like you were made for the job." (Bob Goff)

Father, may I persevere in loving the unlovable. Amen.

St. John Ogilvie, pray for us.

Genesis 12:1-4
Psalm 33:4-5, 18-19,
20, 22
2 Timothy 1:8-10
Matthew 17:1-9

Second Sunday of Lent

ALL IS GRACE

*Bear your share of hardship for the gospel
with the strength that comes from God.*
– 2 Timothy 1:8

I've been serving as a volunteer catechist in public elementary and high schools for the past seven years. I was 53 when I started. With an average of 40 mostly noisy and unruly students in a room, it's challenging and tiring. I have taught up to 16 sections in one school year. But it has stretched my vocal cords that when I once served as lector during a brownout, the person seated near the back of the church could still hear me proclaim the Word of God without a microphone.

A big consolation I get from the school children, especially the little ones, is when they cluster around me as I enter their room. Their smiles, waves and greetings every time they see me outside the school, in the marketplace or on the streets are rewards.

At the end of each day, after spending a lot of energy teaching, I hear Mass and say, "Thank You, Lord, for the grace and strength. I made it through this day. I could not have done this on my own if not for Your grace." *Bella Estrella (blestrella@gmail.com)*

Reflection: Do you commit to continue serving God and others despite hardships and trials?

Father, shower me with the graces and strength I need so that I can rise above any difficulty in serving You. To whom shall I go? You have the words of everlasting life.

Blessed Angela Salawa, pray for us.

MARCH 13
MONDAY

Daniel 9:4-10
Psalm 79:8, 9, 11, 13
Luke 6:36-38

BIRTHDAY GIFT TO THE LORD

"Give and gifts will be given to you."
– Luke 6:38

In the many years the Lord has blessed me with this beautiful ministry of writing for *Didache,* 2017 is the first time I was given an assignment that falls on my birthday today.

I want to give something special to the Giver of life. For the past 12 years, my gift to Him has been the people in the ministry He gave me. I would schedule the Lenten recollection of Basic Ecclesial Community leaders on my birthday. It's a time for confession, talk, sometimes stations of the cross, and Eucharistic celebration. Drawing them closer to Him is the best gift I could think of for Jesus.

But you know what? God cannot be outgiven. The inspiring testimonies of how blessed the experience was, the unforgettable fellowship and bonding we have, the personal and sometimes intimate message from the Lord from the talks or silent moments for reflection make my day! Joy that is "good measure, pressed down, shaken together, and running over" is poured unto me.

When I give something to the Lord, He always doubles it back to me. *Cristy Galang (cristy_cc@yahoo.com)*

Reflection: Do you make sure you are pleasing to the Lord on your birthday? Do you go to Mass and give thanks?

Thank You, Lord Jesus, for the life You have given me. I know You have a beautiful purpose for creating me. I ask for the grace to live that I may fulfill that purpose. Amen.

MARCH 14
TUESDAY

Isaiah 1:10, 16-20
Psalm 50:8-9, 16-17,
21, 23
Matthew 23:1-12

*"You have but one teacher, and you are
all brothers." – Matthew 23:8*

As all 11-year-old schoolers of his day did, Neil postponed doing his book report until the last minute. The night before the deadline, he rushed to the library, and saw the book to be "too thick for speed reading."

The next day, when his name was called for the oral book report, he immediately launched into a "fabricated" story, with all its wonderful details, complete with breathtaking turns, and mind-boggling twists. The teacher and students alike were hanging on the edge of their seats, listening intently to his amazing story.

He got his grade the next day, a huge A+! But underneath this was a note from the teacher that said, "I've read the book you reported on yesterday, and it had absolutely nothing to do with the story you shared. But you're an amazing storyteller. You will do something great with your life. I believe in you."

Neil has grown to be a successful screenwriter. Now on top of his game, he always gives credit to his teacher, who, instead of chewing him out, saw the greatness in him, and made him believe in God's amazing gift.

This is what a great teacher does. *Jon Escoto (faithatworkjon@gmail.com)*

Reflection: My friend, will you be a teacher to someone today?

Lord, teach me how to love and not to judge. Then I'll be able to teach genuinely today. Amen.

Jeremiah 18:18-20
Psalm 31:5-6, 14, 15-16
Matthew 20:17-28

KEEP YOUR FOCUS

"And they will condemn him to death, and hand him over to the Gentiles to be mocked and scourged and crucified."
– Matthew 20:18, 19

I was on the way to Batangas to pick up my 12-year-old son from his summer youth camp. The highway was almost empty because it was a Sunday and Manny Pacquiao also had a boxing match that morning. The skies were clear, the radio played good music and the scenery was peaceful. It was such a relaxing drive that that I missed my toll exit. I had no choice but to take the next exit a few kilometers away to make a U-turn. I lost time and money because I got too comfortable.

I changed my attitude as I reentered the highway. This time, I was more alert so I wouldn't miss the right exit. I arrived at the campsite only a few minutes late.

It's the same with our lives. Sometimes, we forget to focus and we get lost when life gets too comfortable.

If you experience trials and life seems hard, simply be alert and focus on Jesus so you may reach your destination. Jesus also experienced difficulties. He was persecuted, mocked, scourged and crucified. Yet He remained focused on His mission so that we may receive the gift of salvation. *Alvin Fabella (alvinfabella@yahoo.com)*

Reflection: "Don't let your trials blow you down; let them lift you up." (Woodrow Kroll)

Lord Jesus, thank You for showing me the way. You experienced trials and difficulties to save us.

MARCH 16
THURSDAY

Jeremiah 17:5-10
Psalm 1:1-2, 3, 4, 6
Luke 16:19-31

TEST

"I, the Lord, alone probe the mind and test the heart." – Jeremiah 17:10

I had chills the night before and I had a cold so I went to the hospital to know what medicine I should take. It was standard procedure for the nurse in the clinic to take the patient's blood pressure (BP), but she was alarmed that mine was too high. They sent me to the emergency room immediately. My blood pressure was even higher by the time I got to the ER so they moved me to critical care. The doctors took blood tests and X-rays to check my organs. Right up to the moment they hooked me to a drip and admitted me, I didn't feel any panic.

But when I moved to a room and the nurses would come hourly to check my BP, I started to worry. Knowing every BP reading didn't help calm me at all. That's when the fear of dying gripped me. I prayed and asked God for help. I was only able to sleep when I played liturgical songs by David Haas.

That medical condition tested me literally and spiritually. Looking back, I know I should have trusted God more and not worried. I realized He guided me to be in the hospital at just the right time so I could have the medical attention I didn't even know I needed. *Mae Ignacio (maemi04@aim.com)*

Reflection: Do we give up on God during times of trial?

Dear Lord, I pray that through every trial we encounter, we will learn to trust in You and know that You have our backs all the time.

Genesis 37:3-4, 12-13, 17-28
Psalm 105:16-17, 18-19, 20-21
Matthew 21:33-43, 45-46

ONE WOULD SAVE YOU

His purpose was to rescue him from their hands and return him to his father.
– Genesis 37:22

Have you ever felt as if the entire world is out to get you? Maybe there are people who are trying to bring you down. People who say nasty things about you even when you've done nothing wrong. People who'd destroy everything you've worked hard for.

It happened to me before. I didn't have anything against anyone, but there were people who spread bad things about me just so I could be fired from my job. I didn't mind the rumors because they weren't true, but I still felt awful. What kept me going during those bad days were the people who spoke on my behalf. I had great friends who fought for me when I couldn't fight for myself.

It's difficult to keep moving, to keep fighting, to keep going forward when all the odds are against you. But think about this: The devil would send probably 10, 100 or 1,000 people to destroy you. But God has sent the One who fought for you, died for you, won over death for you.

God has sent Jesus. There is nothing more to fear. *Karren Renz Seña (karren.s@shepherdsvoice.com.ph)*

Reflection: Do you feel as if you are pressed from all sides? Call on Jesus. He has overcome.

Lord, when the world is out to get me, remind me that Jesus has already won against all my enemies. In Him, I have overcome. Amen.

St. Patrick, bishop, patron of Ireland and Nigeria, pray for us.

MARCH 18
SATURDAY

Micah 7:14-15, 18-20
Psalm 103:1-2, 3-4, 9-10, 11-12
Luke 15:1-3, 11-32

THE PRODIGAL

While he was still a long way off, his father caught sight of him, and was filled with compassion. He ran to his son, embraced him and kissed him. – Luke 15:20

In the summer of my third year in high school, I became a rebel middle child. At this point in my teenage life, I was lost trying to find myself. I felt unloved. Some of the crazy things I did included downing two bottles of cough syrup containing codeine, baking brownies with poppy seeds, and guzzling five cases of beer with a handful of friends. I knew my mom learned about my dopey moments but never called my attention. I thought that she didn't love me.

I got frustrated and decided to go joyriding to Tagaytay with P1,000 in my pocket. Assuming that no one would look for me, I didn't go home for five days. I managed to live in a *kubo* (native hut), ate two meals a day at the Mahogany market, and used the toilet of the nearby church. I never took a bath and smelled like a pig.

Realizing my dire situation, I called my mom to return home and reconcile. I was ready to be reprimanded and punished. As soon as I rang the bell, she opened the gate. I got the best embrace of my life. *Dean Pax Lapid (happyretiree40@gmail.com)*

Reflection: Have you ever felt unconditional love? Have you given unconditional love?

Father God, forgive me for my rebel ways. I realize that it's only by Your grace and mercy that I can go back to the road of righteousness and rejoicing.

St. Cyril of Jerusalem, bishop and doctor of the Church, pray for us.

MARCH 19
SUNDAY

Exodus 17:3-7
Psalm 95:1-2, 6-7, 8-9
Romans 5:1-2, 5-8
John 4:5-42

Third Sunday of Lent

WITNESS

"We no longer believe because of your word; for we have heard for ourselves…"
– John 4:42

The Gospel today is one powerful conversion story of a sinner — a Samaritan woman turned evangelizer — all because she witnessed Jesus face to face. By the strength of her word, though she was a known adulteress, people believed in Jesus because of her witnessing. Then they themselves heard Jesus and became witnesses, too.

We cannot comprehend whom God can and will use to proclaim His message of love. At times, it comes from the most unexpected messenger.

I am a sinner. Yet, I too am a preacher. Thousands of people regularly listen to me, and by the strength of the words that come out of my mouth, people believe.

But don't let people just dwell on your words, on your experiences, or on your witnessing. They too have to encounter Jesus in a personal way. So that in the end, they will say, "Now we believe no longer because of what you told us; we have heard Him ourselves." And that's when you become a true *witness* for Jesus. *Alvin Barcelona (apb_ayo@yahoo.com)*

Reflection: When was the last time you became a witness for Jesus? When was the last time you let others be a witness and listened to their own personal encounter with Him?

Dear Lord, I pray for the courage to be Your witness, in spite of who I am. Allow others to be witnesses too of how You love them so much.

St. Joseph, husband of the Blessed Virgin Mary, principal patron of Canada and the universal Church, pray for us.

IN A DREAM

He did as the angel of the Lord commanded him... – Matthew 1:24

2 Samuel 7:4-5, 12-14, 16
Psalm 89:2-3, 4-5, 27, 29
Romans 4:13, 16-18, 22
Matthew 1:16, 18-21, 24 (or Luke 2:41-51)

Solemnity of St. Joseph, Husband of the Blessed Virgin Mary

Pope Francis spoke about his great love for St. Joseph during his apostolic visit to the Philippines in 2015. He said, "I have great love for St. Joseph, because he is a man of silence and strength. On my table, I have an image of St. Joseph sleeping. Even when he is asleep, he is taking care of the Church!... So when I have a problem, a difficulty, I write a little note and I put it underneath St. Joseph, so that he can dream about it! In other words, I tell him: Pray for this problem."

Pope Francis' devotion to St. Joseph inspired me to spend time getting to know St. Joseph better. I reflected on the few Scripture passages mentioning St. Joseph. He became so real and human, just like anyone of us facing life's daily challenges. I felt St. Joseph assuring me that just as he watched over Mary and Jesus, he would watch over me. I now have the image of St. Joseph sleeping and I entrust my needs to him. There is a quiet strength knowing that St. Joseph is present daily to keep me from harm. *Beth Melchor (epmelchor6@gmail.com)*

Reflection: St. Joseph is the universal patron of the Church. We can pray to him with confidence that he will obtain the favor we ask for.

Dear St. Joseph, whose privilege it was to carry Jesus in your arms and watch over Him, watch over us and bring us to Jesus.

St. Salvator of Horta, pray for us.

Daniel 3:25, 34-43
Psalm 25:4-5, 6, 7, 8, 9
Matthew 18:21-35

FORGIVEN AND FORGOTTEN

"Since he had no way of paying it back..."
– Matthew 18:25

In the early 90s, a close friend during my college days borrowed a huge amount of money from me. Well, at that time, P15,000 was big enough for me.

He had lost his job in a multinational oil company and had been jobless for three years. Credit card companies were hounding him. His house was at risk of being foreclosed.

His wife, a medical doctor, had just started her practice and could not be expected to help much in solving his financial difficulties.

For many years, my friend kept in touch, sending greeting cards on special occasions, and all the time apologizing that he still could not settle his debt.

I understood that he had no way of paying me back, so I was ready to forget it. But after a couple of years, the wind suddenly blew in his favor. He got a high-paying job in a faraway country. Not long after, he was finally able to pay his debt.

The experience taught me that by embracing the situation of others, I am able to show God's mercy and compassion. And I pray that if ever I find myself in the same situation, I'll receive His mercy and compassion, too. *Tess V. Atienza (theresa.a@shepherdsvoice.com.ph)*

Reflection: How do you treat those who owe you something?

Lord, I pray for people who are in great financial debt. Lead them to the right channel of Your blessings for them.

MARCH 22
WEDNESDAY

Deuteronomy 4:1, 5-9
Psalm 147:12-13, 15-16,
19-20
Matthew 5:17-19

CHILDREN SEE, CHILDREN DO

"But teach them to your children and to your children's children..."
– Deuteronomy 4:9

When I meet parents for coaching, I share with them a life lesson I learned from my sister, a preschool teacher: "Our kids pick up from our actions more than we realize."

There's a video of five-year-old toddlers following every move of their adult companion.

When mom litters, daughter litters.

Dad curses clerk, son curses clerk.

Driving mom gives a dirty finger, son gives a dirty finger.

Dad raises hand at mom, son raises hand at baby.

Children see, children do.

The good side of this is that children learn good things the same way. They learn kindness, respect, forgiveness, humility, caring, love, happiness, celebration, confidence, persistence, aspiration when they see *you* do it.

Whatever we know to be good, to be true, to be kind, to be loving, let's do it even in the simplest way. Smile. Greet good morning. Say thank you. Clean as you go. Let others pass through before you.

Because what people see, people do. *Edwin S. Soriano (edwin@winningcoaching.net)*

Reflection: How can you be a good example to children around you?

Lord, as Your child, let me show Your love through my actions.

St. Nicholas Owen, pray for us.

MARCH 23
THURSDAY

Jeremiah 7:23-28
Psalm 95:1-2, 6-7, 8-9
Luke 11:14-23

CATHOLIC CHRISTIAN

Every kingdom divided against itself will be laid waste and house will fall against house. – Luke 11:17

One challenge I face as a teacher of Christian Living Education is answering delicate questions from young inquiring minds. One such question is, "What's the difference between a Christian and a Catholic?" When that question is raised, follow-up comments emerge from other kids, like, "My mom and dad said I'm Catholic!" and "Mrs. Catral, are you Catholic or Christian?" I explain to them that Catholics are Christians, and while we have certain beliefs that those who call themselves "Christians" don't accept, I tell them that Catholics and Christians alike are all part of God's family. We are all followers of Jesus Christ and we have a shared responsibility of spreading God's love with those who do not know Him. We could choose to focus on what divides us, or we could work together and focus on our common mission of love.

In the Gospel today, Jesus says, "Whoever is not with me is against me, and whoever does not gather, scatters." As we do our part in building God's Kingdom here on earth, let us remember that God's love has no borders, no limits, and that He can use anyone He chooses for His work. *Geraldine G. Catral (catral. geegee@beaconschool.ph)*

Reflection: To be Catholic means to "welcome all." Have you been a true Catholic lately?

Dearest Lord, help me to do my part in building Your Kingdom, and to encourage others who are doing theirs.

St. Turibius of Mongrovejo, bishop, pray for us.

MARCH 24
FRIDAY

Hosea 14:2-10
Psalm 81:6-8, 8-9, 10-11,
14, 17
Mark 12:28-34

"You shall love the Lord your God with all your heart, with all your soul, with all your mind, and with all your strength. The second is this: You shall love your neighbor as yourself." – Mark 12:30-31

How can I love God and others with all my heart, soul, mind and strength when I feel so weak in every area of my life?

I had been asking that question for the nth time during the week. I was sick. I was alone. I was hurt. I felt rejected by the people I love the most. My prayer life was wobbly, too. How do I love in this condition?

As I delved into self-pity, I heard God speak. "Maymay, allow Me to love you. Just let Me love you."

"What, Lord? Didn't You hear me?" I said.

Then one realization hit me: Loving God and my neighbor with all my heart, soul, mind and strength is a call for me to love even if my heart, soul, mind and strength fail. To love with my everything is to love even if I have nothing to give. Sometimes, the best way we can love others is to just receive their love.

So I opened my heart to God and let Him in. Ah! Finally, joy and peace. It's all I need. This is love. *Maymay R. Salvosa (christiane. salvosa@gmail.com)*

Reflection: Take a pause and be in prayerful silence. Let God love you as you are, where you are.

I surrender to Your love, O God. I come to You with all my pains, my weaknesses and shortcomings. Embrace me as You will. Amen.

MARCH 25
SATURDAY

Isaiah 7:10-14; 8:10
Psalm 40:7-8, 8-9, 10, 11
Hebrews 10:4-10
Luke 1:26-38

Solemnity of the Annunciation of
the Lord

GOD'S FAVOR

"Do not be afraid... for you have found favor with God." – Luke 1:30

My family arrived at the airport departure area at about 4 o'clock in the morning for our 7 a.m. flight.

I noticed an immense number of people were massing at the check-in counters of almost all the airlines. It seemed impossible for us to reach the counter in time for the cut-off, as the lines were very long.

I called my friend who was booked at the 6 a.m. flight for the same destination. He arrived at the airport at about 2:30 a.m. but his flight was canceled. No wonder it was chaotic at the departure area.

My family and I prayed that we would easily get our boarding pass. Suddenly, we saw three computer kiosks for online check-in. In less than 10 minutes, we were able to check in and get our boarding passes.

All we could do was exclaim, "This is the favor of God!" Thank You, Lord! *Danny Tariman (dtariman.loj@gmail.com)*

Reflection: The Bible says, "Come! let us go to implore the favor of the Lord and to seek the Lord of hosts" (Zechariah 8:21). Before you leave home for work or any activity, pray for God's favor to be manifested in whatever you undertake for the day.

Lord Jesus, thank You for the grace You have given us to see Your hand moving in our lives. May we see Your favor manifested in us in many more ways.

St. Dismas, pray for us.

MARCH 26
SUNDAY

1 Samuel 16:1, 6-7, 10-13
Psalm 23:1-3, 3-4, 5, 6
Ephesians 5:8-14
John 9:1, 6-9, 13-17,
34-38 (or John 9:1-41)

Fourth Sunday of Lent

HOW'S YOUR SCHEDULE?

Try to learn what is pleasing to the Lord.
– Ephesians 5:10

I've noticed something. When we get busy, the things that get booted out of our schedule are the important stuff. Think about it.

When we have a lot of work and we need to go overtime, don't we forego time with our family?

When our nights are so full, we run out of time to exercise.

Or when we have a lot of things to do in a day, don't we skip our prayer time or Mass?

Martin Luther said, "I have so much to do that I shall spend the first three hours in prayer." This man knew how much he needed God's empowerment for the things he had to accomplish.

Our world is spinning so fast that it's easy to exchange the urgent for the important. Let's guard our time so that we don't waste it on useless activities that don't get us closer to our eternal goal. *Rissa Singson Kawpeng (rissa@shepherdsvoice.com.ph)*

Reflection: "The key is not to prioritize what's on your schedule, but to schedule your priorities." (Stephen Covey)

Lord, help us discern how to spend our time. Teach us to "waste" our time on things that have eternal value. Amen.

Blessed Didacus of Cadiz, pray for us.

GOD HAS A PLAN

No longer shall there be in it an infant who lives but a few days. – Isaiah 65:20

Isaiah 65:17-21
Psalm 30:2, 4, 5-6,
11-12, 13
John 4:43-54

As a mother, I sometimes find myself asking God why He allows little children to suffer; why babies unexpectedly die in their mothers' wombs; why some infants live "but a few days," as it says in the verse above.

I remember when our second child was born in Timor Leste eight years ago. She had to stay in the NICU for a few days, so I stayed with her, too. I remember grieving with one of the moms there when her baby died. He was just a few days old.

I remember the stories of our Timorese brethren from Couples for Christ during one prayer meeting. Some of the mothers shared about losing their young children to illness, and we cried together as we prayed for their kids' souls and for one another.

I may never understand why God allows suffering in this world, but I do believe in His great plan for us. As it says in the First Reading, He is "creating new heavens and a new earth; the former things shall not be remembered nor come to mind."

Let's trust in Him, even during difficult times. *Tina Santiago Rodriguez (trulyrichandblessed@gmail.com)*

Reflection: "The more we are afflicted in this world, the greater is our assurance in the next; the more sorrow in the present, the greater will be our joy in the future." (St. Isidore of Seville)

O Most Sacred Heart of Jesus, I put my trust in You.

MARCH 28
TUESDAY

Ezekiel 47:1-9, 12
Psalm 46:2-3, 5-6, 8-9
John 5:1-16

PHARISAICAL

The Jews began to persecute Jesus because he did this on a Sabbath. – John 5:16

"What was the most unforgettable piece of advice Pope Francis gave you?" Boy Abunda asked Fr. Luciano Felloni, an Argentine missionary, during an interview on his show. When Fr. Felloni was still a seminarian, Pope Francis (who was then the rector of a Jesuit seminary) asked him, "How are the people in your pastoral work?"

"We're trying to teach them, Father, because every time there's a celebration of a saint's feast, they always touch the image of the saint. We need to purify their faith." "When was the last time you cried while praying?" the Pope asked, adding, "If you can't reach that level, don't teach the people. Learn from them." Fr. Felloni never forgot that.

"Sometimes, we laugh at the simple faith of the people shown through kissing or touching of the images," Fr. Felloni said, "but despite the seeming shallowness of such acts, there lies a deep faith.... Ask yourself, 'When was the last time you've reached that level of prayerfulness?'"

We all have our expressions of faith. Sometimes we scoff at what other believers do, considering ourselves to be more spiritually mature. If we do this, we are no better than the Pharisees who persecute Jesus for curing on the Sabbath. *Judith Concepcion (svp_jmc@yahoo.com)*

Reflection: Let not your love for God lead you to self-righteousness.

Grant me the grace to respect the faith expressions of others.

MARCH 29
WEDNESDAY

Isaiah 49:8-15
Psalm 145:8-9, 13-14,
17-18
John 5:17-30

EVEN DOGS NEED MERCY

*For the Lord comforts his people and
shows mercy to his afflicted.*
– Isaiah 49:13

We have a family pet dog named Tuchi and she has been with us since I was a teenager. There was a time when my whole family got so busy that we forgot to take care of her, which eventually led to her getting ticks.

One day, my heart was moved with pity for her suffering. Instead of ignoring this, I made a decision not to give up on her. I suited up for the challenge and made time to remove her ticks one by one. It was a disgusting task but I persevered because of my compassion for Tuchi. All the hard work paid off, and to this day, Tuchi is still in good shape despite her old age.

I thank God for this experience because it reminded me of His compassion for us. If we humans can show dogs what mercy is about, then how much more our merciful God can.

Receive God's mercy today and become His mercy to the lost, the least and the last. *JC Libiran (JCLibiran@ymail.com)*

Reflection: "If you judge people, you have no time to love them." (Mother Teresa)

Lord Jesus, I accept Your mercy and forgiveness today. I also answer Your call to be Your love and embrace to the world. Amen.

MARCH 30
THURSDAY

Exodus 32:7-14
Psalm 106:19-20, 21-22, 23
John 5:31-47

A FATHER'S PLAN
...I will make of you a great nation.
– Exodus 32:10

Becoming a father was one of the most amazing things that happened to me. The moment I first saw my son, Luca Sebastian, in the nursery, I fell in love with him.

Most fathers would say that the first time they saw their child was the same moment they started to think about their child's future.

Not me.

My planning started way before that. It started way before my wife, Guada, conceived. It started way before we got married, way before we got engaged.

It all started when I was still single and trying to be the best version of myself. Ever since I saw where God was leading me, I planned for Luca. I knew him. I saw his bright future. I saw his achievements, his talents, his friends, his successes.

Now that I hold him in my arms, it's only a matter of time. It may be that some of my plans will be futile. But I am confident that God's plans and favor for Luca will surely come to pass.

Stephen I. Nellas (sinfts@live.com)

Reflection: Our God is a personal God. He has a lot of plans and favors for you. Have you asked Him seriously what those plans are? Have you consulted Him about your future lately?

Father, thank You for Your favor that is ever upon me. Without You, I am truly nothing. The plans You have for me are beyond my understanding. May You be praised forever and ever. Amen.

St. Peter Regalado, pray for us.

Wisdom 2:1, 12-22
Psalm 34:17-18, 19-20,
21, 23
John 7:1-2, 10, 25-30

DEATH RECONCILES

*They did not know the hidden counsels of
God... – Wisdom 2:22*

"It is good that I am dying. If not,
this rift (with her son) would have
persisted," lamented a dying mother
in the movie *Everything About Her.*

Vivian was once a homeless kid who worked hard to build a
business empire. On her way to the top, she neglected her family
and drove her son and husband away. Alone at the peak of her
success, she was diagnosed with cancer. Her private nurse, Jica,
secretly exerted every effort to reconnect the estranged mother
and son. While Vivian longed for her son's embrace, he remained
distant. Eventually, he forgave her and rebuilt his relationship
with her. Vivian died a happy mother in peace.

We often neglect God. It is only at our low point or in the
face of death that we seek His forgiveness and return to His
fold. Death is certain but we do not know when it will be for us.

Live a meaningful life as true children of God every minute
of the day, believing we could be called Home anytime. Surely,
we will be at peace in death knowing we are reconciled with
Him in life. *Marie Franco (mariefranco_pie@yahoo.com)*

Reflection: Will you be ready to face your Creator today?

*Grant unto us, Lord Jesus, ever to follow the example of Your holy
Family, that in the hour of our death, Your glorious Virgin Mother
together with blessed Joseph may come to meet us and we may be
worthily received by You into everlasting dwellings: Who live and reign
world without end. Amen. (Prayer for a Happy Death #1)*

QUIT NOW!

"Let us destroy the tree in its vigor…"
– Jeremiah 11:19

Jeremiah 11:18-20
Psalm 7:2-3, 9-10, 11-12
John 7:40-53

Religious people define sin as something that offends God. That's true. But with this definition, some people think God is an uptight King with an immaculate palace — and you walk in with muddy shoes.

Hey, God is a Big Guy. Nothing happens to Him when we sin. The only reason sin affects Him is because it affects you. Sin doesn't violate His holiness as much as it violates His heart — because you are His heart.

As a father of two growing boys, I experience this firsthand. One time, my son came home frustrated over something that happened in his ministry. When I asked him a question, he answered me in a belligerent tone. So I told him gently, "Son, I know you had a rough day, but when you answered me right now, I felt disrespected." Quickly, he said, "I'm sorry, Dad." (I have a fantastic son.)

When he spoke to me in a disrespectful tone, I was hurt, yes. But more than anything else, I felt hurt at what the habit of disrespect will do to his future. It will steal away his relationships, his potential, and his success. And I didn't want that to happen.

I urge you now: Quit sin. Quit bad habits. Quit anything that is destroying your future. *Bo Sanchez (bosanchez@kerygmafamily.com)*

Reflection: What sin or bad habit do you need to cut now?

Dearest Lord, thank You for treasuring me in Your heart. Help me to quit my sinful ways. Amen.

Ezekiel 37:12-14
Psalm 130:1-2, 3-4, 5-6, 7-8
Romans 8:8-11
John 11:3-7, 17, 20-27, 33-45

Fifth Sunday of Lent

WILL YOU?

He cried out in a loud voice, "Lazarus, come out!" – John 11:43

Two years ago, I wanted to get slim fast. So I found this "super diet shake" being sold by a friend who claimed it could slim me down in two weeks, even without exercise!

I remembered all the money I lost and all the warnings of my parents who've also been "victims" of these marketing schemes. But this offer was too good to pass up. So I kept it a secret and bought it. It was the same old ending: The product ran out, I sprang back to my chubby self, I lost a five-digit investment, and I buried myself again in my self-dug grave.

It wasn't until a year later when I seriously wanted to get back in shape. My gym instructor refocused me on my goals. I exerted effort to eat well and exercise religiously. In four weeks, I lost more weight than I expected!

Like the people of Israel, God wants us out of the graves of our sin and stubbornness. But we take the shortcut. We remain comfortable and slack. God opens our graves and calls us out, but we have to take a leap of faith to step into the light. *Migs Ramirez (migsramirez.seminars@gmail.com)*

Reflection: Will you let go of your shortcuts to live a better life?

Mary my Mother, be with me when I am stubborn. Gently nudge me and wake me up from the things I do so complacently. May I follow your Son more closely, especially in these days leading to His passion, death and resurrection. Amen.

St. Francis of Paola, hermit, pray for us.

Daniel 13:41-62
(or Daniel 13:1-9, 15-17,
19-30, 33-62)
Psalm 23:1-3, 3-4, 5, 6
John 8:1-11

TRAFFIC VIOLATION

"I am completely trapped… Yet it is better for me to fall into your power without guilt than to sin before the Lord."
– Daniel 13:22-23

Once, a policeman flagged me down for swerving. It was a questionable violation since I didn't change lanes recklessly. Nevertheless, the traffic enforcer said he would issue me a ticket but was reminding me that I'd have to pay a fine as well as attend a driving seminar because of my violation. In other words, he was giving me the chance to settle my fine in a more convenient way — by giving him grease money.

I immediately told him that I was a practicing Christian and that I don't give bribes. I also told him that if he did think I violated the law, then it's just right that he give me a ticket. Even as I boldly said that, I prayed that the Lord would make the policeman release me without a ticket. After a while, he told me to be more mindful next time and let me go scot-free!

We think we need to compromise our faith if we want to get things done in this country. We forget the power of the Lord that can work in the midst of the darkest of circumstances.

Christians, let's be light to our world. And even if standing up for our faith won't get us off the hook, let's remember what Susanna said in our verse above. *Rissa Singson Kawpeng (justbreatherissa@gmail.com)*

Reflection: "Integrity is doing the right thing. Even when no one is watching." (C.S. Lewis)

Help me, Lord, to live for You no matter what the cost.

Numbers 21:4-9
Psalm 102:2-3, 16-18,
19-21
John 8:21-30

STOP COMPLAINING

"We have sinned in complaining against the Lord and you. Pray to the Lord to take the serpents from us."
– Numbers 21:7

Two years ago, I decided to eat healthy and exercise regularly. My wife and I joined a gym with like-minded people who had the same goal: to be fitter and stronger.

I thought it was easy at first, but every time I worked out, I found myself gasping for air. I would complain and ask, "Why am I even here killing myself with this workout?!" Plus, I'd get sore muscles and body aches days after, not to mention the pain of saying no to pizza, ice cream and crispy *pata*.

Once, I asked God, "Can't You just take away the pain and discomfort of working out?" Instead of answering my prayer, He sent people to encourage me to finish every workout. And because of this, I've persevered in my fitness journey.

We can sometimes be like the Israelites who complained to Moses about their situation. They prayed for God to remove the serpents from their midst, but instead, God gave them a bronze serpent on a pole to heal whoever was bitten.

When God calls you to your Promised Land, you will experience discomfort. Worry not. God may not take away the suffering, but He will surely comfort you in your difficulties until you reach your Promise Land. *Velden Lim (veldenlim@gmail.com)*

Reflection: If God does not calm your storms, ask for the strength to brave through them.

Jesus, let distress teach me to trust in Your ways.

St. Isidore of Seville, bishop and doctor of the Church, pray for us.

APRIL 5
WEDNESDAY

Daniel 3:14-20, 91-92, 95
Daniel 3:52, 53, 54, 55, 56
John 8:31-42

FAITH SO FREE

"You are trying to kill me, because my word has no room among you."
– John 8:37

In my masteral studies at the Loyola School of Theology, I have classmates who are priests from Vietnam, Cambodia, India, Africa, etc. A lot of them share how difficult it is to practice and share their faith in their homeland because of religious persecution. Thus, they have to keep their ministry underground for fear of death.

In the Philippines, Christianity is widely accepted with about 85 percent of the population believing in Jesus. So we're blessed to exercise our faith freely. But don't get fooled by that 85 percent and the religious freedom we enjoy. Because many of that 85 percent no longer go to church and many are choosing atheism. There are many people today who are broken and hurting, who are far away from God.

So, for us who believe and enjoy this privilege of faith, let's gratefully work to reach the lost, least and last. Let's take part in advancing the Gospel and building the Church.

I believe the best way to share our faith is to love people through mercy and kindness, just as Jesus did. *Mike Viñas (mikemichaelfcv@yahoo.com)*

Reflection: Ask God to lead you to someone who needs to hear the Gospel according to you.

Jesus, thank You for the gift of faith that I get to enjoy and share. Amen.

APRIL 6
THURSDAY

Genesis 17:3-9
Psalm 105:4-5, 6-7, 8-9
John 8:51-59

THREE FATHERS

"Abraham your father rejoiced to see my day; he saw it and was glad."
– John 8:56

I was seven years old then and had a fever. Papa said I should not go, but I insisted to join the Brownie camping. Later, my father came to the campsite to see if I was OK. I was and happily survived the one-day camping.

I was 19 and already in college during those turbulent days of the First Quarter Storm, when students marched to Malacañang to protest on issues such as poverty, injustice and tuition fee increases. Papa cautioned me about joining those marches. But I was a student leader, president of the student council, so naturally, I joined those marches, which my parents watched in horror on the six o'clock news.

Late in the evening, as I walked home, I would see Papa standing under the lamppost on our street, smoking his n^{th} cigarette, waiting for me without fail.

Today's readings is about two fathers: Abraham, destined to become a great father of all nations, fulfilled his mandate well; and God the Father Himself who let His Son fulfill His Great Mission of Salvation for all of us. In his own loving way, Papa did his mission to be a father to me. Six days from now, April 12, 2017, would be the 19th anniversary of his death. He succumbed to emphysema. *Chay Santiago (cusantiago@gmail.com)*

Reflection: What's your mission and how are you fulfilling it?

Our Father, Thy Kingdom come!

St. Crescentia Hoess, pray for us.

Jeremiah 20:10-13
Psalm 18:2-3, 3-4, 5-6, 7
John 10:31-42

Memorial of John the Baptist de
La Salle

FRUITS AND ROOTS

*"If I do not perform my Father's works,
do not believe me." – John 10:37*

There is no such thing as overnight success. Don't wish for success and significance today and expect it to happen the following day.

Three of my life principles are: Important things need not be hurried. Slow is beautiful. Success is all about preparation.

You see, an onion plant is full-grown in nine months. But the mighty oak tree is full-grown in 10 years. We don't want to be onion plants that can be easily broken. We have to be mighty oak trees whose shade and fruits can be enjoyed by people and other creatures.

Success and significance are the fruits, but character-building is the roots. If you want fruits, you have to work on the roots. In my 44 years of life, I have only One Character Trainer. Without Him, my life will go berserk with vice, violence and vulgarity. I surrender to my Divine Vine Grower "to perform the Father's work" in my life, watering me with blessing and cultivating me through trials.

I'm still a work in progress. But with His mighty hands and heart, I'm excited for more years of serving Him towards godly success and significance. *Obet Cabrillas (obetcab@yahoo.com /twitter: @daddyobet)*

Reflection: In the garden of God's mercy and grace, even a broken tree bears fruit.

In my heart, Lord, be glorified! In my thoughts, Lord, be glorified! In my words, Lord, be glorified! In my life, Lord, be glorified!

St. John Baptist de la Salle, priest, pray for us.

APRIL 8
SATURDAY

Ezekiel 37:21-28
Jeremiah 31:10, 11-12, 13
John 11:45-56

… and there he remained with the disciples. – John 11:54

Taybeh is a town inside the West Bank in Palestine. It is well-known for a few things. It has a large world-class beer brewery; it is predominantly Christian; and its old name is Ephraim, the town mentioned in today's Gospel where Jesus went to spend time preparing for His coming passion.

We all need a Taybeh in our lives, a place of quiet where we can clearly hear the Spirit's leading. Harassed by threats and surrounded by panic, many of us understand why Jesus needed to retreat to Ephraim. We go through seasons in our lives when we feel the same way and have the same need for silence.

Jesus teaches us what to do in these situations because He often (a) retreated to quiet places, (b) was often accompanied by His mother and disciples, and (c) He spent enormous amounts of time listening to the Father.

This Holy Week, let us seek to find time to prepare as Jesus did to drown out the noise of the world and to listen more intently to God's leading. *Rod Velez (rod.velez@gmail.com)*

Reflection: When you are hungry, you eat. How do you know when your soul is hungry and what do you feed it?

I only have one God and He gave His life to save mine. Teach me, Lord, to spend this week in gratitude.

St. Julie Billiart, pray for us.

FOR SURE

"Surely it is not I, Lord?"
– Matthew 26:22

Isaiah 50:4-7
Psalm 22:8-9, 17-18,
19-20, 23-24
Philippians 2:6-11
Matthew 27:11-54
(or Matthew 26:14-27:66)

Palm Sunday of the Lord's Passion

Today is my sixth wedding anniversary. (Background music… He, he, he.)

When I decided to pursue my wife, Dinah, I was sure about her. I had hurt a few girls in the past by backing out on my word, but this time, I knew it was forever.

I guess that's how the disciples must have felt, too. They had journeyed with Jesus for three years, listened to His teachings, spent all that time with Him and were in His "inner circle." How could they betray Him? Never. And yet, they all did, somehow. Still, they bounced back and continued to follow Jesus, despite their faults and failures.

I'm not a perfect husband. I've failed my wife many times. But despite and in spite of all that has happened, I have not changed my mind about her. And thank God, she hasn't changed her mind about me, either.

I believe God asks us not to be perfect, but that we be committed. We may fail Him, but in the end, we just need to choose Him over and over again. Thankfully, He never gives up on us either. *George Tolentino Gabriel (george.svp@gmail.com)*

Reflection: How committed are you to following Christ?

May I strive to be faithful to You, my faithful God.

St. Casilda, pray for us.

Isaiah 42:1-7
Psalm 27:1, 2, 3, 13-14
John 12:1-11

A MISSIONARY AT ONE

Here is my servant whom I uphold, my chosen one with whom I am pleased, upon whom I have put my Spirit…
– Isaiah 42:1

After seven search-ins and declining to be a religious missionary for the nth time, God spoke to my heart and whispered that He anointed me for His work. My initial reaction was, "Why me?"

I don't like to leave my comfort zone. I detest changes. I'm no Miss Congeniality. I distrust men. I prefer the background, instead of basking in klieg lights. I just want to write and teach children, not preach with my tongue. Wearing a blue habit doesn't suit me because I know I'll represent Christ in my littlest actions.

After attending apologetics classes for over a year, God made me realize, through a lay apologist who taught the *Catechism of the Catholic Church* and *Faith Explained*, that by virtue of baptism, a baptized Christian is a missionary, whether we like it or not. We are anointed to partake in the kingly, priestly and prophetic duties of Christ. That's why a Christian is called a "little Christ."

Now that I'm slowly learning to detach myself from mundane matters, denying and dying to myself every day, swallowing my pride, and embracing my daily crosses, I'm gradually accepting my calling as a missionary. *Ems Sy Chan (leeannesy7@yahoo.com)*

Reflection: Are you doing your duty as a missionary?

Thank You, Lord, for choosing me to be Your daughter, even before I became worthy to be called Your own.

St. Magdalen of Canossa, pray for us.

Isaiah 49:1-6
Psalm 71:1-2, 3-4, 5-6,
15, 17
John 13:21-33, 36-38

NEVER SAY NEVER

*Reclining at table, with his disciples,
Jesus was deeply troubled and testified,
"Amen, amen, I say to you, one of you
will betray me." – John 13:21*

"Lord, I'll never commit that sin."
Boom. Uh-huh. And at the prime
of my leadership in community, I fell to the temptation I swore
I'd never succumb to.

I guess that's how the disciples must have felt, too. They had
journeyed with Jesus for three years, listened to His teachings,
spent all that time with Him and were in His "inner circle."
How could they betray Him? And yes, there was only one Judas
Iscariot, but didn't they all betray Him when they disappeared
once the going got tough? In the same way, I betrayed Him.
Even when I said I'd never do it.

I also used to say, "God will never forgive me for that," but
He did. I thought I'd never be able to forgive myself, but I did.

Does God say never? Only when it comes to Him
destroying, forsaking or leaving us.

Whew! What a relief. *George Tolentino Gabriel (george.svp@gmail.com)*

Reflection: When you say never, are you really in full control?

Lord, empower me to follow You all the days of my life.

St. Stanislaus, bishop and martyr, pray for us.

Isaiah 50:4-9
Psalm 69:8-10, 21-22,
31, 33-34
Matthew 26:14-25

SAVING GRACE

The Lord God has given me a well-trained tongue, that I might know how to speak to the weary a word that will rouse them. – Isaiah 50:4

It was almost three months and I still had no sale. I only had about two weeks left to clinch a deal or else the company will have to let me go. The pressure was building up.

My dry spell left me with little money but I needed to visit prospects and clients. Back at home, my wife and I were not in good terms. Arguments and fighting became a common thing in the house.

Then it happened. I got confined in the hospital after I started to pee blood. I was forced to rest for a week. That sealed the ruin of my career. Almost a month after I had recovered, no one would hire me. I was jobless, penniless and suffering a deteriorating relationship. Alone at home, I cried on my knees and asked God to forgive me and help me.

After sobbing for an hour, I finally felt peace. I realized that Jesus was there with me the whole time. That day, I once again gave my life to Him. And my life was never the same again.

Are you tired of life? Beset by trials? At the end of your rope? What God has done for me, He will do for you. Turn to Him and receive His saving grace. *Edwin Marcelo (imboodoo@yahoo.com)*

Reflection: God is the light in our darkness, the wind beneath our wings and the very air we breathe.

You are my life, Jesus. Let me never forget that.

Exodus 12:1-8, 11-14
Psalm 116:12-13, 15-16,
17-18
1 Corinthians 11:23-26
John 13:1-15

BEFORE I DIE

*Jesus knew that his hour had come to
pass from this world to the Father.*
– John 13:1

In 2012, Candy Chang transformed an abandoned building in her New Orleans neighborhood. She put up a wall that had this lines written: "Before I die, I want to_____." People came by and completed the sentence with their own hopes, dreams and final wishes. Walls like this have been put up in 70 countries.

While there are those who want to travel or go on an adventure, some want to "help a Third World country," "put up an orphanage," or "cure cancer." Others want to "be the best father," "hug my grandkids," and "tell her I love her."

Jesus was clear about what He wanted to do before He died. We saw it in how He lived.

We know how He spent His last day, too. It was with people dear to Him. He prepared them for a life without Him. And although it was not clear to them, He gave them His message of love and service to others during their last meal together.

Until the end, His message and His life was consistent. It was love. *Kitty D. Ferreria (kittydulay@yahoo.com)*

Reflection: How are you continuing Jesus' legacy while you live?

Help us live lives of love and service every day, Lord.

KEEP MY MOUTH SHUT

Isaiah 52:13-53:12
Psalm 31:2, 6, 12-13,
15-16, 17, 25
Hebrews 4:14-16; 5:7-9
John 18:1-19:42

Though he was harshly treated, he submitted and opened not his mouth…
– Isaiah 53:7

I'm the kind of person who isn't afraid to speak her mind, especially when I believe that I am right. When I was still working as part of the HR team of a multinational company, I would reason out and negotiate with our president or the HR director when I thought that they were asking too much from our people.

But there came a time when I experienced being disrespected by people in my own house. Imagine that! It was not only for a brief moment or a day. It went on for days and weeks. It was a big challenge for me to keep my mouth shut and not point out to them how rude they were towards me, the house owner.

You must be wondering why I didn't promptly show them the way out of my house when they were misbehaving. Let me just say that there are some people that you can't just kick out of your house easily even when they treat you badly. I guess those are the people that Jesus wants us to practice forbearance and endurance with, just like what He did when He was being treated harshly. *Teresa Gumap-as Dumadag (teresa@fulllifecube.com)*

Reflection: Can you follow Jesus' example of keeping your mouth shut even when you are harshly treated? Why or why not? What keeps you from following His example?

Lord Jesus, help me to have the strength and humility to endure if it is Your will for me to grow in character in these kinds of situations.

Blessed Peter Gonzalez, pray for us.

APRIL 15
HOLY SATURDAY

Ezekiel 36:16-17, 18-28
Romans 6:3-11
Psalm 118:1-2, 16-17, 22-23
Matthew 28:1-10

OLD WALLET

*Just as Christ was raised from the dead…
we too might live in newness of life.
– Romans 6:4*

I was cleaning my room at the beginning of 2016 when I unearthed an old wallet from my drawer. Although dust had clung to it, the red leather was intact. Inside, I found expired cards, old notes and US$10. "Enough to buy a pair of jeans," I thought. When I checked the mint, they were series 2003, and I saw the pair of jeans slip from my fingers. I may no longer be able to exchange it to pesos.

I realized that had I not kept it in that wallet and allowed the wallet to be buried in the messy drawer, I would have probably enjoyed what that bill could buy.

In the same way, God gave us talents to use to better the world and planted dreams in our hearts to fulfill. However, some of us choose to bury them where they are eventually forgotten and covered by cobwebs.

Friends, let us give life to our dead talents and old dreams. God has created us to reach our full potential, not with a spirit of cowardice or being small. *Osy Erica (osy.erica@gmail.com)*

Reflection: "The glory of God is man fully alive." (St. Irenaeus)

Father, use me until I have nothing left to give. When I grow complacent, remind of the greatness within me that comes from You. Amen.

APRIL 16
EASTER SUNDAY

Acts 10:34, 37-43
Psalm 118:1-2, 16-17, 22-23
Colossians 3:1-4
(or 1 Corinthians 5:6-8)
John 20:1-9
(or Matthew 28:1-10 or Luke 24:13-35)

SHE KNOWS

Think of what is above, not of what is on earth. – Colossians 3:2

I have been a contributor of *Didache* for 10 years. But that is as far as my writing talent goes. Little did I know, our Blessed Mother was preparing me for a bigger purpose.

I was tasked to work on a book project to spread awareness on the events of Her 1948 apparition in Lipa and promote the devotion to Her. My role was to find volunteers to write and edit the material, and source funds to have it printed and distribute 10,000 copies for free.

As things unfolded, the book was published with me as its ghostwriter. Admittedly, I was initially disappointed for the missed chance for credit, even at least as a co-author. But with God's grace, I let the negative thoughts go and focused on being grateful to do something worthy for our Blessed Mother. It was enough that She knows I did it for Her.

The merits from acts of charity are lost when we pursue them for public recognition or tax breaks. Let us quietly do our Christian work here on earth and earn our place beside God's throne. *Marie Franco (mariefranco_pie@yahoo.com)*

Reflection: What is your real intention when you do good deeds?

Create in me a clean heart, O Lord. Fill it with love and compassion. Let me serve my brothers not in my name, but Yours.

St. Bernadette Soubirous, virgin, pray for us.

Acts 2:14, 22-33
Psalm 16:1-2, 5, 7-8,
9-10, 11
Matthew 28:8-15

THE SOLDIER AND THE DAUGHTER

They approached, embraced his feet, and did him homage. – Matthew 28:9

I've always considered myself as God's soldier, His warrior, His champion. I thought that worshiping Him meant working overtime to advance His Kingdom. In prayer, I would always imagine myself kneeling before the throne of God, receiving His orders and anointing, and then I'd go out into the world to do His work.

I worked hard. I served hard. I loved hard. But I didn't know that I was also getting tired. So I asked God for a favor. A few lines from a worship song came to mind: "While I'm waiting, I will serve You, Lord." I felt sad because I thought I had to work harder in order for Him to answer my prayers. But God stopped me mid-tirade. "Karren, you are not only My soldier. You are also My daughter," He said. "You don't have to work so hard. Now, what do you want? Come, tell your Father." His words struck home so hard, I cried. I realized then that I didn't have to work to earn God's love, or anyone else's love for that matter.

God calls us to a deeper relationship with Him because He wants to love us and bless us, not because He wants to give us orders. God loves us as we are, where we are. *Karren Renz Seña (karren.s@shepherdsvoice.com.ph)*

Reflection: God wants nothing more than to love us. Let us receive this truth with joy, trust and faith.

May Your Holy Spirit open us to Your unfailing and unconditional love.

St. Benedict Joseph Labre, pray for us.

Acts 2:36-41
Psalm 33:4-5, 18-19,
20, 22
John 20:11-18

WHO IS IT YOU'RE LOOKING FOR?

Jesus said to her, "Woman, why are you weeping? Whom are you looking for?"
— John 20:15

I'm a goal-oriented person. When I have a dream, I find ways, resources and people that can help me reach that dream.

But there are times when I get so caught up on working for my goals, that I experience anxiety attacks and stress from overthinking. I begin to neglect my family, friends, and even God—those who really matter in my life.

Thank God for The Feast, Light Groups and prayer times that always remind me to pause, take a step back, and see the reason why I'm doing what I'm doing.

Our careers, money and achievements are all important. But let's learn to set our priorities in order. Do they distract us from paying attention to the things that really matter? Yes, I can be busy with a lot of urgent matters, but at the end of the day, I will always cry out and look to Jesus—the reason for my being.

Tintin Mutuc (kristinemutuc@shepherdsvoice.com.ph)

Reflection: Let us always remember that the Lord is always with us, waiting for us to approach Him.

Jesus, may I always look for You amidst the busyness of my every day. You are the only treasure worth searching for.

Blessed James Oldo, pray for us.

Acts 3:1-10
Psalm 105:1-2, 3-4, 6-7, 8-9
Luke 24:13-35

LOOK UP

Their eyes were prevented from recognizing him. – Luke 24:16

The Walk to Emmaus is a favorite opening Bible story of mine every time I give retreats. It never fails to make my retreatants immediately reflect. How on earth could the two not recognize Jesus when they were supposed to know Him well? They were His disciples! They saw Him, followed Him, walked with Him, and lived with Him.

Some scholars say Jesus' appearance changed when He rose again from the dead, a possible reason why the two didn't recognize Him. But you can get a practical answer and clue in the reading itself. They were downcast. They were frustrated and disappointed. Jesus, their only hope, died right before their eyes. They felt depressed and defeated. They thought it was over.

It's OK to feel down and sad. But don't dwell on it too long. Because when restoration comes, when victory happens, when the Resurrected Christ appears in your life — and He will — you might miss seeing Him. Because you got used to "looking down."

Today, start looking up. Because when everything seems to have died on you and there seems no other way to go, that's the time you look up! *Alvin Barcelona (apb_ayo@yahoo.com)*

Reflection: Has something died in your life? A relationship, your finances, your dreams? Don't look down too long. Your resurrection is coming. Prepare to recognize it!

Lord, I believe that like You, I too will be resurrected. Grant me the faith to dwell on the things that will rise and live again. Amen.

St. Gianna Beretta Molla, pray for us.

Acts 3:11-26
Psalm 8:2, 5, 6-7, 8-9
Luke 24:35-48

THE MASS TO ME
*and how they had come to recognize him
in the breaking of bread. – Luke 24:35*

I grew up in a Sunday Mass-going household. Masses were lengthy, boring and irrelevant that I found myself complaining. High Masses made me anything but high. There were more important matters to spend time on, but I was obliged and felt obliged.

When I became an adult, each Mass became an escape from the chaos of daily grind, opium to run away from problems. I needed it to break free.

Then Jesus happened in my life. The Mass grew on me — its importance and relevance. Today, I go to Mass every day. My daily schedule is structured around it.

The boredom I used to experience at Mass has turned to peace. It is my spiritual refreshment in the midst of chaos. It's where I get my needed inspiration.

Mass miraculously stretches my time, making it possible for me to do daily tasks more wisely. I gain wisdom that becomes apparent when senseless decisions are reduced to a minimum.

In the Mass, more than asking for anything, I offer thanksgiving, knowing that He will bless me with more reasons to keep going. *Rene Espinosa (drekki@gmail.com)*

Reflection: "If we only knew how God regards this Sacrifice, we would risk our lives to be present at every single Mass." (St. Padre Pio)

Lord, make me realize what the Eucharist truly is — the source and summit of Christian life, the highest form of prayer and worship.

St. Conrad of Parzham, pray for us.

APRIL 21

FRIDAY

Acts 4:1-12
Psalm 118:1-2, 4, 22-24, 25-27
John 21:1-14

IN JESUS' NAME

It was in the name of Jesus Christ the Nazorean... – Acts 4:10

It was 3 a.m. My mother woke up and she couldn't find my sister, a special child, beside her. She looked all over the house, still no trace of my sister. Fear and nervousness crippled her body. Confused and didn't know what to do, she closed her eyes and prayed hard: "In Jesus' name, please keep my daughter safe from harm." A few minutes later, she saw a security guard in front of our house with my sister.

A prayer is even more powerful if we pray "in Jesus' name." In fact, according to the *Catechism of the Catholic Church,* "Our prayer... has access to the Father only if we pray "in the name" of Jesus" (ccc2664). In this way, we also pray with His authority. Jesus assured us in His last words to His apostles that "All authority in heaven and on earth has been given to Me" (Matthew 28:18). And according to John 14:14, "If you ask anything of me in my name, I will do it."

Pastor John MacArthur, in his book, *The Upper Room,* said that by praying in Jesus' name, we are submitting ourselves to the will of God. I'm also reminded by this Bible verse through a billboard along EDSA that says, "[Jesus] I am the Way, the Truth and the Life. No one comes to the Father except through me" (John 14:6). *Gracious B. Romero (graciousromero@gmail.com)*

Reflection: Have we already realized the extraordinary strength and power which comes in praying through Jesus' mighty name?

Father God, reveal Yourself to us in everything that we do. Let Your will be done in every aspect of our lives, in Jesus' mighty name. Amen.

St. Anselm, bishop and doctor of the Church, pray for us.

BOLDNESS FOR CHRIST

Acts 4:13-21
Psalm 118:1, 14-15,
16-18, 19-21
Mark 16:9-15

"It is impossible for us not to speak about what we have seen and heard."
– Acts 4:20

I've learned that when we try to know Christ deeper, we eventually find ourselves discovering who He really is. He cured the sick, He performed miracles, He loved the lost, and most of all, He sacrificed His life to save mankind.

Now, try to imagine yourself being friends with a superhero like Jesus. It would be really hard not to passionately talk about him, right? That's why Peter and John said, "It is impossible for us not to speak about what we have seen and heard."

The boldness of Peter and John in the First Reading is something we need to imitate as we journey in getting to know Christ. Not only does He deserve all the praise and glory for everything He is and what He has done, but most importantly, because the world needs to know Christ.

Let's pray for the same boldness Peter and John had. Even though they were perceived as uneducated and ordinary men, they didn't miss out on the chance to spread the word about God's goodness. *Erika Mendoza (epaulmendoza@gmail.com)*

Reflection: Grab every opportunity to share your encounters with Christ.

Lord, teach me to be bold just like Peter and John.

FOOTPRINTS

Every day they devoted themselves to meeting together in the temple area and to breaking bread in their homes…
– Acts 2:46

Acts 2:42-47
Psalm 118:2-4, 13-15, 22-24
1 Peter 1:3-9
John 20:19-31

Second Sunday of Easter

At Coron, Palawan, we were going home late in the afternoon from Kayangan Lake, the most serene place I have ever been to. On our way back, another group wanted to view the lake, but the island's indigenous caretakers prevented them from going up the lake. They said that the birds were already sleeping and should not be disturbed. They said that has been their way to preserve the ecosystem. Their ancestors left them with good footprints to follow.

The Holy Mass is one footprint that Jesus left for us to appreciate. Try this prescription from Fr. Bob McConaghy:

• As the priest marches toward the altar, spot a person you feel the Holy Spirit tells you to pray for;

• As the priest kisses the relic at the altar table, choose a saint to help you intercede.

• During offertory, be thankful.

A tradition like the Mass is very beautiful. It is beautiful because the feet that made the footprints are beautiful. *Rolly España (rollyespana53@gmail.com)*

Reflection: Grace will flow out of the sacrament of the Holy Eucharist. Mercy beyond what is needed will follow.

Father, Your grace is sufficient for me. I boast only of Your goodness and love.

St. George, martyr, patron of England, pray for us.

Acts 4:23-31
Psalm 2:1-3, 4-7, 7-9
John 3:1-8

ABOVE ALL ELSE

"Sovereign Lord, maker of heaven and earth and the sea and all that is in them…" – Acts 4:24

"Jesus, embrace her, please," I pleaded between Hail Marys and commands for any ungodly spirit to go away. Right after we finished a small prayer gathering, a friend of mine acted out differently. She wanted to bolt out of the place. She bawled and said she heard horrifying voices. I asked our co-servants to pray the rosary while four of us talked to and prayed over her. She made faces, wailed and struggled against us. It was a long and taxing experience.

Holding on to Jesus for strength, I called to Him in a personal way. "Jesus, we can't do this without You. Please take over. Embrace her. Comfort her. Protect her. You alone have the power over her, Lord. Mama Mary, help us please."

Finally, she rested her head on my shoulder and whispered, "Jesus." Then she fell into a nap. It was over. Thank God!

That experience reminded me that even in our most fearful situation, Jesus emerges victorious. He reigns supreme over anything and anyone else in our world — and even what's beneath and beyond. Jesus is above all else. *Maymay R. Salvosa (christiane. salvosa@gmail.com)*

Reflection: "Your Name is higher. Your Name is greater. All my hope is in You." (from the song "Anchor" by Hillsong)

Jesus, be the Lord of my everything. Even amidst my doubts and hopelessness, I know You are able. Take control, my Lord.

St. Fidelis of Sigmaringen, priest and martyr, pray for us.

1 Peter 5:5-14
Psalm 89:2-3, 6-7, 16-17
Mark 16:15-20

Feast of St. Mark, Evangelist

HOW LOW CAN YOU GO?

"Clothe yourselves with humility in your dealings with one another." – 1 Peter 5:5

I was having a haircut when my barber asked me about my view of a certain politician. I told him that I didn't vote for him because I didn't like him.

I didn't know that someone in the barbershop waiting for his turn heard our conversation. I recognized him as a regular early morning Mass-goer and was an avid supporter of that politician. I was surprised when he butted in on our conversation with an angry comment and started to curse as he defended the politician.

I immediately apologized for offending him with my comment. He pointed his finger at me and tried to pick a fight. I kept my cool and said, "I'm so sorry, sir, but I don't want a fight, especially with you because I respect church people." When he realized that I knew him from church, he slowly lowered his voice and left.

The King of kings and Lord of all left His throne in heaven to show us what humility is about. He was criticized, mocked, and humiliated for our sake. Humility is setting aside who we are and declaring who God is in our lives. *Monty Mendigoria (montymendigoria@yahoo.com)*

Reflection: "Humility is the mother of giants. One sees great things from the valley; only small things from the peak." (G.K. Chesterton)

Lord, teach us to step down from our pedestals and lead a life of humility and peace.

APRIL 26
WEDNESDAY

Acts 5:17-26
Psalm 34:2-3, 4-5, 6-7, 8-9
John 3:16-21

SPREAD THE WORD

When they heard this, they went to the temple early in the morning and taught.
– Acts 5:21

Didache editor Rissa Kawpeng shared with us writers about a conference she attended where she met other Christian writers and publishers. What struck her most, she said, was those who shared the Good News in countries where there was heightened religious persecution. In spite of their circumstance, or maybe because of it, they boldly proclaimed Jesus to others.

This reminded me of *God's Smuggler,* a book narrating the many adventures of Brother Andrew in spreading God's Word in communist Russia in the 1960's. Imprisonment awaited him had he been caught, but the Lord protected him and he survived his mission unscathed.

We don't need to be missionaries and go to an unfamiliar territory to share Jesus' love to others. Right where we are, we can evangelize others. We only need to act on the promptings in our heart. It could be an act of kindness, or saying a prayer or sharing a Bible verse, or inviting someone to a prayer meeting or retreat. Try it. It could be a life-changing moment for the other person, and you as well. *Erwin Roceles (erwin_roceles@yahoo.com)*

Reflection: Get hold of a copy of *God's Smuggler* and be inspired to go out and evangelize!

Lord, give me the strength to overcome any hesitation I have in sharing You with others. As much as You have worked wonders in my life, I pray that others get to experience Your love in an intimate way as well.

St. Pedro de San Jose Betancur, pray for us.

APRIL 27
THURSDAY

Acts 5:27-33
Psalm 34:2, 9, 17-18,
19-20
John 3:31-36

TRUST THE DIRECTOR

*Whoever does accept his testimony
certifies that God is trustworthy.*
– John 3:33

When Leonardo di Caprio gave his speech for winning the Golden Globe Best Actor award for *The Revenant*, he explained that the movie was about trust, and that the best person to give that trust to was their director, Alejandro Gonzales Iñarritu. The movie won Best Director for Iñarritu, and Best Picture for the film.

In the movie of our life, do we trust the Director? Do we trust that He knows the whole script, knows when to put in the sound of happiness, or to shift to the low sound of sadness? Do we think He knows how to highlight the best part of our life's script and how to add in the extras when it looks like it's going nowhere?

Or do we think we are our own best director?

Di Caprio is one of this generation's most popular and critically acclaimed actors and yet he still needs a director. We may become this world's greatest genius or most popular person, but like it or not, we still need a Director.

In the movie of our life, let's choose Jesus as our Director for His other name is The Alpha and the Omega, as well as The Way, the Truth and the Life. We won't find a better One than Him. *Joy Sosoban-Roa (jsosoban@gmail.com)*

Reflection: There are many roads that may beckon, but Jesus is the Way that surely leads to where the best awaits you.

Lord, keep me from directing my own life out of ignorance, fear or greed. Wake me up to the beauty of being guided by You.

St. Louis Mary Grignion de Montfort, pray for us.

APRIL 28
FRIDAY

Acts 5:34-42
Psalm 27:1, 4, 13-14
John 6:1-15

He said this to test him, because he himself knew what he was going to do.
– John 6:6

I don't like "gotcha" questions. These are like surprise pop quizzes that test my knowledge on certain topics in front of other people. Somebody just asked me one a while ago during a conference call. It made me look dumb and I hated it.

But questions have a way of revealing what's truly inside — whether in my brain or in my heart. Great leaders and mentors don't have to know everything but are great in asking questions.

In today's Gospel, the Lord gave Philip a kind of a "gotcha" quiz. Faced with a situation where they needed to feed 5,000 people, Jesus popped a question that revealed the level of his faith. Prior to this, they had already seen Jesus perform miracle upon miracle. Philip's answer reflected that of an honest concern, not an assurance that Jesus had it covered.

So did Philip fail? I don't think that's the point. After that, Jesus performed an amazing miracle in multiplying the loaves. The Lord's question to Philip must've resonated in his heart after these occurrences. His response to Jesus revealed his level of faith and the Lord's actions made it grow.

We encounter daily our own "gotcha" moments. May we maximize its use. *Ariel Driz (adriz77@yahoo.com)*

Reflection: Do you allow yourself to hear the Lord's questions?

Father, thank You for all my gotcha moments. I realize that growth happens when I embrace these times.

APRIL 29
SATURDAY

Acts 6:1-7
Psalm 33:1-2, 4-5, 18-19
John 6:16-21

They wanted to take him into the boat, but the boat immediately arrived at the shore to which they were heading.
– John 6:21

If you live in the south of Metro Manila and commute to Cubao, what do you do?

You find a Cubao bus or jeepney station, right? You find a bus or jeepney with a sign that says "Cubao" in front and on the side of the vehicle, with a person shouting at the top of his lungs, "Cubao! Cubao! Cubao!" And when you approach this barker, what do you ask? "Cubao?"

Friends, life has been showing you many signs. God has been giving you directions. But have you been reading the signs? If you've read them, do you believe them? Have you followed its directions?

Many aren't able to progress in their lives and relationships because they lack trust. Instead of getting on the bus or jeepney and getting on with their lives, they're still waiting at the station, asking, "'Really, Lord?... Cubao?"

Friends, do you want to move forward and achieve your goals? Do you want to "reach the shore?" Take the Lord into your boat. Trust Him. And you will be in your "Cubao" before you know it! Jonathan Yogawin (jyogawin@gmail.com)

Reflection: What is God asking of you? What if you finally trust Him? Like, really! Do it now.

Jesus, I trust in You.

St. Catherine of Siena, virgin and Doctor of the Church, pray for us.

APRIL 30
SUNDAY

Acts 2:14, 22-33
Psalm 16:1-2, 5, 7-8,
9-10, 11
1 Peter 1:17-21
Luke 24:13-35

Third Sunday of Easter

LUNAR ENCOUNTER

With that, their eyes were opened and they recognized him... – Luke 24:31

I have always been enthralled with the full moon. (No, I don't howl when I see one.) A full moon makes me feel like God embraces me and whispers, "I am your sovereign God and I love you."

One summer, my husband and I were in Paris with our three daughters. I was anxious for our safety because of the stories I heard about bad elements lurking around, targeting distracted parents with their kids. So we'd pray the rosary and ask for protection.

We made our way to the Eiffel Tower and arrived there by nightfall. As we emerged from the subway, there it was in all its majestic glory, lit up against the dark sky. But what really gave me goosebumps was the sight of the beautiful glistening full moon right beside the Eiffel Tower. It looked like a postcard! With that, all my anxiety faded away. I knew we would be safe.

Often we allow our problems to overwhelm us and drown us in fear and anxiety. All we need is to encounter God maybe through a song or through nature that will remind us that God is in control. We just have to open our eyes and see that God is present everywhere. *Ronna Singson Ledesma (ronna_ledesma@yahoo.com.ph)*

Reflection: Are you drowning? Open your eyes and see that Jesus is walking beside you on the water.

Lord, thank You for letting me feel Your presence with something as simple as a full moon.

St. Pius V, pope, pray for us.

Genesis 1:26-2:3
Psalm 90:2, 3-4, 12, 13,
14, 16
Matthew 13:54-58
(or John 6:22-29)

Feast of St. Joseph the Worker

REJECTION HURTS

*"A prophet is not without honor except in
his native place and in his own house."*
– Matthew 13:57

I thought that when I grew older, I'd be able to handle rejection better. No such luck. No matter what age, rejection will always be painful. I was already 25 years old when I had a big crush on a pretty girl. I fell in love with her because she had the heart of St. Claire. In a prayer meeting, she had a radar for people who felt the most isolated and unwelcome. In every prayer meeting, she'd search for and sit beside these people who felt unwanted because they were ugly or dirty or filthy. She'd make them feel comfortable. So I courted her all-out. But in the end, she rejected me. Later, I learned why: Because I wasn't ugly.

Just kidding. For some reason, she rejected me. And it hurt like crazy. I wept a bucket of tears.

It hurts when people reject us. Why? Because deep in our soul, we're longing for one thing: acceptance. We're thirsting for someone to recognize our worth, to embrace us "as we are."

Friend, there is Someone who has accepted you — even when you were still in your mother's womb.

God accepts you as you are. And the moment you allow Him to embrace you in your sinfulness, you will have the power to embrace others in their sinfulness. *Bo Sanchez (bosanchez@kerygmafamily.com)*

Reflection: What area of your life have you not accepted yet?

Dearest Lord, help me to be more accepting — not only of others but most especially of myself. Amen.

St. Joseph the worker, pray for us.

Acts 7:51-8:1
Psalm 31:3-4, 6, 7, 8,
17, 21
John 6:30-35

YOU DON'T NEED A SIGN

The crowd said to Jesus: "What sign can you do, that we may see and believe in you? What can you do? – John 6:30

Have you ever seen a street sign that says: *"Bawal Tumawid. Nakamamatay!"* (Do not cross the street, you may die!) There's even a fence and a big overpass for us to know that it's dangerous to cross the street. But what do some people do? They still ignore these signs, find creative ways to destroy the fences, and still foolishly cross these streets.

It's funny that there are times when we ask God for a sign from the biggest to the smallest decisions that we make. A classic example is when we bombard the heavens for signs to point us to our one true love. I'm not saying that God doesn't give signs. He does! Every single day. But more often that not, we ignore them, especially if it's not to our favor.

Friends, instead of looking for signs, isn't it better to just hear God's voice and have a good conversation with Him? If there's uncertainty, especially in difficult moments, let God direct you. Talk to Him in prayer and listen to your heart. In your silent moments, let Him speak to you. *Monching Bueno (ramon_bueno@yahoo.com)*

Reflection: Do you often seek signs from God? Take time today to be at peace with your mind and your heart. Spend some quiet time with the Lord through prayer and let Him speak to your heart.

Father God, forgive us for not trusting You enough. Speak to us every day. Guide us along the way. Amen.

St. Athanasius, bishop and doctor of the Church, pray for us.

MAY 3
WEDNESDAY

1 Corinthians 15:1-8
Psalm 19:2-3, 4-5
John 14:6-14

Feast of Sts. Philip and
James, Apostles

SILENT WITNESS

The heavens declare the glory of God; and the firmament proclaims his handiwork. Not a word nor a discourse whose voice is not heard. – Psalm 19:2, 4

Our home office has a huge window in front of our desk that frames the majestic sky. It's where I often look to for inspiration when I write.

Oftentimes, it's a sunny, clear, blue sky that greets me. It cheers me up. Other times, I see dark clouds rolling in to cover the sun. I see the clouds cover the sun but I know that the sun will win out in the end. When a typhoon comes, the sky is gray and weepy. I know there may be a storm now but it doesn't last forever. At night, the sky is inky black, with hardly any visible stars. But I know that night will give way to the dawn.

Without words, the heavens speak volumes to me.

Most of my service to the Lord involves words — whether written or spoken. Many tell me how my books, articles or talks have impacted them. But more than those, I know that the more powerful witness I can give is the one where no words are spoken or written. When I preach with my life and my actions.

Easy? I'd rather write a 10,000-word essay on the disambiguation of medical abbreviations.

Necessary? Definitely. Otherwise, all my words have no meaning. *Rissa Singson Kawpeng (justbreatherissa@gmail.com)*

Reflection: What do you preach with your life?

Lord, may my life declare Your glory without the need for speech, words or voice.

Sts. Philip and James, Apostles, pray for us.

CHOOSE WHAT YOU EAT

"I am the bread of life." – John 6:48

Acts 8:26-40
Psalm 66:8-9, 16-17, 20
John 6:44-51

In *Kung Fu Panda*, Po, the "dragon warrior," experiences rejection and self-doubts on his first exhausting day of training. To escape the pain of the day's failures, he gobbles all the peaches he can fit into his mouth.

After quietly observing him, the wise Master Oogway interrupts, "I see you eat when you are upset."

I also eat when I am upset. I eat coffee cake, tiramisu or coffee gelato. Or anything sweet. Maybe for you it's pizza, or lots of rice. After the second serving of cake, however, I still feel upset... and bloated.

There are days though that I choose to eat something else. I eat the Bread of Life. I line up, receive Him, and return to my pew. I then just utter, "Have Your way in me." Then I keep my mouth shut. I let Him love me. Before I know it, "the peace that surpasses all understanding" envelopes me. My fears dissolve. My worries crumble. I am full of Life.

Next time you're upset, partake of the Bread of Life. It's not a symbol. It's not a feeling. It's Life Himself in all its fullness.
Marc Lopez (lamblightschool@yahoo.com)

Reflection: How do you see Holy Communion? As a symbol? Or as our Savior Himself?

Jesus, I am hungry. Can You join me for a meal today?

Blessed Michael Giedroyc, pray for us.

DEALING WITH GRIEF

"and I will show him what he will have to suffer for my name." – Acts 9:16

Acts 9:1-20
Psalm 117:1, 2
John 6:52-59

Despite being a writer, I'm always at a loss for words when addressing those who are suffering. I cringe when the best I can muster up is the question, "How are you?" when it's obvious that they are not doing well at all.

So it was extremely helpful when I came across an article written by a mother who had lost her 17-year-old son in a terrible accident. She talked about her heartbreak and how, in her experience, she would prefer people to approach her. She made interesting points such as how she wished she didn't have to hear the phrase "time to move on" from others when she simply wasn't ready yet, or how some people would nervously avoid talking about her son altogether.

"When I speak of his name or relive memories, relive them with me, don't shrink away. If you've never met him, ask me about him. One of my greatest joys is talking about my son," she wrote.

While pain may prolong, valuable memories still exist and help in the healing process. They may be a lesson, a way for us to appreciate what we have, or they can also spark moments of happiness and inspire others who are going through the same experience. *Eleanore Teo (elyo.lee@gmail.com)*

Reflection: How can others help you heal through a crisis?

Heavenly Father, heal me in the light of my suffering and be my instrument of peace.

MAY 6
SATURDAY

Acts 9:31-42
Psalm 116:12-13, 14-15, 16-17
John 6:60-69

WITH HIS BOOTS ON

There was a disciple… completely occupied with good deeds and almsgiving. – Acts 9:36

Eric was the events head of one of Feast Alabang's sessions. He also headed the Creatives Ministry and was always ready and willing to provide the backdrop, props or set needed no matter how difficult it was to make. He was also our main caterer for functions, big or small. He was so kindhearted that the Food Ministry could wheedle big discounts and freebies that he gave for the love of the Lord's hungry servants.

Even if he had a variety of illnesses and had been hospitalized several times, he continued to serve tirelessly. The night before he died, he catered for the wake of a fellow servant's father. When we passed the donation envelope around, I was surprised with the big amount he handed me, I figured it was a big chunk from his earnings that night.

Our community appreciated all his good deeds. At the Mass during his wake, the overflow from the chapel transformed the stairs into a sea of lavender – Feast Alabang servants wearing that year's Lenten Recollection T-shirt to commemorate the major role he played in making the event a success.

Eric died with his boots on, still occupied with God's work.

Lella M. Santiago (lellams88@gmail.com)

Reflection: When it's time to join your Creator, can you show Him a portfolio of your good deeds?

Father, I am Your disciple. Make Your goodness manifest through me.

MAY 7
SUNDAY

Acts 2:14, 36-41
Psalm 23:1-3, 3-4, 5, 6
1 Peter 2:20-25
John 10:1-10

Fourth Sunday of Easter

THE BIGGEST ROOM
"I came so that they might have life and have it more abundantly." – John 10:10

Do you want to know my daily routine, as a family man and Feast builder? Here we go… Prayer and Scripture time at 5:30 a.m. Intercession and workout time (I pray for people while exercising). Cardiovascular training, doing jump-rope or stationary biking for 30 minutes to an hour. My verison of circuit training: power sets of push-ups, pull-ups, lunges and crunches.

Family time follows: daughter Reese's hug and play time, and son Rob's Lesson for the Day sessions. Then it's date time with my wife, Joie. Since her love language is quality time, we do the following: dine and share stories. Plan and pray together. Laugh and cry together. Minister and reach out together.

Then it's mission time: one-to-one discipling; family discipling; giving life-changing inspiration and motivational talks; coaching and counseling; and visualization exercise.

I won't stop growing because I believe that the biggest room in the world is the room for improvement. St. Augustine was right when he said that serving God is the greatest adventure in the world! Wanna live a life of adventure? Immerse yourself in Jesus' fullness of life! *Obet Cabrillas (obetcab@yahoo.com /twitter: @daddyobet)*

Reflection: "We are not human beings having a spiritual experience. We are spiritual beings having a human experience." (Pierre Teilhard de Chardin)

Lord, please bless me, so that I can do what You want me to do.

ANY CONCERN?

*"This is because he works for pay and
has no concern for the sheep."*
– John 10:13

She is a senior vice president of a prestigious company. Of course, with her position comes an attractive salary package. She is efficient and is an effective asset whose expertise is bringing their company to the top of its industry.

But even though she reports early for work, she goes home late at night every single day. She can be disapproving because she easily gets irritated or mad when things are not done the way she wants them. She can be demanding as she wants to get things done at the shortest time possible. She even calls and asks her staff to do something even during lunchbreak or beyond working hours. Unsympathetic, one may say, but if someone is sick, she would still ask that person to deliver the job. She shows no concern for anyone in her workplace. She just lives to work.

I'm glad our God is not like that. He is always concerned about us. He knows our needs and takes care of us. He teaches us and equips us to live life to its fullest. He blesses us with His goodness and mercy. *Sol Saura (sol_saura@yahoo.com)*

Reflection: How do you show concern for the people around you?

O God, please forgive us for the times we are not sensitive to the needs of others. Grant us the grace to be like Jesus to them.

St. Peter of Tarentaise, pray for us.

MAY 9
TUESDAY

Acts 11:19-26
Psalm 87:1-3, 4-5, 6-7
John 10:22-30

GIVING IT UP

"My sheep hear my voice; I know them, and they follow me." – John 10:27

I remember the last job I had back in 2012 before serving full-time in ministry. One day, my boss told me that we will market a men's magazine website.

I had my apprehensions because it was a website that contained material that went against my belief and conviction as a Christian. But not wanting to market the site meant giving up many things: our family's main source of income, a six-figure salary, job and financial security, employee benefits, and more. As my doubts got stronger, God's voice became louder. I felt so much peace when I resigned.

Looking back after almost four years, my life has never been better. I now live the life that God has called me to. The income that I have lost, God has returned a hundredfold not only financially but in many different ways.

Following Jesus means listening to His call. It may be difficult sometimes. It may entail giving up some things in your life. But God promises the reward of eternal life — a life lived to the fullest. *Joel Saludares (joelsaludares@yahoo.com)*

Reflection: Are you ready to follow what God is telling you to do?

Father in heaven, give us the grace to always listen to Your voice and follow what You want us to do.

St. John of Avila, pray for us.

MAY 10

Acts 12:24-13:5
Psalm 67:2-3, 5, 6, 8
John 12:44-50

THE POWER OF PRAYER

They laid hands on them... – Acts 13:3

It was sometime in July 1972 when our landlady invited my dad, Paul Aguas, to a prayer meeting. Dad accepted.

At one point, the American missionary who was leading the prayer meeting asked Dad if he wanted to be prayed over. My father said yes.

The missionary laid hands on Dad.

In a flash, Dad saw his entire life and realized how selfish he was. He prayed, "Lord, I do not love You. Help me to love You." He went away from that prayer meeting a changed man.

That was the start of my dad's ministry. He eventually became a world-renowned preacher and an international leader of the Catholic Charismatic Renewal Movement.

His life was changed. For 21 years, he traveled all over the world, sharing the Good News, which, in turn, touched the lives of thousands of people. This happened because of a man who laid hands over him and prayed for him.

That's the power of one prayer. *Matthew Aguas (jojangaguas@yahoo.com)*

Reflection: Can your prayers actually reach out and touch another person? Let me reassure you it will.

Use me, Lord, as Your instrument to reach out and touch someone. Change their life as You have changed mine.

Acts 13:13-25
Psalm 89:2-3, 21-22, 25, 27
John 13:16-20

MESSENGERS

"My brothers, if one of you has a word of exhortation for the people, please speak."
– Acts 13:15

A few years ago, I joined a contemplative prayer group. Here, I learned to seek the Lord's guidance and to intercede for others. I was the youngest and only single member of this group. I was blessed by these prayerful, mature and wise people who became my spiritual parents.

Once, our leader, *Tita* Ana, and a fellow member, *Tita* Glo, prayed over me. *Tita* Ana shared this with me: She saw in a vision my late father and me, and I held out to him a pair of slippers saying, "Dad, *sige na, lakad ka na* (Go on and walk, Dad)." In another vision, *Tita* Ana saw Mom and me in our living room, holding hands as we picked up broken pieces of pottery together. These images speak of God healing our unforgiveness with the gift of gratitude, she said. I cried tears of thanksgiving and joy that day for God had spoken to me His message of healing, hope, love and of letting go through these women.

Do you sense that the Lord wants to speak through you? Be His messenger. No need to fear or worry — He Himself will give you the words to say. *Dina Pecaña (dina.p@shepherdsvoice.com.ph)*

Reflection: "On the other hand, one who prophesies does speak to human beings, for their building up, encouragement, and solace." (1 Corinthians 14:3)

Holy Spirit, may my words be acceptable and pleasing to You as You hear their sound and know the intent behind them. Amen. (An excerpt from a prayer by Roy Lessin)

St. Ignatius of Laconi, pray for us.

Acts 13:26-33
Psalm 2:6-7, 8-9, 10-11
John 14:1-6

MEANINGFUL WORK

"I am the way and the truth and the life. No one comes to the Father except through me." – John 14:6

My work for the Lord got me involved in various tasks and activities. I work for a company that has ministries for the poor. But my work is predominantly in events and media. In recent years, I fell in love with the art of coaching so I trained in it. Even before I completed the course, I already started coaching people.

I've also written my first book and self-published it. I have another one in the pipeline and one more that's almost finished. I started my online business, and while doing that, I continue to serve the Lord in the music ministry. But even with a very busy schedule, I never forget two important things in my life — to give time to God and my family. They are the primary reasons why I do what I do. By becoming a better me, I help my family by providing for their needs and giving the best for them. The better version of me also blesses the world with my talents and expertise.

We are all pilgrims and our life should lead us to eternity with the Father. With Jesus as our way, everything we accomplish in this world becomes meaningful as they lead us to the Father. *Edwin Marcelo (imboodoo@yahoo.com)*

Reflection: Let the things you do bring you closer to Jesus.

Be glorified, Lord, in everything that I do. Be my Way so that I only go where it pleases You.

Acts 13:44-52
Psalm 98:1, 2-3, 3-4
John 14:7-14

Memorial of Our Lady of Fatima

ACCEPT ACCEPTANCE

Both Paul and Barnabas spoke out boldly and said, "It was necessary that the word of God be spoken to you first, but since you reject it and condemn yourselves as unworthy of eternal life, we now turn to the Gentiles." – Acts 13:46

When I started preaching God's word onstage, I heard a lot of people question why I was chosen for that privilege. People who stood up against me sounded like a noisy gong because they didn't like me. Well, even if it hurt, I could understand them because I had a murky past and didn't fit the mold of an altar boy preacher.

I used a lot of my time and energy to win my detractors' approval but I always ended up heartbroken. I'd still be rejected.

Eventually, I focused on reaching out to people who didn't judge me, and amazingly, I was accepted with open arms. Experiencing this acceptance freed me to grow more and helped me become a better preacher and servant of God.

Decide right now to let go of the opinion of people who reject you and put you down. Focus on the encouragement of loving people who truly accept you for who you are. *JPaul Hernandez (jpaulmh@yahoo.com)*

Reflection: "Everyone has inside of him a piece of good news. The good news is that you don't know how great you can be! How much you can love! What you can accomplish! And what your potential is!" (Anne Frank)

Jesus, thank You for the unconditional love that You have for me. I surrender to its power because I know it's the only force in this world that can truly change my life. Amen.

Acts 6:1-7
Psalm 33:1-2, 4-5, 18-19
1 Peter 2:4-9
John 14:1-12

Fifth Sunday of Easter

SOMEONE SEES YOUR TEARS

"Do not let your hearts be troubled…"
John 14:1

After countless vomits and visits in the bathroom during the weekend, I suddenly burst in tears. I was exhausted, my tummy was searing in pain, and my dizziness almost knocked me unconscious. I wanted to rest. A real rest where I couldn't feel any of that pain anymore.

As I cried, I felt someone wiping away my tears. When I opened my eyes, I saw that it was my close friend. He said nothing, but the love in his eyes assured me that everything's going to be alright.

It calmed me down, and taught me something else.

When we're in pain, we tend to close our eyes and turn our back from the things that hurt. In the process, we think that we are on our own. But God sees our tears. He is concerned with our concerns. Maybe we're just too absorbed by what we are going through that we can't feel His touch, His embrace.

A few days and a deepened hope later, I got well. Indeed, with God at my side, there's no doubt that everything will be alright. *Maymay R. Salvosa (christiane.salvosa@gmail.com)*

Reflection: "So we're not giving up… Even though on the outside it often looks like things are falling apart on us, on the inside, where God is making new life, not a day goes by without his unfolding grace" (2 Corinthians 4:16-17, MSG).

Strengthen my hope, O God! I put my faith in You. Amen.

St. Matthias, Apostle, pray for us.

MAY 15
MONDAY

Acts 14:5-18
Psalm 115:1-2, 3-4, 15-16
John 14:21-26

LEAD SOMEONE TO JESUS TODAY

... where they continued to proclaim the Good News. – Acts 14:7

I know a couple from the north of Manila who wanted to bring some of their relatives to a prayer gathering. However, these relatives live in the south of Manila. They knew that it would not be practical to bring them to their prayer group that meets in the north. So they brought their relatives to our prayer meeting in Alabang. They traveled at least 30 kilometers and endured several hours of traffic so they can personally accompany them. They stayed till the end of the prayer meeting, not minding the long travel going back to Quezon City. Their relatives have been regular attendees since then.

You might have witnessed or heard of similar stories. God will meet us where we are. However, as Jesus' followers, it is also our role to bring people to where they can meet God.

Evangelization requires our time, effort and a lot of patience. It's challenging but it is our duty as Jesus Christ's followers.

How "far" would you go to evangelize? *Alvin Fabella (alvinfabella@yahoo.com)*

Reflection: When was the last time you led someone to Jesus?

Lord Jesus, I pray that I may have the courage to evangelize. I ask for Your grace to be willing to sacrifice so that more people may encounter You in their lives.

St. Isidore the farmer, pray for us.

Acts 14:19-28
Psalm 145:10-11, 12-13, 21
John 14: 27-31

BECAUSE OF LOVE

"Peace I leave with you; my peace I give to you. Not as the world gives do I give it to you. Do not let your hearts be troubled or afraid." – John 14:27

Last year, my wife decided to resign from her job.

It was tough.

She was actually working for a good company, with a good boss, and a good team. She was on the verge of a promotion and a salary increase.

But still, she decided to be a stay-at-home mom to spend more time with our baby.

Even if there were more offers after she expressed her resignation, she had inner peace.

She was afraid, but she remained trusting — that God will work out everything.

There are difficult decisions that we need to make in our life.

But whatever decision we make, as long as it is done out of love and because of love, God's peace will rest on us.

So no need to be troubled or afraid. Just trust and just love, and surely, peace will reign. *Paolo Galia (pgalia@gmail.com)*

Reflection: Are all the things that you're doing now done because of love?

Dear Lord, help me in my decisions. May they all be motivated by love so that Your peace will be upon me.

St. Margaret of Cortona, pray for us.

Acts 15:1-6
Psalm 122:1-2, 3-4, 4-5
John 15:1-8

ASK, WAIT, RECEIVE

"Ask for whatever you want and it will be done for you." – John 15:7

A year ago, I was restless. There were many doors before me, and though I knew my destination — towards God — the paths that lead to that door varied. I was waiting for something that lay beyond my control. I was waiting for the answer to a question that I couldn't even voice out.

But God's voice was clear: "Love. Just love. Just work. Do your work with love. I can see everything. I know everything. I know what you do, and I know what you have to do. So just go do what you do best."

So I just loved. And I served. The answer came when I least expected it. It actually felt like a sudden blow that took my breath away. Just when I'd already let go of the very thing I was praying for, it was handed to me on a golden platter.

God answers our prayers when we least expect Him to. Sometimes He answers immediately, but in some cases, He answers when the dream has died down, or when the heart has settled, or when we've learned to let go. God thinks He's funny like that. We wait and wait for our own version of His answer. But His version is so awesome, it blows our mind away. *Karren Renz Seña (karren.s@shepherdsvoice.com.ph)*

Reflection: Are you waiting for answers? Just love while you wait.

Dear God, we wait in joyful hope for Your best version of the answers to our prayers. We are ready to receive, Lord! In Jesus' name. Amen.

REBUILDING RUINS

"... from its ruins I shall rebuild it and raise it up again." – Acts 15:16

Acts 15:7-21
Psalm 96:1-2, 2-3, 10
John 15:9-11

One day I received this letter: "I just lost my dad, lost my boyfriend of four years, and my business is going downhill. I am lost. I have faith in God but why is this happening to me? He has forgotten me."

After a month, she wrote again: "I was so distraught, and felt like the universe was on my back so I decided to attend the The Feast. It felt funny because it seemed that the preacher was talking to me alone! He said that we are saved and healed by the grace of God. That I will climb up from that pit where I am, and then I will believe He loves me."

This woman continued to attend The Feast every week. At every meeting, her faith grew by leaps and bounds. "My devastation and depression soon turned to joy and hope," she wrote adding, "I held my head high because I knew that God will not allow me to stay ruined but raise me up again to glorify Him."

Indeed, God's grace will raise us from rock bottom in His perfect time. *Chelle Crisanto (ellehcmaria@gmail.com)*

Reflection: Yes, I am lost, but the Lord has found me. I will not despair.

I am often down in the pits with my problems, Lord. Hold my hand and lift me up from where I am. Give me the grace to stand strong, loving You no matter what.

St. John I, pope and martyr, pray for us.

"I no longer call you slaves…I have called you friends…" – John 15:15

Acts 15:22-31
Psalm 57:8-9, 10, 12
John 15:12-17

Do you realize what being God's friend means? I've got rich and famous, powerful and popular friends — celebrities in showbiz, politics, business, and yes, even in church.

I was a nobody. But now I can say I became somebody. And one main reason is because of these "big" friends of mine. I got big breaks because of them. Most of the time, just being with them makes me instantly big, too.

Yet, no big shot on this planet or in the entire universe can even come close to the bigness of God. He created and owns the universe. Even the richest, most powerful, most famous person on earth is a speck of dust to Him. And this big God calls you *friend!*

Chances are, the big shot you brag about as your friend doesn't really know you, or doesn't really care for you, or won't stand by you in times of failure, trouble or shame. But Jesus gave His life for you while you were a sinner and a nobody. That's a true Big Friend who, in your smallness, loves you.

I am a friend of God… And that makes me big! *Alvin Barcelona*
(apb_ayo@yahoo.com)

Reflection: Are you feeling small? Come to Jesus, your One True Big Friend who will truly love you big-time!

Lord, thank You that in my sinfulness, in my smallness, in my nothingness, You see me and You truly love me. Thank You for making me big in Your loving eyes. Amen.

St. Theophilus of Corte, pray for us.

MAY 20
SATURDAY

Acts 16:1-10
Psalm 100:1-2, 3, 5
John 15:18-21

WHAT'S YOUR NAME?

*"And they will do all these things to you
on account of my name." – John 15:21*

According to an article of Wilson Lee Flores in *The Philippine Star* some years back, some of the most powerful businessmen in the Philippines are Lopez, Cojuangco, Zobel de Ayala, Pangilinan and Aboitiz. They are not only wealthy but said to be able to exert influence on political and government leaders as well. Imagine, if your surname was any of the aforementioned, I am sure landing a job will be a breeze unlike if you were the child of Juan de la Cruz. Doors will open wide for you. HR may even waive a lot of their requirements. All these happen just because you are the child of some big shot.

You are no different from them. Yes, you may not be the COO (child of the owner) but you are a COG (child of God).

You are the child of the King of kings, the Lord of lords!

You have a Father who is more powerful than any of these men.

Never ever forget your identity. *Reng Morelos (norina morelos@gmail.com)*

Reflection: "We know what we are but not what we may be." (William Shakespeare)

Lord, may I always be aware of my identity as Your child so that I may become a person after Your own heart.

FOREVER PARENT

"I will not leave you orphans."
– John 14:18

Acts 8:5-8, 14-17
Psalm 66:1-3, 4-5, 6-7,
16, 20
1 Peter 3:15-18
John 14:15-21

Sixth Sunday of Easter

"So we're now orphans," I thought to myself, as we prepared for the wake of my father in January 2016.

I'm writing this reflection three months after his death. And yes, I could feel the void that his and my mother's passing away had created in my life.

It's different when you go home and they're no longer there to welcome you. There's no one to give you a blessing before you leave the house and no one to check on you if you've reached your destination safely.

It's been pretty sad the first few months (and years, in the case of my mother), and my six sisters and I can only comfort one another — through photos with our parents, through remembrances of happy times, through get-togethers.

But there comes a time when one really has to face the fact that these things cannot fill the void. There comes a time when one has to accept that the loss cannot be replaced. There comes a time when the best thing to do is surrender to the only One who is our eternal parent: God. *Tess V. Atienza (theresa.a@shepherdsvoice.com.ph)*

Reflection: What is God's role in your life?

Dearest God, may my life be filled with Your presence each and every day.

St. Cristobal Magallanes and Companions, pray for us.

Acts 16:11-15
Psalm 149:1-2, 3-4, 5-6, 9
John 15:26-16:4

DREAM COME TRUE
The Lord opened her heart to pay attention... – Acts 16:14

Woohoo! I was approved for an insurance shoot as an on-cam talent! But wait, I've already agreed to serve for free at a certain event on the same date.

I chose the shoot. After making that decision, I got a call from a different agent saying I was approved for a fast-food shoot with a bigger budget, also on the same date. It broke my heart to turn it down.

To make everything even more confusing, I received a message that the budget for the insurance shoot was slashed and the shoot date was rescheduled.

I paused. I prayed to God to open my heart so I could pay attention to what He was telling me.

I was greedy. God told me to serve at the event. I did. I surrendered the two projects. I was at peace.

Finally, my heart was in the right place. God orchestrated everything. God wanted my character to be fit to receive those blessings. After realigning my priorities to put Him first, I received more projects that enabled me to shoot three TV commercials and three online advertisements without any conflicts in my schedules. *Carlo Lorenzo (carloflorenzo@yahoo.com)*

Reflection: Are there opportunities coming to you but challenges seem to block the way? Pause. Pray. What is God telling you?

Lord God, open our hearts to help us pay attention to what You are telling us.

St. Rita of Cascia, pray for us.

Acts 16:22-34
Psalm 138:1-2, 2-3, 7-8
John 16:5-11

FIRE STARTER

"Believe in the Lord Jesus and you and your household will be saved."
– Acts 16:31

My nephew was a reluctant Christian when my husband and I started mentoring him in his career. We shared how God demonstrated His blessings upon us and invited him to join us every Sunday at The Feast, our community gathering at the Philippine International Convention Center, to discover for himself how he will also be blessed.

He came every Sunday and even brought friends. When he resigned as an employee and ventured into business, he brought his employees with him. He then started to organize marathons and he would begin the events with a full band leading the worship. He would donate the proceeds to ministries for the poor.

Being on fire with the Spirit, he convinced his parents — old as they were — to get married in church because he firmly believed in God's blessings. He witnessed to his brothers and sister about the blessings from his personal encounters with Jesus. The Lord put a fire in his heart and he spread it to his household, friends and business. And the Lord honored his heart by prospering him. *Donna España (donna.espana@yahoo.com)*

Reflection: "A true disciple is constantly ready to share the love of Jesus with others and this can happen unexpectedly and in any place." (Pope Francis)

Lord, let your Holy Spirit work through me so I can reach out to those around me.

St. Gregory VII, pray for us.

MAY 24
WEDNESDAY

Acts 17:15, 22-18:1
Psalm 148:1-2, 11-12,
13, 14
John 16:12-15

WHAT LOVE CAN DO
*"We should like to hear you on this some
other time." – Acts 17:32*

"I don't know what to do anymore.
I'm hopeless!"

My friend cried inside the coffee shop. Just a few minutes after the office hours started, she was already sobbing in front of her computer. Then I received an internal message from her, "Can we talk?"

We weren't that close. We would go out once in while but that was it. She thought I was the religious kind because I'd invite her to Mass or prayer meetings. But she would always say, "Next time." So I was surprised when she opened up to me. She had hit rock bottom with a breakup and a financial problem. I listened to her until she calmed down. Her ending question startled me. "Can I join you at Mass tonight?"

She did. She also attended our prayer meeting. And long after I left that job, I learned that her relationship with God continues to grow.

I realized one thing: People will reject teachings and sermons, but they can never resist love. Once they experience Jesus in us, it's impossible for them not to come home to Him. Love has the power to win people back to God. *Maymay R. Salvosa (christiane.salvosa@gmail.com)*

Reflection: "We have been sent to inspire courage, to support and to lead others to Jesus." (Pope Francis)

Teach us to love, Jesus. Grant us the grace to never give up on the people we love. Amen.

St. Mary Magdalene de Pazzi, pray for us.

MAY 25
THURSDAY

Acts 18:1-8
Psalm 98:1, 2-3, 3-4
John 16:16-20

MOURNING TO MORNING

"You will grieve, but your grief will become joy." – John 16:20

I saw in my Facebook page a group called "Mourning to Morning." What a beautiful catchword!

I don't know the group but it seems a good description of how we, Christians, should handle frustrations, defeats and problems. While we mourn our situations, we should look forward to "mornings" which signify a new day, a new hope.

A few years back, my overseas work contract abruptly ended because of a change in management. I was not bitter, but I was saddened of this development in my career. I had lost substantial earning capacity.

I kept my faith in the Lord. I held on to His word that He is the "God who richly provides us with all things for our enjoyment" (1 Timothy 6:17). I was not able to get a job immediately after I went home, but this gave our family more bonding time after years of being away. We went to beaches and islands, explored mountains and volcanoes, and toured many places. Meanwhile, consulting jobs came in and God prospered us.

God turned my sadness into joy! *Danny Tariman (dtariman.loj@gmail.com)*

Reflection: "Rejoice in the Lord always. I shall say it again: rejoice! Have no anxiety at all, but in everything, by prayer and petition, with thanksgiving, make your requests known to God." (Philippians 4:4,6)

Lord Jesus, thank You for all the blessings. I pray that You will meet all my needs, and even my dreams, for my enjoyment.

St. Bede the Venerable, priest and doctor of the Church, pray for us.

Acts 18:9-18
Psalm 47:2-3, 4-5, 6-7
John 16:20-23

Memorial of St. Philip Neri, priest

FOOLS FOR CHRIST

"Do not be afraid. Go on speaking, and do not be silent, for I am with you." – Acts 18:9-10

I have three spiritual communities that give me strength. One is the Light of Jesus that allows me to write about God's blessings, healings and miracles in this devotional you are reading. They have many other publications that bless millions of people as they continue to speak of God's love for us. They also have The Feasts that provide a sacred space for the unchurched. Their mercy ministries are loudspeakers of God's love for the least, the last and the lost.

Second is the Regina Rosarii Contemplative Association, lay partner of the contemplative-in-action Dominican Sisters of the Regina Rosarii. Theirs is a story of miraculous growth. The founding sisters could not contain their message of being still and silent in order to know God more.

Third is the Couples for Christ where I am in the ministry of the Handmaids of the Lord. Some of them were introduced to God because some believers couldn't help but share their conversion.

All these communities came into being because of their "foolishness" for Jesus. No matter what they go through, they don't give up for they know God is with them. *Grace Princesa (grprincesa@yahoo.com)*

Reflection: As we continue to spread the Good News to the ends of the earth, God remains with us and protects us as He has promised.

God, my Shield, may I never be afraid to be a fool for You to the ends of the earth, reassured that no one will be able to harm me.

St. Philip Neri, priest, pray for us.

MAY 27
SATURDAY

Acts 18:23-28
Psalm 47:2-3, 8-9, 10
John 16:23-28

THE BOOK FOR ME

He was an authority on the Scriptures.
– Acts 18:24

There is a Christian children's song that has the following lyrics: "The B-I-B-L-E, yes that's the book for me. I stand alone on the Word of God, the B-I-B-L-E!" I remember singing it when I was a child, and now, as a mom, I sing it with my kids. It's a simple song but it has a deep meaning — it reminds us of the importance of God's Word as revealed through Holy Scripture.

Sadly though, many Catholics — myself included — sometimes forget the importance of reading the Bible and studying the Scriptures. We prioritize the things of the world over God's Word. We busy ourselves with Facebook and don't face His Book. We are at a loss when Christians from other denominations quote Bible verses from memory. We do not know the scriptural basis for our rich Catholic beliefs and traditions.

This need not be the status quo. It's never too late to study Scriptures! Reading devotionals like *Didache, Companion* and *Sabbath* is one way to get started. Let's ask the Holy Spirit to help us as we dig into God's Word every day. *Tina Santiago Rodriguez (trulyrichandblessed@gmail.com)*

Reflection: "Ignorance of Scripture is ignorance of Christ." (Saint Jerome)

Come, Holy Spirit. Fill my heart with love for God's Word.

St. Augustine of Canterbury, bishop, pray for us.

Acts 1:1-11
Psalm 47:2-3, 6-7, 8-9
Ephesians 1:17-23
Matthew 28:16-20

Solemnity of the Ascension of the Lord

PROMISE FULFILLED

"... to wait for 'the promise of the Father about which you have heard me speak.'"
– Acts 1:4

"God will use you and your hands to bring hope, love and compassion. You'll bring these to strangers to win the world," said Bro. Walter, a foreign missionary, while he pointed his finger at Armie, singling her out from among the Feast attendees. A week before that, Armie asked the Lord to confirm if her decision to work as a physical therapist in the U.S. was His will. Everything was set but she feared starting a new life alone. When she heard Bro. Walter's prophecy, she felt peace and flew to the U.S.

But she started to doubt again when her employer sent her back to the Philippines and told her to wait until they had processed her working visa extension. After two months, she went back to the U.S. and new problems arose: delay in the release of her license, shortage of funds, and frustrations in her work. But God was merciful and sent her lifelines.

Armie has been working as a therapist for several years now, using her hands to bring hope, love and comfort to strangers who are broken physically and otherwise, just as the Lord told her. When God speaks, rest assured that He will fulfill what He promises. We just need to wait and trust. *Judith Concepcion (svp_jmc@yahoo.com)*

Reflection: "So shall my word be that goes forth from my mouth; it shall not return to me void, but shall do my will, achieving the end for which I sent it." *(Isaiah 55:11)*

When clouds of doubt overwhelm me, increase my faith, Lord.

Venerable Pierre Toussaint, pray for us.

MAY 29
MONDAY

Acts 19:1-8
Psalm 68:2-3, 4-5, 6-7
John 16:29-33

NO MORE FEAR, JESUS IS HERE

"In the world you will have trouble, but take courage, I have conquered the world." – John 16:33

We live in a world where fear and terror are everywhere. We feel unsafe not just outside but even inside our homes. Because of this, we are paralyzed and we feel helpless.

Do you want to live life in fear or are you ready for courageous living?

This is no time for cowardice and half-heartedness. We need a new generation of courageous men and women to take on the challenge of living not for the world but for the Lord, living life in its fullness.

We need courageous men and women to stand up for what is right at home, in the workplace, in our communities, and to be followers of Jesus to conquer the world with love.

This may sound impossible but take courage because you are not alone in this battle. This is what Easter is all about. Remember that Jesus Christ has already conquered sin and death. God has already won for us. Have no more fear because Jesus is here. *JC Libiran (JCLibiran@ymail.com)*

Reflection: "Be strong and courageous. Do not be frightened, and do not be dismayed, for the Lord your God is with you wherever you go." (Joshua 1:9)

Jesus, You are my shield and protection. I am courageous not because of my strength but because I have You by my side. Amen.

MAY 30
TUESDAY

Acts 20:17-27
Psalm 68:10-11, 20-21
John 17:1-11

CALL ON YOUR FATHER

*"and everything of mine is yours and
everything of yours is mine."*
– John 17:10

As I write this reflection, my son Luca is just over a month old.

Since I'm a motivational speaker, I'm so excited to hear him speak his first word.

Something in me wants his first word to be "Papa," but I don't want to take away my wife's joy.

Right now, what comes out of his mouth are just murmurs and giggles. But even if those are just unintelligible sounds, my wife and I revel in them. I could only imagine how it would feel when I finally hear him say, "Mama" — and especially when he calls me "Papa." That would mean the world to me!

I often imagine the days when he'd finally call on me for his needs. How gladly I would give whatever is good for him!

In the Gospel reading, Jesus was so passionate when He addressed His Father. Did you know that God is excited for you to call Him Father, too? He awaits for you to speak to Him and tell Him your needs. And I can just imagine how excited He is to grant your prayer. Stephen I. Nellas (sinfts@live.com)

Reflection: Talk to your God. Have a heart-to-heart talk with your Father. Tell Him what you feel, what you need, or even just how your day went. He longs to speak with you.

Abba, You are my Father and Your eyes are upon me always. May You never take Your presence away from me.

St. Joan of Arc, pray for us.

TRUE LOVE

Let love be sincere. – Romans 12:9

Zephaniah 3:14-18
(or Romans 12:9-16)
Isaiah 12:2-3, 4, 5-6
Luke 1:39-56

Feast of the Visitation of the
Blessed Virgin Mary

"I married her soul, her character, and she's the only woman who will continue to fulfill my dreams." This was the declaration of a gentleman when asked if he ever thought of leaving his girlfriend.

In 2015, the social network carried the love story of a beautiful ex-model and her handsome boyfriend. The woman figured in a fire accident. Sixty-five percent of her body, including her face, was burned and she lost the fingers and thumb on her right hand. Instead of leaving, her boyfriend quit his job and took care of her. They remained a strong couple in love in spite of her disfigured appearance.

Men naturally choose the beautiful, sexy and intelligent woman. When her body becomes fat and saggy, her facial lines appear, and her character flaws surface, men find a reason to find a new partner.

How much do we love God? Is it only up to the point where His commandments are easy to follow and everything seems to be going our way? We may be fickle with our love for God, but His love for us is unconditional. He will remain with us forever in spite of our disfigured character. *Marie Franco (mariefranco_pie@yahoo.com)*

Reflection: There are five languages of love – words, touch, gifts, presence and service. How do you express your love to your significant other? How do you show your love to God?

Lord, I am not worthy of Your unconditional love. But the promise of it fills my heart and makes me confident to face life.

St. Mechtildis, pray for us.

Acts 22:30; 23:6-11
Psalm 16:1-2, 5, 7-8,
9-10, 11
John 17:20-26

BE A BLESSING

"I pray not only for these, but also for those who will believe in me through their word…" – John 17:20

I like the story of Elijah and Elisha. Next to Moses, Elijah was the greatest Old Testament prophet. Elisha was his disciple, his understudy. Think Robin to Batman.

One day, the great prophet said to his disciple, "Ask what I shall do for you before I am taken away from you." I love what Elisha replied: "I pray that I get a double portion of your spirit."

How daring! If there were people around who heard Elisha's request, perhaps some of them would have said, "How dare he ask that way? How arrogant!" But Elijah asked for a double portion not so that he would be greater than his teacher. He asked so that he could serve more.

There are times when we pray for something, and then we stop because we feel that it's a selfish prayer. "It's just for me," we think. And so we reject the blessing of God that was supposed to be not for us, but to be used as a blessing for many others.

Here's a key principle you have to understand: God wants to bless others through you, but He has to bless you first. *Bo Sanchez (bosanchez@kerygmafamily.com)*

Reflection: Are you ready to be blessed? Ask God for a double portion of the blessing that you need.

Dearest Lord, please use me as a channel of Your blessings to others. Amen.

St. Justin, martyr, pray for us.

JUNE 2
FRIDAY

Acts 25:13-21
Psalm 103:1-2, 11-12,
19-20
John 21:15-19

EVERYDAY MARTYRDOM

"But when you grow old... someone else will dress you and lead you where you do not want to go." – John 21:18

Nanay Remy was my foster mother when I spent two weeks in the mountains of Batangas on an immersion camp in college. She was a spirited elderly woman, with hair grayed by age, legs toughened by walking, hands calloused by labor, and face wrinkled by smiles. Each day, I accompanied her as she went around to do chores. Among many tasks, I would carry the buckets of water, collect the wood for cooking, and occasionally pound some corn for chicken feed. She was a busy woman, wrapped in the poverty of life.

I couldn't forget how she spoke with much dignity and wisdom. "I'm a native of Pampanga," she said. "I grew up in a well-off family, and I had a future ahead of me. But then I met Banoy, who was a farmer here in Batangas. We fell in love. He uprooted me from that life and brought me here. Many times, I regretted that decision. I wasn't ready for this poor life. I would complain, but I still held on. Now I have no regrets. My family is here, and so my heart is here."

That's martyrdom. It's dying to yourself every day because you know what is really important. *Migs Ramirez (migsramirez.seminars@gmail.com)*

Reflection: Are you comfortable jumping into the unknown, with only God's love to catch you? It's easier said than done.

Mama Mary, saying yes to God wasn't easy but you did it. Teach me to say yes and follow Jesus closer even during my trials.

Sts. Marcellinus and Peter, martyrs, pray for us.

JUNE 3
SATURDAY

Acts 28:16-20, 30-31
Psalm 11:4, 5, 7
John 21:20-25

NOT YOUR WAYS

He received all who came to him, and with complete assurance and without hindrance he proclaimed the Kingdom of God and taught about the Lord Jesus Christ. – Acts 28:31

Paul had always known the Lord wanted him to go to Rome to preach.

But sometimes we interpret God's will for us differently from what He actually has in mind.

Paul must have thought he would go to Rome under pleasant circumstances, "with joy by the will of God and be refreshed together with you" (Romans 15:32). But who would have known that he would indeed reach his destination, not as a preacher but as a prisoner, with hands bound and awaiting trial?

But God's purpose can't be thwarted. Yes, Paul came to Rome as a prisoner. That's how God made it possible for him to get there. But he was also able to fulfill his mission.

In today's reading, we learn that Paul stayed there for two years in a house where people came to see him. And there he was able to preach about Jesus "without hindrance."

Is your life unfolding in a way that's not according to your plan? Don't worry. Yield to God's plan. He knows what's best. His ways are far better than ours. *Rissa Singson Kawpeng (rissa@shepherdsvoice. com.ph)*

Reflection: "For my thoughts are not your thoughts, nor are your ways my ways—oracle of the Lord. For as the heavens are higher than the earth, so are my ways higher than your ways, my thoughts higher than your thoughts." (Isaiah 55:8-9)

Lord, I trust in Your ways.

JUNE 4
SUNDAY

Acts 2:1-11
Psalm 104:1, 24, 29-30, 34
1 Corinthians 12:3-7, 12-13
John 20:19-23

Solemnity of the Pentecost

LANGUAGE OF LOVE

And they were all filled with the Holy Spirit and began to speak in different tongues, as the Spirit enabled them to proclaim… yet we hear them speaking in our own tongues…. – Acts 2:4,11

I thought that knowing English was enough for a preacher since it's the universal language. But there were times when I found it hard to communicate in other countries because of the language barrier. But here's what I noticed. Wherever I go, a hug is a hug. A kiss is a kiss. A handshake is a handshake. A bow is a bow. A smile is a smile. I realized that English is not the universal language — love is.

On this day of Pentecost, the Holy Spirit descended upon the Apostles. They began speaking in their own tongues, speaking differently, yet they understood each other and were more united than ever. Why? Because the Holy Spirit is present. And where the Spirit of the Lord is, there is love. There is unity. There is understanding.

Is there misunderstanding in your home, office or community? Maybe respect, compassion and trust are not present. You may speak the same language or dialect, but unless you love, you will never break the barriers of division, hatred and selfishness.

Just love. And you will understand. Then, hopefully, you will be understood. *Velden Lim (veldenlim@gmail.com)*

Reflection: In your most difficult relationship, what gets in the way? Is it pride? Selfishness? Hatred? Unforgiveness?

Lord, teach me to love even if it doesn't seem fair or even make sense.

JUNE 5
MONDAY

Tobit 1:3; 2:1-8
Psalm 112:1-2, 3-4, 5-6
Mark 12:1-12

CORNERSTONE

"The stone that the builders rejected has become the cornerstone..." – Mark 12:10

In buildings, a cornerstone is the first stone set in laying the foundation. The cornerstone is important because all other stones will be set in reference to this stone. It becomes the base that determines the position of the entire structure. In other words, it is the cornerstone that upholds the whole structure together.

Friend, what is the cornerstone of your life? What is your foundation? On what have you built your life upon? People? Prestige? Power? Popularity? Plans?

All these things will at one point fall, fail and fade away. If you build on worldly things as your foundation, your life will come crumbling down when troubles come.

So let me encourage you: Build your life on the foundation of a Person – Jesus Christ. Establish Him as your Sure Foundation, your Cornerstone on whom the structure of your life stands firm. For in Him all things hold together. He will never be shaken. *Mike Viñas (mikemichaelfcv@yahoo.com, @mikevinas)*

Reflection: "Christ alone, cornerstone. Weak made strong in the Savior's love. Through the storm He is Lord, Lord of all." (from the song "Cornerstone" by Hillsong Worship)

Jesus, You are my Cornerstone. Uphold my life and elevate my existence to be all that You want it to be. Amen.

St. Boniface, bishop and martyr, pray for us.

A GIFT OR A BRIBE?

"Where are your virtuous acts?"
– Tobit 2:14

Tobit 2:9-14
Psalm 112:1-2, 7-8, 9
Mark 12:13-17

I am a media practitioner. I also had the chance to teach Journalism in college where one of the subjects was Media Ethics.

One day, I had to tackle a common test on a journalist's integrity: to discern whether a gift is a bribe.

I told my students that gifts, like sample products, are given for you to be able to try the products so you can determine whether they are what the manufacturers claim them to be, and you can report the truth about your observations.

Now, if you are given not only samples, but tons of the products, those may already be considered as bribes. For them, it's like you are already being paid so much, you can't help but endorse the product already.

Every day we face tests on our integrity— like in today's Gospel where Jesus was asked whether one should pay taxes.

The key to preserving our integrity, as Jesus taught, is to have the grace to stand up for the truth and do what is right. *Chay Santiago (cusantiago@gmail.com)*

Reflection: How true are you in everything you say and do?

Lord, grant me the grace to choose You always, for You are the Truth.

JUNE 7
WEDNESDAY

Tobit 3:1-11, 16-17
Psalm 25:2-3, 4-5, 6,
7, 8-9
Mark 12:18-27

A LESSON ON FIERCE DECISIVENESS

"He is not the God of the dead but of the living." – Mark 12:27

Here's a case study on decisive living. Warning: the following discussion might be highly cerebral for some. Here it is…

> *Eensy weensy spider went up the waterspout.*
> *Down came the rain and washed the spider out.*
> *Out came the sun and dried up all the rain*
> *Now the eensy weensy spider went up the spout again.*

Whoa! What fierce decisiveness! Our courageous spider has to go somewhere important. He accepted the challenge as big as the waterspout. But the waterspout unleashed the momentum of the downpour full strength upon Eensy Weensy.

But he held on. He dug in his heels and clung to dear life. He persisted! Water poured and flowed mightily… until it was over.

"Out came the sun and dried up all the rain."

Resilience paid off! Eensy Weensy Spider went up the spout again.

What about us? Do we possess the same inner strength to accept life's challenges? Do we have the same spirit of determination when times get rough?

We need the resilience of Eensy Weensy when troubles come raging in on us. *Obet Cabrillas (obetcab@yahoo.com)*

Reflection: When the going gets rough, the tough gets tougher!

Lord, may we not be overcome by the gigantic challenges before us but instead be empowered by Your power within us!

St. Willibald, bishop and missionary, pray for us.

ALIVE!

"…He is One and there is no other…"
– Mark 12:32

Tobit 6:10-11; 7:1, 9-17;
8:4-9
Psalm 128:1-2, 3, 4-5
Mark 12:28-34

A retreat master once asked a group of novices who their role model was. The only condition was that the role model was to be someone living in the present time. When the answers were read out, it was a hodgepodge of family members, famous celebrities, politicians, humanitarians and religious personalities. No one had written "Jesus" as a role model. Is it a wonder?

When we say we "love" the Lord, we declare it in the present tense because it is active, because He is, quite simply, alive. More alive and more real than your neighbor, or your boss, or even yourself. We sing it, we put it up on posters, we print it on our T-shirts, and we hear it declared in the streets: Jesus *is* alive.

The blessing of our generation is that "we have not seen and yet believed." The fact that Jesus is alive is not just a sound byte or a feel-good phrase we post on Instagram or Facebook. It is the anchor of our faith and we need to believe it, live it, and make it active and real in our lives. *Rod Velez (rod.velez@gmail.com)*

Reflection: Who is your role model and why? Condition: He or she has to be alive in the present time.

Reveal to us, O Lord, the times and the ways we take You for granted. Teach us to make You more real than what our senses tell us.

Tobit 11:5-17
Psalm 146:1-2, 6-7,
8-9, 9-10
Mark 12:35-37

TO BE UNITED AGAIN

Then Tobit went back in, rejoicing and praising God with full voice… Tobiah told to his father that the Lord God had granted him a successful journey…
– Tobit 11:15

Last January 10, we celebrated the 72nd birthday of my Papa. I've been physically away from him for seven years, yet I believe that our hearts are still connected. Unfortunately, in my seven years of spiritual mission far away from home, Papa hadn't attended our prayer meetings.

Oh, did I mention that Papa is already gone? Two days from now, it will be his seventh death anniversary. It pains me to remember that I wasn't there during his last breath, yet I'm thankful that I was able to deepen my relationship with him for the last year of his life.

I believe that he is rejoicing and praising God with full voice every day. While I'm serving at our weekly Feasts, I believe that my earthly father is celebrating and serving in the eternal Feast of our Heavenly Father. I can't wait for the right time for us to be reunited and tell him that my journey on earth had been a success.

Do you spend quality time with your loved ones? Make sure you do before it's too late. *Aben Garlan (mail@abengarlan.com)*

Reflection: "Family is not an important thing. It's everything." (Michael J. Fox)

Lord Jesus, teach me how to love the people that matter most in my life. May I deepen my relationship with them. Amen.

St. Ephrem, deacon and doctor of the Church, pray for us.

Tobit 12:1, 5-15, 20
Tobit 13:2, 6, 7, 8
Mark 12:38-44

MY BEST BIRTHDAY EVER

"Those who regularly give alms shall enjoy a full life…" – Tobit 12:9

I usually celebrate my birthdays with parties or vacations abroad. Last year, I chose to have a quiet birthday. I just called a few friends, bought a hundred burgers and juices, and wrote simple Post-it notes to go along with the snacks. We roamed the streets of Manila on a sunny afternoon, and gave food to street vendors and less fortunate brothers and sisters.

It was a different kind of birthday treat. I thought I just wanted to give back. But each time I extended my hand outside the car window, I knew I was the one who received more. Each time we waved at them and gave them the burgers they were surprised to get, our hearts were warmed with their joyous smiles. I've never heard *"Salamat po"* spoken so genuinely. One man was even in tears as he pointed skyward when he held the food on his hands, praising the Lord for the gift he didn't expect to receive.

When we give, we don't only bless the people who will receive, but we're even more blessed because of it. That's the miracle of giving — of loving. *Ruby Albino (r_jean07@yahoo.com)*

Reflection: Be a miracle to someone today. Visit a charity, give alms, donate to your parish, help the elderly.

Lord, use me today so I may be a blessing to the world. Bless the works of my hands so I can always give more to Your Kingdom here on earth.

Blessed Joachima, pray for us.

JUNE 11
SUNDAY

Exodus 34:4-6, 8-9
Daniel 3:52, 53, 54, 55
2 Corinthians 13:11-13
John 3:16-18

Solemnity of the Most Holy Trinity

MERCIFUL JUDGE

The Lord, the Lord, a merciful and gracious God, slow to anger and rich in kindness and fidelity. – Exodus 34:6

"You need not fear judgment if you know the Judge." That was one lesson I took home from an advent retreat I attended several years ago. And I have heard it preached over and over again: No sinner is beyond God's mercy. God forgives even the most grievous sin. God's love is perfect and He loves us unconditionally. These truths about God I know in my mind, but do I believe them in my heart and soul?

I imagined myself standing before God on Judgment Day, a wide screen behind me that showed every moment of my earthly life, including both the good and bad I've done. Nothing remains hidden – every single thing about me is exposed for the Lord to see. I bow my head and close my eyes, bearing the guilt but also harboring hope. How will He judge the way I lived my life? Only God knows.

Indeed, I do not have to be afraid of God's judgment if I truly believe that He is "gracious and merciful, slow to anger and abounding in love and fidelity." And if there is one faithful soul who intercedes for me, just as Moses did for the stiff-necked Israelites, I believe God will hear his plea and will let His grace and love prevail. *Dina Pecaña (dpecana@yahoo.com)*

Reflection: Do you fear God's judgment?

"Holy God, Holy Mighty One, Holy Immortal One, have mercy on us and the whole world." (from the Divine Mercy Prayer)

St. Barnabas, Apostle, pray for us.

JUNE 12
MONDAY

2 Corinthians 1:1-7
Psalm 34:2-3, 4-5, 6-7,
8-9
Matthew 5:1-12

HEALED TO HEAL

… encourage those who are in any affliction with the encouragement with which we ourselves are encouraged by God. – 2 Corinthians 1:4

I met her during a personal retreat. She reminded me of myself 10 years ago. God prompted my spirit to give my book to her. While I was in bed, I told myself, *OK, I'll give it tomorrow.* But God encouraged me, "No, give it now." So I knocked on her door that night and gave it to her.

She was leaving when I saw her again. This time she was with her retreat director. He shared that during his prayer time, God told him to tell his retreatant that she must learn to love herself. But before he could tell her this, she told him about the book that I gave her the night before. When he saw the title of the book, *Love Yourself as God Loves You,* he was amazed. I had goosebumps while he was recounting the story. It is amazing how God works and affirms His message for us.

Ten years ago, I was sad because I didn't love myself. I made a lot of wrong choices because of my unhealed wounds. Through the years, God restored me to wholeness. He inspired me to write that book to share what I had learned. Today, the book continues to encourage those who need to love themselves as God loves them. He heals us so that through our healing, others may also be set free. *Marjorie Ann Duterte (marjorie.travels@gmail.com)*

Reflection: Your wounds will one day be a source of healing for others.

Thank You, Lord, for healing us and using our stories to heal others.

Blessed Jolenta (Yolanda) of Poland, pray for us.

JUNE 13
TUESDAY

2 Corinthians 1:18-22
Psalm 119:129, 130, 131, 132, 133, 135
Matthew 5:13-16

PARASAILING

... the one who gives us security with you in Christ. – 2 Corinthians 1:21

My husband, Raul, and I went first. We were strapped to a harness attached to what looked like a huge bright-colored parachute connected by a rope to the boat.

The boat began to move, the rope started to unwind from the spool, and we were blown away by the wind to the skies. It was then that I realized how unprepared I was for this adventure.

I knew we were several hundreds of feet above the sea when our son Peevee was hardly visible on the boat. I was gripped with fear. I could stay frozen that way for the rest of the 15-minute flight or I could let go and embrace the whole experience. Knowing that there was absolutely nothing I could do at that point, I chose to surrender and let the Lord take control.

And then it happened. I was overtaken with an overwhelming sense of peace and serenity. I was like a bird gliding on air, relishing a panoramic view of the pristine waters of Boracay. I felt secure. My favorite passage came to life: "Then the peace of God that surpasses all understanding will guard your hearts and minds in Christ Jesus" (Philippians 4:7). *Mari Sison-Garcia (mari_sison_garcia@yahoo.com)*

Reflection: Is anything bothering you today? Surrender all to Jesus.

Lord, take control of my life that I may have peace and security in my heart.

St. Anthony of Padua, priest and doctor of the Church, pray for us.

2 Corinthians 3:4-11
Psalm 99:5, 6, 7, 8, 9
Matthew 5:17-19

FROM UNQUALIFIED TO QUALIFIED

Not that of ourselves we are qualified to take credit for anything as coming from us; rather, our qualification comes from God. – 2 Corinthians 3:4-5

I was invited to be a guest in a radio program last year. I got excited when I was told that the topic would be hands-on parenting because the book I was writing then is titled *How to Be a Hands-On Parent While Earning*.

I chose to embark on this new book project to share some of the lessons I learned about parenting and working smart. I do not claim to be a parenting expert. I simply want to help strengthen families in a way I know how. Thus, I was surprised when the hosts of the radio program introduced me as a parenting expert.

The interview went well. A reporter from the same radio network even wrote about my interview in their website. I also got e-mails, both from people I know and I don't know, giving me positive feedback for it. They said that I answered the questions well and confidently. I believe that it was God who granted me wisdom and confidence so I could help the program's listeners. I may not feel qualified to be called an expert, but God made me qualified by His anointing. *Teresa Gumap-as Dumadag (teresa@fulllifecube.com)*

Reflection: When was the last time you felt unqualified to do something and God made you qualified? How did you feel?

Lord, thank You so much for qualifying those whom You have called to serve You. We are truly honored to respond positively to Your call.

St. Albert Chmielowski, pray for us.

JUNE 15
THURSDAY

2 Corinthians 3:15-4:1, 3-6
Psalm 85:9, 10, 11-12, 13-14
Matthew 5:20-26

TIMELY TRANSFORMATION

All of us… are being transformed into the same image…as from the Lord.
– 2 Corinthians 3:18

Gab was a college friend. On our first year, a professor invited us to join a Catholic youth group. I did, but Gab politely refused. She wasn't into the religious thing. Relationships were also discouraged in the youth group, and Gab had a boyfriend then. Her refusal saddened me, but I couldn't force her. I sincerely thought she was a lost cause.

After graduation, we went on to build our careers and eventually lost touch. A reunion a few years later ended the disconnection. Gab came with her new boyfriend, whom she met at work. She shared that Miko is active in a Catholic community and joked that she now attends prayer meetings, the very thing she avoided in college. She also joins small groups, shares her personal testimony of God's love, and sings for the worship team.

I welcomed her news with amazement at how God has transformed her. I realized that God's plan to change her was right on track, not a minute too early or too late. No matter how seemingly long it took, His transformational love cannot be denied. He has His own timeline. *Osy Erica (osy.erica@gmail.com)*

Reflection: Do not give up on a loved one or a friend. God is transforming their characters, and He is doing the same with you.

Father, I know You are transforming me every day. Change me so I can reflect Your face to the world. Amen.

St. Marguerite d' Youville, pray for us.

2 Corinthians 4:7-15
Psalm 116:10-11, 15-16,
17-18
Matthew 5:27-32

BREAK POINT

We are afflicted in every way, but not constrained; perplexed, but not driven to despair. – 2 Corinthians 4:8

It still haunts me to this day. And people have a hard time picturing me every time I tell them that point in my life when I experienced a breakdown.

Have you ever gone through the same thing?

Where everything is just so dark, and light seems out of sight?

Where the pain is just so unbearable, and relief seems out of reach?

Well, I have. And I believe that everybody else has, in varying degrees.

Life has taught me that during such times, we just need to hold on.

To have faith that we can still carry on and keep taking the next step.

To have hope that everything works out at the end and keep moving forward.

To have love that lights our way and keep giving our best.

And before we know it, our break point becomes our breakthrough point. *Orange Garcia (orange.garcia@outlook.com)*

Reflection: When was the last time a break point became your breakthrough point?

Lord, please give me the courage to do what is right, no matter what the cost.

JUNE 17
SATURDAY

2 Corinthians 5:14-21
Psalm 103:1-2, 3-4,
9-10, 11-12
Matthew 5:33-37

FREE, FINALLY

God was reconciling the world to himself
in Christ... and entrusting to us the
message of reconciliation.
– 2 Corinthians 5:19

I used to write to my absentee father all the time. Some letters were forgiving, some were loving. But many were sad, angry or disappointed. It was my way of trying to make sense of his absence, of trying to find answers to one lingering question: "Why weren't you there as I grew up?" Just because he stopped being my mom's husband didn't mean that he should also stop being my father.

I reached out to him for many years but more often than not I was unsuccessful. I became angry, bitter and resentful without me knowing it. Forgiving him was necessary, not because I wanted to.

Thank God for the gift of mercy. Through the help of great mentors and friends, as well as the enduring and unconditional love of my mother, I was finally able to truly forgive my father. The Cross was the greatest symbol of mercy, of love. If God sent His only Son to die so that I could be reunited with Him, who am I to withhold the same mercy to the people who hurt me?

So I wrote my father one last letter, but this time, it was a letter of forgiveness, and a letter asking for forgiveness. And when I signed my name, I was finally free. *Karren Renz Seña (karren.s@shepherdsvoice.com.ph)*

Reflection: For God so loved the world that He gave His one and only Son, that whoever believes in Him shall not perish but have eternal life. (John 3:16)

Jesus, help us to forgive, to be merciful, to be loving — just like You.

St. Joseph Cafasso, pray for us.

JUNE **18**
SUNDAY

Deuteronomy 8:2-3, 14-16
Psalm 147:12-13, 14-15, 19-20
1 Corinthians 10:16-17
John 6:51-58

Solemnity of the Body and Blood of Christ (Corpus Christi)

PUZZLE PIECE

"Your God has directed all your journeying in the desert."
– Deuteronomy 8:2

Have you ever asked God why you are where you are?

I have always believed that there are no coincidences in life. We had to go through experiences in the past to prepare us for now and for the future. That agonizing breakup led into meeting the lifetime partner God has prepared for you. You had to let go of a great job for something uncertain at the time, then you realized it was definitely better than the previous one.

Every life experience is a small puzzle piece that fits into a bigger and beautiful picture. Can we see the bigger picture? Probably not. What we only see is our circumstance right now. And yes, maybe we complain because it is not what we imagined it to be or what we prayed to happen. But remember, God makes all things work for our good! This is only a piece of the puzzle.

God created the bigger picture. He is holding your hand as you journey in the wilderness. Trust that He has nothing but the best ending for your life. *Lala Dela Cruz (bella.delacruz@gmail.com)*

Reflection: What is the Lord teaching you right now, in the circumstance you are in?

Lord, do not let go of my hand. I trust that You are with me in this journey.

Venerable Matt Talbot, pray for us.

2 Corinthians 6:1-10
Psalm 98:1, 2, 3, 3-4
Matthew 5:38-42

'SAYANG!'

We appeal to you not to receive the grace of God in vain. – 2 Corinthians 6:1

There is not one English word translation for the Filipino word *sayang*. Loosely, it means "what a waste."

Here are samples of how you apply this word: When you are served with so much food on the table in an expensive restaurant, and you have more leftovers than what you ate, *"Sayang!"* When you have a happy family and then you fall into the temptation of an extramarital affair that breaks up your marriage, *"Sayang!"* When you are blessed to receive a huge amount of money, and then lose it all on gambling or a vice, *"Sayang!"*

When God gives His all to you, sending His only begotten Son who dies on the cross to show you how much He loves you, and you reject this love, *"Sayang!"* Yes, God loves us all with no exceptions and conditions. His grace is for everyone. But this grace can be in vain if rejected, ignored and wasted.

Today, God is pouring out His grace and mercy, blessings and miracles so you can live your life to the fullest. Don't waste it. Don't go back remembering this day only to say, *"Sayang!"*

Alvin Barcelona (apb_ayo@yahoo.com)

Reflection: Today, resolve to do something that you will not regret tomorrow. Receive God's grace now and avoid disgrace in the future.

Dear Lord, let me not receive Your grace in vain, but in deep gratitude and humility, give it full value by living my life for You and others.

St. Romuald, abbot, pray for us.

2 Corinthians 8:1-9
Psalm 146:2, 5-6, 6-7, 8-9
Matthew 5:43-48

IMAGINARY HAND

"But I say to you, love your enemies, and pray for those who persecute you."
– Matthew 5:44

She was someone I encountered almost every day and I didn't look forward to these encounters.

Her mouth spewed invectives and was painted on her face. I would cringe every time I heard her speak because she always had a bone to pick with someone. If I could, I would steer clear of her path so I wouldn't have to deal with her.

In one of my prayer times, this verse reminded me of her. From then on, I decided to pray for her. I would even lift my imaginary hand and pray over her in silence during the times I would hear her curse or when I would have a chance encounter with her.

And the unbelievable happened.

She began to temper her language and became nicer to the people around her.

The power of my imaginary hand must have taken effect.

More accurately, God's hand moved in her life to change and transform her. It's a reminder to me that nothing moves the hand of God more powerfully than when we pray. *Rissa Espinosa (rissa_d_espinosa@yahoo.com)*

Reflection: How do you deal with those who persecute you?

Lord, may I never give up praying for those who are difficult to relate with.

JUNE 21
WEDNESDAY

2 Corinthians 9:6-11
Psalm 112:1-2, 3-4, 9
Matthew 6:1-6, 16-18

BLESSED ARE THE NAMELESS

"And your Father who sees what is hidden will repay you." – Matthew 6:18

I am a silent worker in our office. Even after two years in my current job, I'm still not used to our office culture of everyday meetings and detailing the things I do and have worked on. For me, as long as my supervisor knows what I am doing, I'm OK with it.

I also happened to meet someone who is planning to enter the seminary. During a search-in session which I attended, he shared that he always brings a piece of bread or biscuit in his bag. Not for him, but to give to a beggar who enters the jeepney or bus he is riding in. And even if I had not seen him since then, I fondly remember him for such a kind act. I knew there and then that he would be a good fit for priesthood.

I also greatly admire those who donate church pews without revealing their names. They're the ones who believe that their reward is not in this earth, but in heaven.

Indeed, blessed are those who are humble and do not boast for they will receive God's greatest blessing. *Gracious B. Romero (graciousromero@gmail.com)*

Reflection: "Consider this: whoever sows sparingly will also reap sparingly, and whoever sows bountifully will also reap bountifully." (2 Corinthians 9:6)

Lord, help us to be cheerful givers. Amen.

YOU ALREADY HAVE IT

"Your Father knows what you need before you ask him." – Matthew 6:8

I needed a laptop to review for the medical board exams and to access online documents easily.

I didn't have the funds yet, but I was saving and praying for it.

One day, I candidly mentioned it to my mom. She smiled and said, " I was wondering when you would ask for it. You'll have your laptop fund by next week."

Wow! The money had already been prepared for me. All I had to do was ask. And when I got the money, I even got more than enough to pay for the laptop that suited my needs.

Oftentimes, we fret and worry even before we pray and ask the Lord for our needs. We forget that He knows all things, including our needs. He's countless of steps ahead, preparing the way for us.

Since then, whenever I need anything, my first prayer is to be thankful for the provision that is already on its way.

In His best time and in His best way, I trust that my Father will meet my every need. *Didoy Lubaton (didoymd@gmail.com)*

Reflection: "The cautious faith that never saws off a limb on which it is sitting, never learns that unattached limbs may find strange unaccountable ways of not falling." (Dallas Willard)

Lord, I trust that You know and will provide for my every need in Your perfect way and time.

JUNE 23
FRIDAY

Deuteronomy 7:6-11
Psalm 103:1-2, 3-4, 6-7,
8, 10
1 John 4:7-16
Matthew 11:25-30

Solemnity of the Most Sacred Heart
of Jesus

WHERE DO YOU RUN?

*"Come to me, all you who labor and are
burdened, and I will give you rest."*
– Matthew 11:28

I know of a man whose dad was sick. After a long day at work, this man would come home, eat dinner with his small family, and then visit his dad late at night after his wife and child were asleep. Night after night, he gathered to say the rosary with his dad, his mom, and his sisters, to ask for healing and grace to overcome the burdens that came with being sick. When his dad was in the hospital, this man watched over him, bought the meals that his dad requested, and spent time by his bedside. He spoke with the doctors, coordinated with the insurance companies, comforted his mother, and continued praying. In all that time, he continued to be a responsible and loving husband and father.

This man is one of many who, at some point in their lives, selflessly endured heartache and exhaustion in the name of love. Their efforts do not always result in the healing of their loved ones, but they are rewarded with the peace of knowing they have loved.

Today we celebrate the Solemnity of the Most Sacred Heart of Jesus. Let us pray for those who carry a heavy load, that in the heart of Jesus, their pain may be soothed, hurt be healed, sadness be overcome, and peace be found. *Geraldine G. Catral (catral. geegee@beaconschool.ph)*

Reflection: When overwhelmed with the burdens of life, run to Jesus.

Sacred Heart of Jesus, I place my trust in You.

St. John Fisher, pray for us.

Isaiah 49:1-6
Psalm 139:1-3, 13-14,
14-15
Acts 13:22-26
Luke 1:57-66, 80

Feast of the Nativity
of John the Baptist

ONLY GRACE

I will make you a light to the nations, that my salvation may reach to the ends of the earth. – Isaiah 49:6

When I talk to young people or hear about those who suffer from low self-worth and hopelessness, I can't help but empathize with them. I was like them ages ago — and it sprang from fear. I was afraid of how other people saw me. So I asked God how I could extend His love to those people even in the simplest way I can. I wanted to shine His light to the hearts dimmed by hopelessness and fear.

God's answer came in one of my personal retreats. During one of my prayer times, I began scribbling non-stop. It ended up as a book outline. For the following weeks, I kept writing even when I didn't feel like it.

The book *Status Confused* came out a year ago and I thank God for embracing many people through its message. I can't claim the glory. My stories reflected my flaws and failures. But one thing filled the empty spaces and restored the broken pieces — God's grace.

I believe that God's relentless grace will keep on shining and saving lives — just as He did with mine. And He continues to do it through us to the ends of the earth. *Maymay R. Salvosa (christiane. salvosa@gmail.com)*

Reflection: Your life is a light that others need to illuminate their path.

Use me, Jesus, to show forth Your grace and Your glory.

St. John the Baptist, pray for us.

JUNE 25
SUNDAY

Jeremiah 20:10-13
Psalm 69:8-10, 14, 17,
33-35
Romans 5:12-15
Matthew 10:26-33

NANAY ISING
"So do not be afraid"
– Matthew 10:31

I attended a New Year's Day Mass at 11 a.m. with my family and friends. An old lady sitting alone in front of us caught my attention. Then a crazy idea came to my mind. I thought of inviting her for lunch.

After the Mass, I asked my companion to invite her to have lunch with us at a nearby restaurant. I was happy she agreed. We introduced ourselves to each other and interviewed her.

Nanay Ising is 70 years old, four feet tall, single, living with her two other single sisters, both in their 60's. They manage their own *sari-sari* store. *Nanay* Ising would iron clothes of her former employer once a week. While listening to her, I wondered how they could live a decent life with their meager earnings.

Before we parted, we gave her some money. She thanked us and happily went home.

There's something special about *Nanay* Ising. Despite her seeming material lack, she looks calm, happy, content and unafraid. I believe that this can only come from a deep faith and trust in God who loves us and provides for all our needs.
Meann Tee (meanntytee@yahoo.com)

Reflection: Are you worried, anxious, stressed and afraid? Be not afraid. Have faith. Let go and let God.

Father, I surrender to You all my fears, worries and anxieties. I believe that You will be with me and will provide for all my needs. Amen.

Blessed Jutta of Thuringia, pray for us.

Genesis 12:1-9
Psalm 33:12-13, 18-19,
20, 22
Matthew 7:1-5

COMFORT IN THE UNCOMFORTABLE

"Go forth from the land of your kinsfolk and from your father's house to a land that I will show you." – Genesis 12:1

Creating marketing plans, analyzing market research data, collaborating with advertising agencies on a communication strategy, managing and developing products. I thrived in these aspects of my career until 10 years ago. Moving abroad changed all that. Now, I'm in a totally different field, reinventing myself and learning new skills set. The key was adapting to the opportunities the Lord opened for me instead of insisting on the familiar when very little of it was available.

When discerning and following God's plan for us, sometimes we will be asked to do something outside of our comfort zone. Naturally and understandably, there will be reluctance, doubt, fear and whatever emotion we can conjure to justify why we should say no. But we need to trust that He desires nothing less than what is best for us and that He will equip us with what we need to be successful in our new pursuits.

With that in mind, I wonder what God will make me do next? *Erwin Roceles (erwin_roceles@yahoo.com)*

Reflection: "As you move outside of your comfort zone, what was once the unknown and frightening becomes your new normal." (Robin S. Sharma)

Lord, give me the courage and strength to overcome my doubts and fears when it comes to trying something new.

JUNE 27
TUESDAY

Genesis 13:2, 5-18
Psalm 15:2-3, 3-4, 5
Matthew 7:6, 12-14

NOT ONLY IN LITERATURE

"Please separate from me. If you prefer the left, I will go to the right; if you prefer the right, I will go to the left."
– Genesis 13:9

The love and loyalty of Sam Gamgee of *The Lord of the Rings* trilogy to his friend and boss and the story's main protagonist, Frodo Baggins, is heroic and touching. He encouraged Frodo and cared for him on their long and perilous quest to Mordor. He even carried Frodo up in the Mount of Doom so Frodo could throw away the ring there.

Self-sacrifice is not limited to literature. For aren't we all a product of someone's self-sacrifice? Perhaps a parent who had to work abroad to provide for the kids. Or a mother who juggled job, home and children. Or a brother or sister who dutifully sent their hard-earned money every payday to the family.

Self-sacrifice is a noble trait to have. It's something that can only come as grace from above. Let us do what we can to practice self-sacrifice in our lives so that we, too, can love others.

Then we will each become living witnesses of the Lamb of God who was slain. *Joy Sosoban-Roa (jsosoban@gmail.com)*

Reflection: "Amen, amen, I say to you, unless a grain of wheat falls to the ground and dies, it remains just a grain of wheat; but if it dies, it produces much fruit." (John 12:24)

Dear Lord, thank You for Your great sacrifice. Thank You that I have a chance now to imitate your example. Let me love You, Lord. Amen.

JUNE 28
WEDNESDAY

Genesis 15:1-12, 17-18
Psalm 105:1-2, 3-4, 6-7,
8-9
Matthew 7:15-20

INTIMACY

Every good tree bears good fruit, and a
rotten tree bears bad fruit.
– Matthew 7:17

I know of a politician who had an elaborate collection of religious images. He was even shown in the papers kneeling down in prayer. Then he was convicted for the heinous crime of rape and murder. How ironic.

After more than 20 years, I met a high school classmate whom we used to call "very reverend" because of his desire to become a priest. He told me that he did enter the seminary in the U.S. but went out because the "holy" people he was following molested him. Today he's still following the Lord but not in the Catholic Church. Sad!

Today's Gospel reminds me that my relationship with God must manifest into action. Striving to do religious acts and attaining religious positions by themselves don't necessarily make us holy in God's eyes.

Today's Gospel calls us to be good trees. Any experienced farmer will tell you that the health of a tree or plant starts with its roots. The roots absorb all the nutrients that help produce abundant fruit. As Christians, we know that we need to be rooted in Christ. His Word is nourishment for our soul and His presence empowers us to live in God's love. *Ariel Driz (adriz77@yahoo.com)*

Reflection: Are you deeply connected with Jesus?

Father, thank You for calling me to be intimate with You. Use me, Lord,
that I may produce good fruit that endures for Your glory.

"And upon this rock I will build my Church." – Matthew 16:18

Acts 12:1-11
Psalm 34:2-3, 4-5, 6-7, 8-9
2 Timothy 4:6-8, 17-18
Matthew 16:13-19

Solemnity of the Sts. Peter and Paul, Apostles

"Termites!"

This was my sad experience when I noticed one day that my book cabinet had some dirt. I wondered why in the world was there soil on my shelves?

It was only when I stepped back and looked at the whole cabinet that I realized that rows of books were covered with soil. It was utterly horrific!

How is it possible for termites to invade my condo unit nine floors above the ground?! After getting over my initial shock, slowly, the answer came. My condo building was quite old and mostly made of wood rather than cement. The building seemed as strong as stone, but was actually weak as wood. It didn't stand a chance against the termites.

Friends, what is the building of your life made of? Is it built with stone — strong, stable and enduring? Or does it give way when difficulty, doubt and suffering attack? I believe that like stone, faith is the best material we need to build our lives with. It will withstand whatever life throws at us. And we will endure.

No wonder Peter and Paul endured till the very end. Their faith was as strong as rock. May we choose to live the same way. *Jonathan Yogawin (jyogawin@gmail.com)*

Reflection: Step back and identify areas in your life where stone has turned to wood. It is never too late to change and believe again.

Lord Jesus, help me build my life upon You.

JUNE 30
FRIDAY

Genesis 17:1, 9-10, 15-22
Psalm 128:1-2, 3, 4-5
Matthew 8:1-4

THE MASTER'S TOUCH

"Lord if you wish…" He stretched out his hand, touched him, and said, "I do will it." – Matthew 8:2-3

My son's bloodcurdling scream was enough for me to know that he was really in pain. When I saw his twisted right leg and felt the knee cap jutting out, my own knees wobbled like jelly. We immediately rushed him to the hospital.

The orthopedic surgeon ordered an X-ray that revealed his right knee was badly dislocated. He needed to fix it right away under general anesthesia.

Surgery was scheduled at 3:00 a.m. I texted my sisters and daughters to pray the rosary for him. I was worried because of his history of seizures. I felt that the anesthesia might put him at risk. I prayed to God, "Lord, just one touch from You and all will be well. If you will, Lord, please stretch out Your hand and heal him. But if not, then let the procedure go well."

One hour before the nurse was to prep him for the operating room, his knee cap miraculously went back to its proper place and my son could now move his leg normally without pain! Even the doctor could not believe it. Yes, Jesus still wills our healing and stretches His hand to touch us today! *Ronna Singson Ledesma (ronna_ledesma@yahoo.com.ph)*

Reflection: If you think that God can't do it, then you have a small God. Jesus, thank You for willing our healing and stretching out Your hand to us.

Jesus, touch Me like only You can do.

The First Martyrs of the Holy Roman Church, pray for us.

30 TAKE THE -DAY CHALLENGE!

TAKE THE
-DAY
CHALLENGE!

MANY YEARS AGO, I DROVE DAD'S CAR.

It was a 16-year-old Mitsubishi Galant. I loved that car. But pretty soon, it was showing its age. Soon, it was conking out on me. (I noticed that it would conk out on me whenever I thought of replacing it. When I told this to my friend, he said, "When you're inside your car, never think about replacing it. Because your car can read your thoughts. *Magtatampo 'yan.* It will feel hurt — and it'll malfunction more."

What can I say? God has blessed me with very weird friends.

But what else should I expect? Like attracts like.

Each time I'd bring the car to the repair shop, the mechanic would fiddle under its hood, and after a day or two, I'd drive it off again. But after a week or so, something else will break down. (Yes, even if I tried mentally shooing away ill thoughts of replacing the car.)

One day, I brought it back to the shop. This time, the mechanic opened the hood, shook his head, and said, "Bo, your car needs an overhaul."

When I heard the word "overhaul," I sighed deeply. I knew that meant a gigantic amount of money.

He took out a piece of paper and wrote down a list of parts that needed to be replaced. He said, "Your engine is leaking. We need to replace the core of your engine."

One month later, when I picked up the car, it was like brand new. And I drove it for a few more years and thousands of miles.

Friend, is there an area in your life that you want to overhaul?

Is there an area in your life that you want fixed?

Repaired?

Today, I'm praying that God will do a massive overhaul in your life. I'm praying that God will make you brand new!

ARE YOU READY TO CHANGE?

Are you ready to change a specific area in your life?

Perhaps you want to be a more affectionate spouse.

Or you want to remove complaining from your life.

Or you want to wake up earlier each day — so you can exercise, pray, or write on your journal.

Or you want to quit smoking.

Whatever change or new habit you want to acquire, the 30-Day Challenge can make it happen for you.

7 RULES OF THE 30-DAY CHALLENGE

Haven't you noticed?

Some people are always making money, while some people are always broke.

Some people are always on time, while some people are always late.

Some people always create happiness wherever they go, while some people create conflict wherever they go.

Some people always achieve their dreams, while some people never achieve their dreams.

Why?

It's habits. Success and failure aren't actions.

They're habits.

By the way, here are 7 Rules of the 30-Day Challenge.

Rule 1: Select One Habit

Don't try to change 19 things in your life.

Just choose one habit. Choose something simple.

Because it's the simple things that will cause a massive difference in your life.

Perhaps you want to compliment your spouse every day for the next 30 days.

Or spend 15 minutes with your child daily for the next 30 days.

Or eat more veggies each day for the next 30 days.

I repeat: Pick one habit only!

Whatever you pick, make a commitment to do it for 30 days. Here's the magic of this program: If you can make one change in January, you can make another habit in February, and the another one in March...

Do you get the picture? That way, you could make 12 fantastic changes in the year. Isn't that awesome?

Write down the new habit that you want to acquire NOW.

Rule 2: Seal It for 30 Days

It has to be for 30 days.

If you miss one day, promise to go back to Day 1 and start over.

Why 30 days? Two reasons.

First, because that's how long it takes to learn a new habit. According to psychologists, it takes 21 days to create a new pattern in your life. It takes 21 days to create a mental pathway in your brain, so that it becomes easier for you to do it.

So why not call it the 21-Day Challenge instead of a 30-Day Challenge? I don't want to take chances.

21 days is the passing mark. 30 days is the honor mark!

Here's the second reason for 30 days only: It's doable.

If someone tells you, "Can you read one hour a day for the rest of your life?" That can be overwhelming.

But if someone tells you, "Can you read one hour a day for the next 30 days?"

All of a sudden, it seems more doable.

Write down your starting date and your ending date... NOW.

Rule 3: Strive to Do It Daily

Developing a new habit requires that you do it daily.

I repeat: You have to do it daily. Not three or four times a week. This is crucial. If it's an activity that can't be done daily, then try to choose an "alternate" activity that you can do at the same time.

For example, if you hit the gym every 5 p.m. to 6 p.m. on Tuesdays, Thursdays and Saturdays — why not take a walk around your village at that same time on Monday, Wednesday, Friday and Sunday? That way, it's still a daily experience.

Rule 4: Schedule an Exact Time

Don't just say, "I'm going to walk daily."

Say instead, "I'm going to walk at 6 a.m. daily." That'll be more powerful.

Don't just say, "I'm going to make 20 sales calls a day."

Say instead, "I'm going to make 20 sales calls a day from 10 a.m. to 12 p.m."

Doing this little tweak will quadruple your chances of sticking to the habit.

If applicable, write the time you will do this daily.

Rule 5: Switch to Your New Habit

Empty space won't remain empty for long. If you remove a bad habit, there'll be an empty space in your life. If you don't fill that empty space, the bad habit will come back.

So don't just try quitting a bad habit. Be sure to replace it with a good habit. In other words, switch.

For example, if you want to quit watching mindless TV shows, what will you do during those three hours of primetime? Read a book? Learn to play a musical instrument? Start a business? Take a sport? Serve in a ministry?

Rule 6: Study about Your New Habit

Study about the new habit you want to acquire.

Let's say you want to be more grateful in the next 30 days. Then Google about gratitude. Read articles about it. Look for books on the topic. Talk to friends about the power of gratitude.

And finally...

Rule 7: Support Your New Habit

Surround yourself with people who are already doing your new habit.

If you want to exercise daily, get your friend or spouse who will do it with you. If you can afford it, get a physical trainer.

My friend used to smoke three packs a day. Her addiction was so bad, she'd wake up at 3 a.m. just to smoke two sticks — and then she'll fall back to sleep.

Talk about addiction!

But one day, she really felt it was time to cut the habit. She told me. She told her best friends. She told her small group at The Feast — which I happened to lead.

And we prayed for her.

Recently, she texted me, saying that she's been "smokeless" for three years now.

Write down the name of your support group.

START AGAIN

I heard this inspiring story from Les Brown.

One day, two guys were retrenched. And these men went looking for a new job — but the economy was so bad, there were no job openings.

One guy got discouraged, watched TV, drank beer, became toxic with his wife, and talked negative stuff with his other negative unemployed friends, with topics like...

How the economy is going to the dogs.

How the rich are robbing us blind.

How politicians are destroying the country.

But the second guy kept applying for a job. Yet no matter what he did, he was still rejected. The most common reason they told him was, "You're overqualified for the job."

But he never gave up. He kept knocking on doors.

One day, in desperation, he said to one of the bosses he was talking to, "Look, you don't have to pay me. I just want to be useful."

The boss said, "OK, but don't expect me to pay you."

He came to work every day. He was the first guy to come in and the last guy to leave. Even if he wasn't paid.

Four weeks later, the top manager quit. The owners looked for a replacement. And they remembered that they had this "volunteer" working in their office. They hired him — and that man now runs the company.

Here's the key to success: Don't stop moving.

When you start and fail, start again.

The old formula for success was Ready, Aim, Fire.

Today, we're realizing that the real formula for success is Ready, Aim, Fire, Aim, Fire, Aim, Fire...

In other words, don't aim for perfect execution but persistent execution.

Friend, go ahead.

It's now your turn to make revolutionary changes in your life.

May your dreams come true,

Bo Sanchez

*Excerpt from How to Change Your Life in 30 Days. Available at **www.kerygmabooks.com***

JULY 1
SATURDAY

Genesis 18:1-15
Luke 1:46-47, 48-49,
50, 53, 54-55
Matthew 8:5-17

JUST DO THE RIGHT THING

"'Do this,' and he does it." – Matthew 8:9

Have you ever wondered why the Philippines never ran out of problems? Just look at our history. From 1521 to 1945, we were always a conquered nation. And if it's not another country that's conquering us, it's a natural disaster.

But perhaps our biggest problems are man-made: corruption, poverty, heavy traffic. We could ask, "Lord, why did You abandon us?" I understand that feeling. Many years ago, I remember staring at the ruins of my *eighth* failed business. I asked God, "Lord, why are You doing this to me? I've given You my life since I was a kid. I've sacrificed for You. Why don't You bless my business?"

At one point in our lives, we all go through these doubts and questions. But didn't you notice? God never answers our whys. Instead, God says only two things: *"Trust me. Do the right thing."* Perhaps right now, you too are asking, "Lord, why? Why have You abandoned me?" Maybe you're tempted to do the wrong thing. But I urge you — no matter what storms you're facing, just do the right thing. Because you know that God will reward you. *Bo Sanchez (bosanchez@kerygmafamily.com)*

Reflection: Are you tempted to quit doing good because nothing's come out of it so far? What is God telling you to do?

Dearest Lord, grant me the grace to obey Your will, that I may continue to do the right thing even if nothing seems to be happening. Amen.

JULY 2
SUNDAY

2 Kings 4:8-11, 14-16
Psalm 89:2-3, 16-17,
18-19
Romans 6:3-4, 8-11
Matthew 10:37-42

SURPRISE ME!

*"This time next year you will be fondling a
baby son." – 2 Kings 4:16*

Today, my wife and I have three beautiful daughters, but we've been praying for a baby boy ever since we got married. It's been a long prayer now — 11 years and counting. I'm still optimistic though in having boys whom I can call sons. Yet a part of me feels that maybe God has other plans. Maybe He wanted me to have a volleyball team instead of a basketball team! That's why I fell off my chair when I read the Bible passage assigned to me: *"This time next year you will be cradling a baby son!"* Hallelujah!

The Lord knows the deepest desires of our hearts. Being a dad, I'm sure God loves to give whatever we ask of Him — as much as possible.

I learned two reasons why some of our prayers haven't been answered yet. One: now's not the right time; and two: He has a better option.

I'm not sure if we'll have a baby boy next year. But I know in time, if it's God's will, it will come. God works in our favor. He knows best. I'm excited for His surprises! *Monching Bueno (ramon_bueno@yahoo.com)*

Reflection: Spend time with the Lord today. Let Him know the deepest desires of your heart. Ask Him to speak to you and to surprise you.

Lord, I believe that all things work for the good of those who love and serve You. Surprise me today!

GOD'S FACE
"We have seen the Lord." – John 20:25

Ephesians 2:19-22
Psalm 117:1, 2
John 20:24-29

Feast of St. Thomas, Apostle

I've been in the Charismatic Renewal since I was 14 years old.

I've served in countless Life in the Spirit Seminars, retreats and recollections.

I've seen thousands of people experience a personal encounter with Jesus.

I've witnessed the lame walk in healing services and hardened hearts melt in God's presence.

In my decades in ministry, you can say I've seen how God moves in ordinary people's lives than most people. I was trained to see God in the supernatural.

But in recent years, I've seen God in the natural.

I see God's face when my husband looks tenderly at our daughters.

I see God's face when my firstborn discovers a new skill, and with pride exclaims, "I did it, Mama!"

I see God's face when my youngest hugs me and says, "You're the best mommy ever!"

We can see God everywhere, anytime, all the time. We just have to train our eyes to see Him.

Have you seen Him lately? *Rissa Singson Kawpeng (justbreatherissa@gmail.com)*

Reflection: "You tell us that to love God and neighbor is not something abstract, but profoundly concrete: it means seeing in every person the face of the Lord to be served, to serve him concretely. And you are, dear brothers and sisters, the face of Jesus." (Pope Francis)

Jesus, open my eyes that I may see Your face everywhere I turn. Amen.

St. Thomas, Apostle, pray for us.

JULY 4
TUESDAY

Genesis 19:15-29
Psalm 26:2-3, 9-10,
11-12
Matthew 8:23-27

FAITH WEAKENS FEAR

*"Why are you terrified, O you of little
faith?" – Matthew 8:26*

It was time to conduct my own seminar in February 2012. I was 22 years old. Even if speaking is one of my passions, I still get huge nerve-racking butterflies in my stomach. What's more frightening was it's my first time as a paid speaker. Can I give back their money's worth?

"What if I fail? What if my audience won't like my message? What if I run out of words to say? Should I just return their payments?" These negative thoughts fed my system before I showed up. I was terrified.

But despite these destroying thoughts, I still did great that day. My audience thanked me for a great talk. Some of them even asked for my signature and e-mail address. These things never happened before.

How did I do it? Let me share it with you: Each time I give a talk, even if I feel some chills down my spine, I let the Holy Spirit do the work. I do my passion lovingly. I embrace my fullest potential and increase my faith not just in myself but most importantly in God. *Sem. Kein Harvey P. Chito (kein.chito@gmail.com)*

Reflection: "Feed your fears and your faith will starve. Feed your faith, and your fears will." (Max Lucado)

Loving Father, each time I feel terrified, please do not give up on me. Increase my faith so that my fears will starve to death.

JULY 5
WEDNESDAY

Genesis 21:5, 8-20
Psalm 34:7-8, 10-11,
12-13
Matthew 8:28-34

POWER TO CHOOSE

"Arise, lift up the boy and hold him by the hand; for I will make of him a great nation." – Genesis 21:18

In one of my theology classes, my peers were in a heated debate about whether an individual's personality was predestined from birth (nature) or shaped by one's environment (nurture).

"Look at Eric," said someone, pointing to a student running for valedictorian of our batch. "He's been top of his class since he was in nursery. He must have been gifted since birth. Obviously, he's naturally smart." Another student said, "We're all a product of how we're raised by our parents and influenced by experience. Whatever our natural inclination is can always be changed."

Everyone turned to our professor for an answer. "You're all correct," he said. "When we're brought into this world, we have different natural talents, strengths and weaknesses. Then the people who care for us make decisions that lead us towards or away from our good or bad nature. As we grow older, we start making decisions for ourselves and take responsibility for our success and failures. Just like how we were born in the image of Christ. We are all destined for great things but sometimes we choose to sin. God is the caregiver who nourishes us towards greatness and away from evil. He does it first through others before eventually putting our fate in our own hands." *Eleanore Teo (elyo.lee@gmail.com)*

Reflection: What helps to nurture your natural strengths and talent?

Lord, thank You for holding my hand and leading me. I walk in confidence with You.

St. Anthony Zaccaria, priest, pray for us.

JULY 6
THURSDAY

Genesis 22:1-19
Psalm 115:1-2, 3-4, 5-6,
8-9
Matthew 9:1-8

MOUNTAIN INTO MOLEHILL

"On the mountain the Lord will see."
– Genesis 22:14

It's horrific to deal with government agencies and all the red tape. It's high-blood-inducing to deal with someone fuming because of time pressure. Imagine these two stressors volting in and giving my peaceful world a shake, rattle and roll.

There I was, trying to gather documents for my late husband's estate needed for the sale of his family's property. I was already harassed by the broker's piecemeal method of telling us what documents were needed. Added to my anxiety was that I couldn't find an important document, one that would bring all negotiations to a standstill if I couldn't produce it. It seemed like I was at that point Abraham was when asked to sacrifice Isaac. It was the end of all hope.

But on that mountain of problems, God provided a way out. A contact at the BIR provided an alternative to the lost document. I can refile my husband's estate tax and pay for something I had already paid for years ago. But at least we got things moving. And it was a legitimate alternative. No under-the-table deals. Just God sending His provisions. *Lella M. Santiago (lellams88@gmail.com)*

Reflection: It's difficult to trust when things are not going your way, but keep the faith. God always comes through.

Thank You, Jesus. Your grace comes just when things are looking hopeless.

Genesis 23:1-4, 19;
24:1-8, 62-67
Psalm 106:1-2, 3-4, 4-5
Matthew 9:9-13

GOD'S STRATEGY

"Those who are well do not need a physician, but the sick do.... I desire mercy, not sacrifice. I did not come to call the righteous but sinners."
– Matthew 9:12-13

God embraced Adam with his earthly nature, enabled him to be the Paradise Caretaker, and empowered him to go, multiply, fill the earth and subdue it.

God embraced Abraham in his old age, enabled him to father Isaac, and empowered him to be Father to all nations;

God embraced Moses after saving him from slaughter, enabled him to live as a prince, and empowered him to lead the exodus to the land flowing with milk and honey;

God embraced David as a shepherd boy, enabled him to be minstrel-soldier-general, and empowered him to be a great king after God's own heart.

God embraced Peter with his impulsive tendencies, enabled him to be the leader of the Apostles, and empowered him to be the first pope.

And God embraced me with my inferiority complex, enabled me to rebuild my self-worth, and empowered me to bring out the best in people.

Friend, allow God to embrace, enable and empower you to be the person He designed you to be. *Obet Cabrillas (obetcab@yahoo.com)*

Reflection: How will you hear His call when you don't admit your weakness?

Lord, I give You full permission to embrace, enable and empower me.

JULY 8
SATURDAY

Genesis 27:1-5, 15-29
Psalm 135:1-2, 3-4, 5-6
Matthew 9:14-17

THE BLESSING
"…blessed be those who bless you."
– Genesis 27:29

Pagmamano is done by taking the hand of an older person and placing it against your forehead as a sign of respect and request for a blessing.

When I was a child, I would *mano* during family reunions. It was a duty performed under the watchful eyes of my parents. When there were many relatives present, I'd take a succession of hands to my forehead without looking at the owners' faces, just to get it done quickly.

Now that I am much older, the *mano* has been replaced by the *beso* or kiss greeting. But during a few occasions, I've experienced a child taking my hand to his or her forehead, and I've felt the impact and beauty of the ritual. It's uplifting to be transformed into an instrument of good will — asking God to bless a young person.

Yet, it's not only children we bless. We can bless anyone and everyone through our generous actions and kind words. That's the way to pass on the blessings we've received from our elders. And in gratitude, we must remember to bless God, too — the origin, meaning and purpose of our lives. *Gina J. Verdolaga (mgjver@yahoo.com)*

Reflection: "God loves to bless us, but He loves even more watching His children imitate their Father by reaching out and blessing others." (Bruce Wilkinson)

Oh, God, grant me a humble, loving heart so that I may serve others better and glorify You.

St. Gregory Grassi and Companions, pray for us.

JULY 9
SUNDAY

Zechariah 9:9-10
Psalm 145:1-2, 8-9, 10-11, 13-14
Romans 8:9, 11-13
Matthew 11:25-30

LEARN FROM HIM

"Take my yoke upon you and learn from me, for I am meek and humble of heart…"
– Matthew 11:29

Have you ever gotten yourself into a stressful situation because of pride and haughtiness? I have, so many times.

I once went head-to-head with an officemate by sending an angry e-mail out of pride. She responded angrily as well. After reading her reply, I realized I was the one at fault. I had misjudged her. And I so wished I hadn't sent that e-mail in the first place.

It got so uncomfortable for several days and I was so burdened. I kept praying, "Lord, please fix this situation." But now I realize He must've been silently saying, "Learn your lesson first."

We finally resolved the situation, but I walked away much wiser because of it. I learned that it's not good enough to just give our cares to Jesus. He wants us to learn to be like Him so that we don't get into burdensome situations unnecessarily. *George Tolentino Gabriel (george.svp@gmail.com)*

Reflection: About to do something out of pride? Take a breath and give it a second thought.

Lord, let me become more like You.

ONLY THE BEST

The land on which you are lying, I will give to you and your descendants. – Genesis 28:13

Genesis 28:10-22
Psalm 91:1-2, 3-4, 14-15
Matthew 9:18-26

My wife, Gina, was offered to work in COJ Catholic Progressive School in 2012. She was content with her role as a housewife but felt that God was calling her for a mission. She wanted to stay in her comfort zone and bargained with God, giving Him conditions before she would say yes.

In prayer, God lovingly reminded her: "What you ask of Me is nothing compared to what I have planned for you." Convicted, she relented and accepted the position. And the Lord gave her much more than what she asked for.

It is natural to go after what we think is good for us. However, we need to remember that God delights in giving us the best; we only need to follow His leading. When we make decisions on our own, we receive a paltry of what God has in store for us. But when we listen and surrender to His will, He blesses us abundantly.

Trust that God will be faithful to His promises to you, just as He was with Jacob, Moses, Joseph, Mary and Gina — even when you can't see what's ahead. *Jun Asis (mabuting.balita@gmail.com)*

Reflection: How much effort do we put in discerning God's promises for us?

Lord, You know what is best for me. May I always trust in Your leading even when I can't see the way clearly.

St. Veronica Giuliani, pray for us.

MAGNIFICENT DEFEAT

"I will not let you go until you bless me."
– Genesis 32:27

Genesis 32:23-33
Psalm 17:1, 2-3, 6-7,
8, 15
Matthew 9:32-38

Jacob had one struggle after another – conflicts with his father, Isaac, and his brother, Esau, and ill treatment by his father-in-law. Overwhelmed by his problems, he ran away and left everything and everyone behind. He arrived at the Jabbok River exhausted and fell asleep. And that was when his real struggle began. God, in the form of angelic being, visited Jacob and they wrestled all night. Jacob lost when God broke his hip bone and disabled him.

I can relate with Jacob's experience. Over the years I, too, have struggled with habitual sins, broken relationships, a dysfunctional family, a recurring depression, unpaid debts and other problems. But more than these problems, I "wrestled" with God because I was stubborn and proud and did not want to relinquish control over my life to Him. In the end, as with Jacob, I lost the match, broken, wounded and weary.

I believe it is not God's intention to hurt us when He allows us to experience difficulties and hardships. Through it all, He remains with us and sustains us by His grace. But He brings us to our lowest point, holding us down just like a victorious wrestler, until we "tap" the floor in humble surrender, and accept this "magnificent defeat" in His hands. Like Jacob, let us say, "I will not let You go until You bless me." *Dina Pecaña (dpecana@yahoo.com)*

Reflection: "Surrender to what is. Let go of what was. Have faith in what will be." (Sonia Ricotti)

I surrender to Your will, Lord. Take over and I will follow. Amen.

St. Benedict, abbot, pray for us.

JULY 12
WEDNESDAY

**Genesis 41:55-57;
42:5-7, 17-24**
Psalm 33:2-3, 10-11,
18-19
Matthew 10:1-7

ENVY VS. INSPIRATION

*"Go to Joseph and do whatever he
told them." – Genesis 41:55*

Envy led the brothers of Joseph to sell him as a slave. It was also envy that led to Jesus' crucifixion. Today, envy leads to the killing of one's reputation and good name. When people are envious, they kill their brother and sister with their tongues or with their words through malicious gossip.

We need to guard our hearts for envy can creep to us subtly. We can be tempted to envy our brother or sister when they are promoted, when they do better than us in their families and careers, when they receive the things we want for ourselves.

Instead of feeling envious, we should be inspired. These people deserve their reward because of their hard work, faithfulness and obedience. They are blessed because they follow God's will for their lives. The Holy Spirit teaches us to be happy for other people when they are blessed. Their success are good examples for us to follow. When we do our best in what God has called us to do and when we follow His ways, He also has His own reward in store for us. *Marjorie Duterte (marjorie.travels@gmail.com)*

Reflection: "I too, invite myself — and everyone — to see if, in my heart, there is any jealousy, any envy, which always leads to death and doesn't make me happy; because this sickness always leads us to regard the good others possess as if it were against us. And this is an ugly sin. It is the beginning of many, many crimes." (Pope Francis)

Lord, protect us from envy. Keep our hearts close to You. We trust in Your good plans for us.

St. John Jones, priest and martyr, pray for us.

JULY 13
THURSDAY

Genesis 44:18-21, 23-29; 45:1-5
Psalm 105:16-17, 18-19, 20-21
Matthew 10:7-15

A WILLING SOUL

Whatever town or village you enter, look for a worthy person in it. – Matthew 10:11

After spending 13 years of my life serving the parish to build "small churches" in the neighborhood, half of the parish is still untapped.

Although we've had Masses in these areas, we haven't been successful at building cells of Bible sharing groups that meet regularly. I admit that this cannot materialize unless there is even just one willing soul to be an area leader.

A previous parish priest verbalized his belief that this activity is only for the depressed areas. But by now, we have already three subdivisions with regular cells because a willing soul agreed to be an area leader there. Colleagues working in other parishes succeeded in building cells in condominiums and high-rise subdivisions — because a willing soul was there to serve.

After all these years, I still believe in my heart that it's not yet time to "shake the dust from my feet" in any area. Who knows, a willing soul to be an area leader will still emerge. *Cristy Galang (cristy_cc@yahoo.com)*

Reflection: This year 2017 is dedicated to the church program of Basic Ecclesial Communities. Other sects are knocking door to door to spread their faith while many Catholics find comfort in driving all the way to a church building to serve. Listen to the Spirit. He may be calling you to be active in Basic Ecclesial Communities.

Open my heart, Lord, to serve where You are calling me. Wherever it is, Lord, with Your grace, my answer is yes.

St. Henry II, pray for us.

JULY **14**
FRIDAY

Genesis 46:1-7, 28-30
Psalm 37:3-4, 18-19,
27-28, 39-40
Matthew 10:16-23

THE PRICE IS RIGHT

"You will be hated by all because of my name, but whoever endures to the end will be saved." – Matthew 10:22

I was just learning the ropes of my first job. The president of one key account hosted a dinner meeting. The venue was too dark for a dinner. Eventually, half-naked girls came in. Dancing as they "artistically" took their clothes off to the beat of the music, all were ready to do what they were paid to do.

I stood up and told our host politely but straightforwardly, "I'm sorry, sir. I mean no disrespect. But I don't do these kinds of things. Please don't take this against me. I believe I should leave now."

I was sure I lost this huge business at that point. "Ignorance in the ways of doing business in the world" is a career killer. The days that followed were of scary silence from the customer.

I decided to pay him a visit. I was prepared for his tirade, but he welcomed me with a genuine smile instead. "You know, Jon, I was impressed with what you did that night. A person who can't be dishonest with his wife can't be dishonest with me. I respect that. I'm doing business with you."

Loving Jesus can be scary. It has a price. But believe me, it is worth it. *Jon Escoto (faithatworkjon@gmail.com)*

Reflection: If your old friends still enjoy you the way they enjoyed the "old" you, perhaps there is still no "new life" in you.

Lord, give me the strength to stand up for You. Your love is my reward.

St. Kateri Tekakwitha, pray for us.

Genesis 49:29-32;
50:15-26
Psalm 105:1-2, 3-4, 6-7
Matthew 10:24-33

THE TRUTH WILL SET YOU FREE

"Nothing is concealed that will not be revealed, nor secret that will not be known." – Matthew 10:26

Dave looked like a regular guy to his acquaintances. The truth is, he was living a double life. He was addicted to drugs and was in deep debt. Even his wife, Jackie, was clueless about his dark side.

But as he was leaving a drug session, he told a friend, "If Jackie calls you, tell her we had to go far to look for a drink." But Dave had accidentally dialed Jackie's number and she heard the conversation. Dave rushed to their place to find his wife and son about to leave. She vowed to file for legal separation.

Dave found himself alone in the following days. His isolation led him to pray. His prayers were answered when he found Jackie by their doorstep after several days. He asked for her forgiveness and vowed to change. Jackie decided to give him another chance.

Dave now lives a clean life. God blessed him and Jackie with another son. He also has his own business. He enjoys a renewed relationship with God. Dave initially thought that his addiction to drugs brought him happiness. He later realized that his true desire is a relationship with God and his family.

Jesus is the light. Go to Him now that He may overcome any darkness present in your life. *Alvin Fabella (alvinfabella@yahoo.com)*

Reflection: Go to Jesus now and let His light dispel your dark side.

Lord, may my life always reflect Your light.

JULY 16
SUNDAY

Isaiah 55:10-11
Psalm 65:10, 11, 12-13, 14
Romans 8:18-23
Matthew 13:1-23

PURPOSE

"My word shall not return to me void, but shall do my will, achieving the end for which I sent it." – Isaiah 55:11

The passage above reminds me of how my kids handle their toys. It's not often that we can give away toys, and it's not because I do not want them to share. It's because most of their toys are worn out by the time they're through with them. And it doesn't matter if the toy is inexpensive or fancy.

As one of those who give them their toys, I'm glad in a way that their playthings get worn out because I know they enjoyed playing with them. The toys served their purpose and were not for viewing purposes only.

Events and people come and go in our lives for a purpose, too. There are events in our lives that make us happy. There are events that make us realize how vulnerable we are and we get hurt or feel sad. We meet people whom we are able to affect in a positive way and we feel good. We meet people who break our hearts and we feel devastated.

Don't think that these are wasted moments. Events and people may not be permanent in our lives but by making an impact on us and making us better people, they have served their purpose. *Mae Ignacio (maemi04@aim.com)*

Reflection: Are we serving God's purpose in the lives of the people around us?

Lord, we thank You for sending people who give positive impact to our lives. May we also be Your instrument to make others know You.

JULY 17
MONDAY

Exodus 1:8-14, 22
Psalm 124:1-3, 4-6, 7-8
Matthew 10:34-11:1

STAND BY GOD

"Do not think that I have come to bring peace upon the earth. I have come to bring not peace but the sword." — Matthew 10:34

"What do I do?" my friend asked me one time during dinner. "Everyone in my organization is promoting this New Age event, and because I'm one of the leaders, I have to promote it, too."

I looked at my friend in the eye and asked, "You do know the Church's stand against New Age, right?"

She said yes and that she wanted to speak up and let the entire organization know that they shouldn't support the event, but she couldn't.

Even the leaders were lobbying for it, and big money was involved. I just prayed for my friend and her organization, with the hopes that God, the Sovereign King, would give us all the strength and courage to fight the good fight for His kingdom.

It's hard to stand by what's right, especially when the entire world doesn't even bat an eye against the many evil things that happen around us. It's hard to make a stand when anyone can shoot you down at any given moment. But we have to. Because all things in this world will pass, but God's judgment will last until eternity. *Karren Renz Seña (karren.s@shepherdsvoice.com.ph)*

Reflection: "Do not conform yourselves to this age but be transformed by the renewal of your mind, that you may discern what is the will of God, what is good and pleasing and perfect." (Romans 12:2)

Lord, give us the courage to go against the grain, to go against the world to follow You.

St. Francis Solano, pray for us.

JULY 18
TUESDAY

Exodus 2:1-15
Psalm 69:3, 14, 30-31,
33-34
Matthew 11:20-24

RECOGNIZE YOUR SIN

Jesus began to reproach the towns where most of his mighty deeds had been done, since they had not repented.
– Matthew 11:20

Forty-seven years ago in Quiapo, Manila, my *Tatay* succumbed to cancer of the liver. He was just 32 years old and I was just entering Grade 5. The big C was his own doing — drinking "gin *bulag*" (literally, "blind gin" because of the belief that drinking too much of the stuff will cause blindness) till the wee hours of the morning with his gang. He started this vice in his twenties.

My mom had been praying for a miracle early on in their marriage. The prayer was for *Tatay* to change his ways. During the last months of his life, the whole family prayed for a miracle of healing but the miracle never came.

Admittedly, during *Tatay's* wake, I questioned God why He didn't answer our prayer for healing. As I walked in faith, I realized that *Tatay* made his reconciliation with our Lord but the consequence of his drinking took his life.

Repentance is not just a New Year's resolution. It means to stop going in the wrong path or abandoning a vice that can have serious consequences for yourself and your family. It means completely turning around and redirecting your life to good and to God. *Dean Pax Lapid (paxlapid@it-spac.com)*

Reflection: "If today you hear His voice, harden not your hearts." (Hebrews 3:7-8)

Almighty God, mold me into the person You want me to be. Continue to shield me from impending danger that could lead to destruction.

St. Camillus de Lellis, pray for us.

Exodus 3:1-6, 9-12
Psalm 103:1-2, 3-4, 6-7
Matthew 11:25-27

CHILDISH-CHILDLIKE

"You have hidden these things from the wise and the learned, you have revealed them to the childlike." – Matthew 11:25

Childish is being immature, selfish, overly sensitive, troublesome, reckless and irresponsible. Childlike is being open, humble, grateful, joyful, perennially at awe.

When Jesus hides things from the wise and learned, it's because they think they don't need it. They think they know better or know it all. On the contrary, children and the childlike people are sponges, always ready to absorb what life has to offer them.

As a teacher and preacher, I am forever a student who always has much to learn from someone or something. I need to listen more, read more, study more, and observe more. And the only way I can do this is by being a "child" who continually thirsts and hungers for more.

The moment you think you have arrived is the moment you stop journeying… and stop learning. While you're still alive, the journey isn't over. And the learning continues.

Be childlike. Enjoy the journey. Learn more. *Alvin Barcelona (apb_ayo@yahoo.com)*

Reflection: When conversing, do you talk more or listen more? By talking more, do you also learn more or learn less?

Dear God, grant me the grace to be Your child, forever dependent on Your love. Let me be open and attentive to what You continue to tell me. In Jesus' name. Amen.

St. Mary MacKillop, pray for us.

Exodus 3:13-20
Psalm 105:1, 5, 8-9,
24-25, 26-27
Matthew 11:28-30

SPIRITUALITY IN ADVERSITY

"Come to me, all you who labor and are burdened…" – Matthew 11:28

I've always wondered what "casting burdens" meant. This problem or difficulty – how do I lay them down at His feet, pray tell?

I wanted answers and God made a way — through a death in the family.

When our beloved godmother Dely died last year, the family felt the loss big-time. *Ninang* Dely was a second mother to many of us, that's why losing her was difficult, not to mention it happened in Christmas time. But we felt that it was God's time that she is finally rested after a lingering illness.

In difficult times like death, when life turns suddenly hopeless, when nights are darkest, we all have a choice between being emotional — feeling sad and resigned — and being spiritual — expecting a miracle.

When *Ninang* left us, we chose to be spiritual.

Henry van Dyke is spot on in his poem "Gone from My Sight": "Just at the moment when someone says, 'There, she is gone,' there are other eyes watching her coming, and other voices ready to take up the glad shout, 'Here she comes!' And that is dying." *Rene Espinosa (drekki@gmail.com)*

Reflection: Feeling resigned in desperation? Choose to be spiritual. Know that a miracle is on its way.

Lord, make every difficult situation in my life an opportunity to strengthen my faith in You.

St. Apollinaris, pray for us.

JULY 21
FRIDAY

Exodus 11:10–12:14
Psalm 116:12-13, 15,
16, 17-18
Matthew 12:1-8

THE BLOOD OF THE LAMB

The blood will mark the houses where you are. Seeing the blood, I will pass over you ... no destructive blow will come upon you.
– Exodus 12:13

"Jesus, cover this vehicle with Your precious blood."

I can't remember from whom I learned this prayer that I utter whenever I walk away from my parked car. When I leave our house, I ask Jesus the same, for Him to cover our belongings. When I board a plane or ride a jeepney, or when I'm walking in the middle of the night, or whenever I am afraid, I call on the Blood of the Lamb to cover me from head to foot. And then I feel safe. I am assured that nothing will harm me, and I imagine myself enveloped by a shield that protects me from any element of evil. This shield is Jesus.

But beyond material possessions and external factors, Jesus is our shield from inner struggles, sins and temptations. If we only call on Him and rely on His saving grace, He will protect us and wash us clean, and we will be given a new chance at life. *Osy Erica (osy.erica@gmail.com)*

Reflection: The Blood of the Lamb protects us and washes us clean.

Jesus, cover me with Your precious Blood — from the tip of my hair to the soles of my feet. Protect me from anything that isn't Yours. Amen.

JULY 22
SATURDAY

Exodus 12:37-42
Psalm 136:1, 23-24,
10-12, 13-15
John 20:1-2, 11-18
(or Matthew 12:14-21)

Memorial of Mary Magdalene,
disciple of the Lord

'I HAVE SEEN THE LORD!'

Mary of Magdala went and announced to the disciples, "I have seen the Lord."
– John 20:18

Some people are caught up with the troubles of life that they fail to see the beauty of the Lord's creation.

Many years ago, I went to Batanes. It was a glorious experience being engulfed in the magnificence of God's creation. I could see God's love in all the colors of the sky, the ocean and the trees. I could feel God's love in the warmth of the sunlight and the cool embrace of fresh air.

When I got back to Manila, I felt a sensory overload. My first thought was: "Everything around me in Manila is man-made, noisy and not as glorious as God's creation."

Later in my years, I started seeing "man" — God's ultimate creation — in a different light. In the compound where I live, I began to enjoy greeting and connecting with young parents, kids, grandparents, driver, nanny or maintenance staff. At the mall, I nod at others and smile. Many people reciprocate.

And when a client comes in for a coaching session, I see God in this person's eyes. I want my clients to feel God's love through me as I listen to them, as I accept them for who they are and commit to help them in the best way I can. *Edwin S. Soriano (edwin@winningcoaching.net)*

Reflection: What has the Lord prepared along your path today?

Lord, open my eyes, my ears, my heart, that I may see, hear and feel Your presence as You guide me in life.

St. Mary Magdalene, pray for us.

Wisdom 12:13, 16-19
Psalm 86:5-6, 9-10,
15-16
Romans 8:26-27
Matthew 13:24-43

NOTHING HAPPENS BY ACCIDENT

"There is no god besides you who have the care of all…" – Wisdom 12:13

I was driving my brand-new car. At the Calamba toll exit, I slammed hard onto the car waiting to pay toll in front of me. The back of the car I bumped was a total wreck. My German-made car proved its safety features and suffered only a minor dent on the fenders. The car promised to give me not just safety on the road but, quite frankly, prestige as well.

In my younger days, I would have thought that crashing my car was my punishment for being vain in having a luxury car. But I know God now, without doubt, to be a caring God. I was profusely thankful that no one get injured in the accident.

Of course, I had my worrisome moments about the repair expenses, but that was erased by the thought of God as my provider. I believe that He doesn't just want to keep me from harm but also enjoy a divine luxury — of being physically and mentally at peace. Accidents like these are reminders that He cares.

Yes, He does care a lot more than we think He does. *Rolly España (rollyespana53@gmail.com)*

Reflection: "No eye has seen, no ear has heard of what God has in store for us" — because He cares.

Thank You, Lord, for keeping me safe in Your arms and for holding me always in the palm of Your loving hands.

OUR BATTLE IS THE LORD'S

"The Lord himself will fight for you; you have only to keep still." – Exodus 14:14

Exodus 14:5-18
Exodus 15:1-2, 3-4, 5-6
Matthew 12:38-42

"Why is this happening? How can our finances be enough? What if…?" These were the questions of *Ate* Conie, my eldest sister, when her husband, *Kuya* Joseph, was dignosed with kidney cancer and had to be operated on immediately in December 2014. During his checkup after the surgery, cancer cells were found in his rib bone and lungs. He began his medication. He diligently took care of his food intake, his body and his spirit.

He started reflecting on the Scriptures each morning. He prayed the rosary and the Divine Mercy chaplet daily. My sister and the rest of our family, together with friends, prayed for him. Where human strength was short, we turned to God's strength.

Oh, how God responded! He sent financial help to cover much of the monthly expenses. He made *Kuya* Joseph's body respond positively. He inspired him to spend more time in prayer.

When we encounter dead ends in our lives, we just have to be still and trust that God will fight our battle for us. *Ma. Luisa Dela Cruz (theessence_byluisa@yahoo.com)*

Reflection: What problems burden your heart and mind? Have you allowed God to move in your life through them?

Dear Lord, I surrender my troubles to You. Let Your peace be upon me as I entrust all to You. Amen.

St. Sharbel Makhlouf, pray for us.

DOWN BUT NOT CRUSHED

We are afflicted in every way, but not constrained... struck down, but not destroyed. – 2 Corinthians 4:8-9

2 Corinthians 4:7-15
Psalm 126:1-2, 2-3, 4-5, 6
Matthew 20:20-28

Feast of St. James, Apostle

He underwent a gallstone operation last month. His sister was hospitalized two weeks later. His mother, too, was recently hospitalized for a couple of days. Then early this week, he was back again in the hospital for dengue.

While I watched him at the hospital, his wife called in the middle of the night telling him that their little girl had a fever. "Her fever will be gone," I heard him whisper on the phone.

It's easy to give up in situations like these. These are the times when our faith as believers of Christ are put to the test.

The Bible says, "No trial has overtaken you that is not faced by others. And God is faithful: He will not let you be tried beyond what you are able to bear, but with the trial will also provide a way out so that you may be able to endure it" (1 Corinthians 10:13).

As we waited for his blood test results, he continues to hold on to his hope. He is down, but he is not beaten. He will come out victorious from all his trials! *Danny Tariman (dtariman.loj@gmail.com)*

Reflection: "They that hope in the Lord will renew their strength, they will soar on eagles' wings; they will run and not grow weary, walk and not grow faint." (Isaiah 40:31)

Lord Jesus, You are my hope. You are my strength. I lift up to You my situation. I am almost crushed. Hold my hand and take me out of this.

St. James, Apostle, pray for us.

JULY 26
WEDNESDAY

Sirach 44:1, 10-15
(or Exodus 16:1-5, 9-15)
Psalm 132:11, 13-14, 17-18
Matthew 13:16-17
(or Matthew 13:1-9)

Memorial of Sts. Joachim
and Anne, parents of the Virgin Mary

WHAT IS THIS?

*"What is this?" for they did not know what
it was. – Exodus 16:15*

How many times in our life have we asked God, "What is this?"

A rebellious child in the family. "What is this?"

A relationship gone sour. "What is this?"

A business bleeding money. "What is this?"

My moment of asking came when my family was on the brink of being broken apart by my infidelity. And even if I knew that it was my fault, I couldn't understand what was happening. I was crying. My wife was hurt. My child was oblivious to our situation. And the question in my heart was, "God, what is this?"

God uses all things — even the bad ones — for our benefit if we love Him. And oftentimes, it's the bad things in our lives that He uses to lift us up. This way, we have no reason to boast that we are good, but instead, point to Him and say, "God is good!"

The Lord has used my adversity to restore me. I have no doubt He will do the same for you. *Boggs Burbos (boggsburbos@yahoo.com)*

Reflection: What difficult circumstances are you facing right now? Ask God, "What is this?"and wait for His loving answer and embrace.

Lord, I entrust to You my difficulties today, knowing that You are mightier and bigger than them. In due time, use my challenges to lift me up.

Exodus 19:1-2, 9-11, 16-20
Daniel 3:52, 53, 54, 55, 56
Matthew 13:10-17

EVERYONE HAS SPECIAL NEEDS

"Blessed are your eyes, because they see, and your ears, because they hear."
— Matthew 13:16

When you see a blind person or a group of deaf people communicating to each other in sign language, what's the first thing that comes to your mind?

Do you feel sorry for them?

Do you pity them?

Or do you find yourself praying for them?

Or maybe even thanking God that all *your* senses are intact?

The truth is, while our blind and deaf brothers and sisters have special needs — just like other persons with different abilities (that's my own definition of PWD) — so does every person who is 100 percent sound in body.

All of us have some sort of handicap, and these are not necessarily of the physical kind.

In fact, many of us may be "blind" and "deaf" in spirit — when we refuse to see the hand of God in our lives, and choose not to hear Him. When we close our eyes to the needs of others and we let the cries of the poor fall on deaf ears.

God doesn't want us to be like this though. He wants us to see and hear as He does. Let's ask Him for the grace to do so.

Tina Santiago Rodriguez (trulyrichandblessed@gmail.com)

Reflection: "To love another person is to see the face of God." (Victor Hugo)

Open the eyes and ears of my heart, Lord. Use me as You will.

Blessed Antonio Lucci, pray for us.

JULY 28
FRIDAY

Exodus 20:1-17
Psalm 19:8, 9, 10, 11
Matthew 13:18-23

DOING THE OPPOSITE

*"One who hears the word of the Kingdom
without understanding it…"*
– Matthew 13:19

To all mothers out there (and to those who deal with babies): How often do you mistake your baby's cry for something else? Your baby is trying to tell you something but you don't understand so you end up getting frustrated.

Priscilla Dunstan, an Australian mom with a gift for sound, claims to have discovered the universal secret language of babies. She tested her baby language theory on more than 1,000 infants all over the world. She said that babies zero to three months old speak the same language regardless of race or culture. She recommends parents to listen for these five "words" or aptly called sound reflexes in a baby's pre-cry before the baby cries hysterically: "Neh" means "I'm hungry." "Owh" means "I'm sleepy or tired." "Heh" means "I feel discomfort." "Eairh" means "I have lower gas." "Eh" means "I need to burp."

God's Word is also universal. His message remains the same. But at times we don't understand it and give it different meanings so we end up doing just the opposite of what He says. Let's cultivate the soil of our heart so when God speaks, we can hear Him with understanding, respond to it appropriately, and produce fruit abundantly. *Judith Concepcion (svp_jmc@yahoo.com)*

Reflection: Do you twist God's Word to suit your needs and preferences?

Lord, grant me the grace to accept Your Word, especially those that convict me of my wrongs, knowing that You discipline those You love.

St. Leopold Mandic, pray for us.

Exodus 24:3-8
Psalm 50:1-2, 5-6, 14-15
John 11:19-27
(or Luke 10:38-42 or Matthew
13:24-30)

Memorial of St. Martha,
disciple of the Lord

WORK AND WORSHIP YOUR WORRIES AWAY

"You are anxious and worried about many things. There is need of only one thing…"
– Luke 10:41-42

Worrying means thinking of things that you don't have control over. The reality is we will never run out of things to worry about. We will always have bills to pay, piles of work to do, and the list goes on.

One antidote is when you work more, you worry less. When you work at things you can control and do the best that you can, then you don't need to worry too much. And when there's nothing you can really do about it, then it's time for you to entrust everything to God and worship Him.

For five years now, my wife, Emelyn, and I have been praying to have a child but until now, we're still waiting for God's perfect time. We made a decision to work for it and find ways to prepare for our pregnancy even as we wait in surrender and worship the God who knows what is best for us.

What are you worried about now? Work on it and worship your worries away with God. *JC Libiran (JCLibiran@ymail.com)*

Reflection: "Come to me, all you who labor and are burdened, and I will give you rest." (Matthew 11:28)

Jesus, I surrender all my worries, my doubts and my fears. May Your love reign in my life. Amen.

St. Martha, pray for us.

JULY 30
SUNDAY

1 Kings 3:5, 7-12
Psalm 119:57, 72, 76-77,
127-128, 129-130
Romans 8:28-30
Matthew 13:44-52

BEYOND CALVARY

We know that all things work for good for those who love God, who are called according to His purpose. – Romans 8:28

In 2006, my son was diagnosed with cancer. The C-word hammered an ominous feeling of finality in my mind.

RJ was fresh out of college and had just begun working on his dreams. Was it the end of the road for him? The thought was devastating!

My heart seemed to explode. My mind struggled to understand the sense of it. Burdened, I sought comfort in prayer. In front of Mary with the Child Jesus in her arms, I cried my heart out. I told Mary my fears, asked her to help me see my son's illness as bravely as she faced her Son's suffering on the cross. I felt oneness with her, then an assurance that everything we were going through was blessed by God's hand. I realized, too, that if He took us to this, He'd surely lead us through it. I thanked Him for my son, for the gift of being his mother, for using me as an instrument of His love.

Our cancer experience taught us to "see beyond Calvary." That period was a sacred time – an invitation to seek God, an opportunity to grow in faith. *Marie G. Ferrer (smgferrer@gmail.com)*

Reflection: Suffering brings us down to our knees, to total and humble dependence on God.

Lord, teach me to accept my hardships as pathways to peace, taking as You did, this sinful world as it is and not as I would have it, trusting that You will make things right if I surrender to Your will. (Serenity Prayer)

St. Peter Chrysologus, bishop and doctor of the Church, pray for us.

Exodus 32:15-24, 30-34
Psalm 106:19-20, 21-
22, 23
Matthew 13:31-35

Memorial of St. Ignatius of Loyola, priest

HER EYES OF FAITH

"The kingdom of heaven is like yeast that a woman took and mixed with three measures of wheat flour until the whole batch was leavened." – Matthew 13:33

I would often see her sitting in the front rows of The Feast, our weekly prayer meetings. You won't miss her because of her beauty, her height and her long black hair.

One Sunday, she approached me after Mass and asked if we could talk. She was instantly in tears as we found a quiet corner. She narrated that her husband left their family to be with another woman. He just packed his bags and brazenly admitted falling out of love with her after more than a decade of marriage. His accusations were crushing. His reasoning was absent. His heart was stone-cold. He left without explanation and without leaving any money for her and their four children.

After all was said, this abandoned wife gripped my hands and looked at me intently. She then said with her soul, "I will move on. He will come back to us. I do not know when or how, but he will. My children will grow up with a dad. We will make it. We will survive."

They say faith can move mountains. That day, I saw that indeed, it does. *Lallaine Gogna (lallygogna@yahoo.com)*

Reflection: What circumstance in your life now do you need to see with the eyes of faith?

Dear Lord, grant that I may see Your hand in all things. You never leave me or forsake me. Your right hand upholds me. You are with me always and forever.

St. Ignatius of Loyola, priest, pray for us.

Exodus 33:7-11; 34:5-9, 28
Psalm 103:6-7, 8-9, 10-11, 12-13
Matthew 13:36-43

We live in a noisy world, yes, but the loudest noise comes from inside us. It's called stress. Friend, the secret to living a stress-free life is to learn the rhythm of work and trust.

Do all you can. But at regular times, stop and surrender. Because unless you give yourself space and time, you won't hear God's voice of assurance and comfort.

We all have big problems and small problems. But let me tell you: Trust that there is no problem too big for God's power or too small for God's concern. What matters most is not whether the problem is big or small, but *how long you carry it in your mind*.

If I ask you to carry a glass of water for an hour, you'd be able to do it. You'll feel a little discomfort, but not much. But if I ask you to carry that same glass of water for 12 hours, you'd still be able to do it, but your arm will ache like crazy.

Worry is "carrying" your problem in your mind. It may be a small problem but if you worry about it for a long time, it can kill you. You need to put your problem down… by giving it to God.

Then listen to what He is trying to tell you in your heart. *Bo Sanchez (bosanchez@kerygmafamily.com)*

Reflection: Is there something that occupies your mind and heart that you can hardly listen to God? Pause now and listen with your heart.

Dearest Lord, speak to me in the silence of my heart. Amen.

St. Alphonsus Liguori, bishop, pray for us.

AUGUST 2
WEDNESDAY

Exodus 34:29-35
Psalm 99:5, 6, 7, 9
Matthew 13:44-46

THE SCENT OF GOD

*He did not know that the skin of his face
had become radiant while he conversed
with the Lord. – Exodus 34:29*

While leading worship one night, I asked God to bless me in a special way. In the past, God would always save me in small ways: He supplies my words at the right moment. He gives me the breath to reach high notes. He even gives me the energy to jump, despite my heavy tummy!

But this night was an ordinary night. There was nothing in particular that I wished for. But as I was jumping up and down, everything suddenly went slow-mo. A breeze of sweet perfume touched my nose. It was the smell of fresh breeze within a sea of sweat and song.

I lingered. I stopped singing and took it all in. I didn't know who sprayed perfume, but one thing was sure: this was God. And when I picked up the mic, a new breath embraced the sound. There was a new life, a new energy filling my bones. God was saying: "I am pleased." That night wasn't ordinary after all. Better yet, in that ordinary night, God made His presence known.

Just like how God manifested in Moses' radiant face. It was evident. It was unmistakable. Through the light of his face, everyone knew that God had spoken. And God loves to show Himself in the ordinary, if only to tell us, "I love you." *Migs Ramirez*
(migsramirez.seminars@gmail.com)

Reflection: How has God shown Himself to you today?

Jesus, let me see You in the ordinary things of today. Amen.

St. Eusebius of Vercelli, bishop, pray for us.

AUGUST 3
THURSDAY

Exodus 40:16-21, 34-38
Psalm 84:3, 4, 5-6, 8, 11
Matthew 13:47-53

READ INSTRUCTIONS!

Moses did everything just as the Lord had commanded him. – Exodus 40:16

There's one unforgettable test I flunked in high school. We had only three minutes to answer a long exam, so I dove into answering the questions even if the instructions told us to read the entire test paper before answering.

I was pressured as one girl and then another raised their hands proudly, signifying they were done. It hadn't been even a minute yet! Only a handful of girls were able to complete the entire exam. How could they have done it so quickly?

If I had been careful to follow instructions and read to the end of the paper, I would have seen the last line that said, "No need to answer any of the questions. Just write your name, the date and put a star on the upper right-hand corner of your paper."

We're so used to doing things our way that we overlook the value of obedience. This is true even when it comes to our relationship with the Lord. We pick and choose which among His commandments we want to follow, not knowing that obedience to Him unlocks the blessings we desire.

God's commandments are there to lead us towards the path of blessing and not to make our lives difficult. Obey and reap the blessings! *Rissa Singson Kawpeng (justbreatherissa@gmail.com)*

Reflection: Obeying God is listening to Him. It is having an open heart to follow the path that He points out to us.

Lord Jesus, help me to follow Your footsteps closely. Open my eyes to the blessings of obeying You. Amen.

St. Peter Julian Eymard, pray for us.

AUGUST 4
FRIDAY

Leviticus 23:1, 4-11, 15-16, 27, 34-37
Psalm 81:3-4, 5-6, 10-11
Matthew 13:54-58

A WELCOMING HOME

"A prophet is not without honor except in his native place and in his own house."
– Matthew 13:57

I love being home. There, I can be my truest self. I don't need to dress up. I can be in my favorite cotton shirt filled with holes. At home, I can bare everything, including my flaws and weaknesses, and still be loved unconditionally.

But because our home has known us with all our flaws, our family might also find it hard to believe in us. So while we find our greatest acceptance at home, sometimes we can also find our greatest rejection in it.

Jesus experienced the same thing. People from His hometown couldn't believe that the carpenter's little son they used to know had grown to be a man of wisdom. Sadly, they weren't able to experience mighty deeds from Jesus because of this. It's not that Jesus didn't want to do miracles. He could have but they just failed to recognize them because of their unbelief.

How about you? Do you believe in the people in your home? Many of us take for granted the spouse, child, parent or friend God has given us. Who knows? Greatness might be in your midst. Start seeing beyond their flaws. Believe in them.

Make your home a little less unwelcoming. And you will begin to receive the miracles your family needs. *Velden Lim (veldenlim@gmail.com)*

Reflection: In your home, who needs to hear the words, "I believe in you"?

Jesus, give me the grace to believe in others the way You believe in me.

St. John Vianney, priest, pray for us.

AUGUST 5
SATURDAY

Leviticus 25:1, 8-17
Psalm 67:2-3, 5, 7-8
Matthew 14:1-12

COW DIVIDED

"Do not deal unfairly, then; but stand in fear of your God. I, the Lord, am your God." – Leviticus 25:17

Butch and Bill were young when their parents died. The brothers inherited a cow and proceeded to divide it. Butch said, "I will be fair with you, Bill. You take the front portion of the cow as your share. I will take the hind. Each one gets its profit from his share."

Bill fed the cow well. It became healthy and produced a lot of milk. Now, Butch got all the milk and sold it for a good profit. But he did not share the money with Bill. When Bill asked for his share, Butch said, "I got the milk from my side of the cow."

So the next day, while Butch was milking the cow, Bill beat the cow on its shoulder. The cow started kicking with its hind legs at Butch. He said, "You fool! Why did you beat the cow? Don't you see I'm milking it?" Bill said, "The front portion of the cow is mine. I can do anything with it. That's our agreement."

The sibling rivalry got so bad that they decided to divide the cow and get their fair share. Each got half a ton of meat, but after selling that, they had no more source of income.

When we treat the other person with fairness and honor, both parties come out the winner. But when we choose to act out of selfish rivalry, we all lose. Fairness begets fairness. Honor begets honor. *Mike Viñas (mikemichaelfcv@yahoo.com)*

Reflection: "Love one another with brotherly affection. Outdo one another in showing honor." (Romans 12:10, ESV)

Jesus, teach me to honor people with justice and grace.

St. Addal, pray for us.

AUGUST 6
SUNDAY

Daniel 7:9-10, 13-14
Psalm 97:1-2, 5-6, 9
2 Peter 1:16-19
Matthew 17:1-9

Feast of the Transfiguration of the Lord

A RAINBOW TO COMFORT ME

"This is my beloved Son, with whom I am well pleased." – Matthew 17:5

How blessed is Peter that he witnessed the transfiguration of Jesus as we read in today's Gospel. It's one of the most amazing, if not the one true proof, that Jesus is the Son of God.

I must admit, the human me still needs to have proof from time to time that God is real. One of the signs I ask for is the rainbow. That's because God said in Genesis 9:13, "I have set my rainbow in the clouds, and it will be the sign of the covenant between me and the earth."

And God still patiently gives me proof of His Presence, especially when I am troubled.

Like when I resigned from my job. I felt bad because I lost a substantial salary. And I needed assurance from God that I did the right thing.

A few days after, I went to the market in the morning to buy the day's food. The sun was up, but there was a drizzle, and there it was in the clouds: a rainbow!

Peter may have the transfiguration but God's rainbow is OK enough to comfort me. *Chay Santiago (cusantiago@gmail.com)*

Reflection: What proof do you need to feel God's Presence?

Lord, grant me the grace of faith to trust You even when I don't see or feel You.

Numbers 11:4-15
Psalm 81:12-13, 14-15,
16-17
Matthew 14:13-21

HEART OF THE CHURCH

When Jesus disembarked and saw the vast crowd, His heart was moved with pity for them, and He cured their sick.
– Matthew 14:14

When I was young, I'd describe Church as a place where stiff people sit together in pews. An unengaging presider leads an alienated congregation. Pouting people pray together yet are indifferent to each other. People stand-sing-sit-listen-stand-listen-kneel. Old men brandish expensive watches, older women talk in whispers, lovers snuggle, young ones glance at their crush, and kids make noise even when they're shushed.

The good news is that the present Church is cool! And it's continuously blessing and refreshing God's people. A cool Church is where God's people unwind in His presence as family and friends. The presiding priest energetically leads the equally responsive congregation. Smiling and loving people pray together. It's a full house yet everyone knows each other by name. People learn God's Word, worship in the Holy Mass and sing praise songs.

What is in the heart of the Church? U R! You are in the heart of the Church! You are in the heart of God. Go and bring His heart of love to the world! *Obet Cabrillas (obetcab@yahoo.com)*

Reflection: Don't complain that church bores you if you don't contribute to its liveliness.

Shepherd of my soul, I give You full control, wherever You may lead, I will follow.

AUGUST 8
TUESDAY

Numbers 12:1-13
Psalm 51:3-4, 5-6, 6-7,
12-13
Matthew 14:22-36
(or Matthew 15:1-2, 10-14)

LEAVE YOUR BOAT

He said, "Come." Peter got out of the boat and began to walk on the water toward Jesus. – Matthew 14:29

Myrna was drowning when she saw Jesus at the end of the pool just watching her. She shouted, "Why aren't You helping me?" Jesus replied, "Because I know you know how to swim." And then Myrna woke up from her dream.

It was a friend's dream that saved me from turning my back on God. I left my corporate job to have more time to serve in ministry. To sustain myself financially, I took online jobs. It paid me well until I lost clients because of an over-supply of online freelancers.

I questioned God, "Is this how You bless me after deciding to serve You more?" I stopped praying. God became just a concept. But God sent Myrna to tell me about her dream. And then I knew He was asking me to leave my current boat and walk on water again, for He has already equipped me for the call He gave me.

Now I am an events host and singer. I get to do what I love, and most of all, I get to serve Him more.

What's your boat? Is He asking you to leave your boat and walk on water? *Veia Lim (veiallim@gmail.com)*

Reflection: "You can't walk on water if you don't get out of the boat." (Anonymous)

Jesus, give me the faith and courage to walk on water. I believe Your hands will hold me when I let go.

St. Dominic, priest, pray for us.

Numbers 13:1-2, 25-14:1,
26-29, 34-35
Psalm 106:6-7, 13-14,
21-22, 23
Matthew 15:21-28

LIVE MY LIFE

"I was sent only to the lost sheep of the house of Israel." – Matthew 15:24

"The good news is your disease is not life-threatening!" my rheumatologist said. I responded with a bemused smile. I couldn't find it in me to celebrate.

It's not uncommon for people with autoimmune diseases to say, "I wish I had cancer." It's not only because the disease makes daily living difficult, but more because of the lack of understanding and empathy from doctors, friends, and even family members.

"You keep thinking you're sick that's why you get sick!"

"Just choose to be happy and you won't be depressed!"

"I'm sure you can do better if you just try!"

I only wish people were more understanding that we are doing the best we can under the circumstances.

Jesus didn't limit His compassion to those of His own kin. He extended healing to the Canaanite woman. I wish everyone would choose to reach out and empathize with people who are different. What a change of perspective we'll have if we can live each other's lives, survive each other's traumas, and experience each other's fears. After all, we are doing the best we can, under our unique circumstances. *Cecil Lim (cez_lim@yahoo.com)*

Reflection: "Mercy is entering into the chaos of another person's life." (Fr. James Keenan, SJ)

Lord, grant me the gift of understanding others, even as I strive to understand myself.

St. Teresa Benedicta of the Cross, pray for us.

AUGUST 10
THURSDAY

2 Corinthians 9:6-10
Psalm 112:1-2, 5-6, 7-8, 9
John 12:24-26

Feast of St. Lawrence, deacon, martyr

A FOLLOWER WHO DOESN'T STAY PUT

"Whoever serves Me must follow Me…"
– John 12:26

As a petite and lean lady who can do a walkathon for up to four hours, it took me 14 years of unsteady faith walk — with a lot of stumbling and trying to rise up again and walk — to realize that Christian life is not a bed of roses but a crown of thorns.

Now I can understand why a lot of people choose secularism, materialism and relativism, among others, over the Christian life. Because Christianity is no joy-ride. It's a long and winding road, a 42-kilometer marathon to the finish line, where one becomes a champion and permanent resident in heaven.

I came to a point when I was hesitant to embrace my everyday crosses of thorns because it was painful and tiring to lead a simple and upright life, especially when I just rely on my own strength and stamina.

But at the end of the day, I ask myself this question: "To whom shall I go, Lord? You alone have the words of eternal life. I will search for You until my weary heart and soul rest in You." *Ems Sy Chan (leeannesy7@yahoo.com)*

Reflection: Have you found your God and followed Him? Know Him, love Him, and serve Him first.

Lead the way, my Lord, and I will follow You to the ends of the earth and heavenward.

St. Lawrence, deacon and martyr, pray for us.

Deuteronomy 4:32-40
Psalm 77:12-13, 14-15,
16, 21
Matthew 16:24-28

PRUNED

"Whoever wishes to come after me must deny himself, take up his cross, and follow me." – Matthew 16:24

My father is a farmer. To make trees bear more fruit, he would often need to do some grafting, pruning or trimming. That is painful to the tree but it ends up being sturdier, healthier and definitely more fruitful.

When we signed up to become Christians, we told God we wanted to change. Then God started pruning, trimming, and grafting at our lives. That's when the complaints started; "not this part, Lord" or "work on this later" or "please don't do that!" So what happens? Nothing. Absolutely nothing. We're stuck.

And then at some later time, we go back to God and accuse Him, "Lord, I prayed that you change me, what's taking so long?" But one thing that God will never do is to change us without our consent. He says to us, "…must deny himself," which basically means we sign up to become a better version of who we were by giving up the old self.

God will never give us anything we cannot bear. And like the Israelites in our First Reading, God wills for us to be blessed but we have to do our part, too. *Rod Velez (rod.velez@gmail.com)*

Reflection: What will it take for you to realize that you no longer have to be in bondage of that recurring sin that you confess so often?

Master, I cannot change alone. Please send me friends who will remind, encourage, admonish, and pray for me because I truly want to be a better Christian.

GOOD TIMES

"Take care not to forget the Lord, who brought you out of the land of Egypt, that place of slavery." – Deuteronomy 6:12

Deuteronomy 6:4-13
Psalm 18:2-3, 3-4, 47, 51
Matthew 17:14-20

A man used to travel from his home in Novaliches to Our Lady of Lipa in Batangas to ask God to heal him from his serious illness. God answered his prayers and extended his life.

A few years later, he was in Batangas for a business trip and passed by the church. He hesitated to drop by but his wife reminded him of the many times he went there to pray for healing. It was only then that he stopped at the place where his prayers had been answered.

It's easy to remember God when we are hurting. We run to church on our own. We go to great lengths to attend a healing Mass. But when we are healed and happy, we tend to forget God.

As the Israelites were about to enter the Promised Land, Moses reminded them not to forget the Lord who brought them out of slavery. We are also reminded not to forget the Giver of our blessings as we enter into good times and prosperity. Let us learn from the lone leper who returned to Jesus to give thanks after realizing he had been healed. The other nine forgot God in their happiness. They forgot the Giver of their gifts. May we not suffer the same spiritual amnesia. *Marjorie Ann Duterte (marjorie.travels@gmail.com)*

Reflection: "Bless the Lord, my soul; and do not forget all his gifts, who pardons all your sins, and heals all your ills." (Psalm 103:2-3)

Thank You, Father! May we never forget You when we are in need and most especially when we are delivered from it.

St. Jane Frances de Chantal, pray for us.

AUGUST 13
SUNDAY

1 Kings 19:9, 11-13
Psalm 85:9, 10, 11-12,
13-14
Romans 9:1-5
Matthew 14:22-33

SAVE DAD

Immediately, Jesus stretched out his hand and caught Peter. – Matthew 14:31

When Dad got dengue, I was scared of losing him. It was the first time I saw him looking weak. Dad was always in control and handled crises for us. That time, though he still gave instructions, we had to do the legwork. Especially when he needed transfusion.

My worry increased each time the blood test results came back with single-digit platelet counts. He needed platelet transfusion immediately. We were in constant coordination with the lab technicians who tried to source it from other hospitals and blood banks. We had to look for donors when the availability of ready platelets was limited. Foolishly, I thought all hospitals had a supply of this and it wasn't that hard to find.

Desperate and worried, I called on Jesus, "Save Dad. We need platelets."

Immediately, we found contacts to blood banks. Some friends and family members, even strangers, volunteered to donate their blood. Prayers poured out for Dad. We found just enough platelet when we needed it.

Jesus was so near. He caught Daddy. He caught me. *Kitty D. Ferreria (kittydulay@yahoo.com)*

Reflection: The Lord is always near, standing always by your side.

Lord, I'm calling out to You. Help me be fearless.

AUGUST 14
MONDAY

Deuteronomy 10:12-22
Psalm 147:12-13, 14-15,
19-20
Matthew 17:22-27

Memorial of St. Maximilian Mary Kolbe,
priest and martyr

AWESOME

*"He is your glory, he, your God, who has
done for you those great and terrible things
which your own eyes have seen."*
– Deuteronomy 10:21

My devotion to the Holy Eucharist started when I was still in high school. Since then, I did my best to go to Holy Mass daily or as often as I can.

Then, when I discerned that I would get married, I wished that one day I would have children with whom I can share my devotion to God and the Holy Eucharist. I dreamt of going to Holy Mass daily with them.

That dream came true when God miraculously gave me children and made a way for us to move to our current house, which is near a church. But God did not stop there. He paved the way for our eldest son to be inspired to play the piano when he saw a pianist serve regularly in the daily Masses we attended.

On October 17, 2015, I did not only celebrate Holy Mass with my family. I also witnessed my seven-year-old son play the piano during Mass for the first time. Since then, I've had the awesome privilege to witness my eldest son serve as pianist in our parish daily and on Sundays during the children's Mass.
Teresa Gumap-as Dumadag (teresa@fulllifecube.com)

Reflection: What are some of the great and awesome things God has done in your life? Take time to praise and thank Him for these.

"Great and wonderful are Thy wondrous deed, O Lord God the Almighty. Just and true are all Thy ways, O Lord. King of the ages art Thou." (From the song "Great and Wonderful" by Stuart Dauermann)

AUGUST 15
TUESDAY

Revelation 11:19;
12:1-6, 10
Psalm 45:10, 11, 12, 16
1 Corinthians 15:20-27
Luke 1:39-56

Solemnity of the Assumption
of the Blessed Virgin Mary

A FINISHED SONG
*"What was spoken to you by the Lord would
be fulfilled." – Luke 1:45*

A powerful photo of Pope Francis embracing a man disfigured by a rare skin disease compelled me to write a poem stating my guilt on how much lighter my burdens are compared to him. I posted the poem on Facebook, along with the link to the image, and a long-time writer-friend from the media ministry at church commented that he could put a melody to it. I then realized he was not only a writer but also an excellent guitar player.

Upon this eureka moment, I remembered I had written a song on God's love about five years before, and I have yet to find someone to help me finish it. *Kuya* Mike was my guy, and next thing I knew, he was working on the guitar chords. The song soon found its way to the recording studio – a dream that I have long prayed for.

A photo led to a poem, which led to an offer for help and a finished song after five years. God orchestrated everything.

When you offer your dreams to God, rest assured He will fulfill them however He puts the pieces together. Trust Him. *Osy Erica (osy.erica@gmail.com)*

Reflection: God is putting each piece of the puzzle of your life one after another. Your dreams will come true in His time and in His ways.

Your hands are constantly at work, Lord. When the waiting is long, shower me with grace to trust You. Amen.

Deuteronomy 34:1-12
Psalm 66:1-3, 5, 8, 16-17
Matthew 18:15-20

THORN ON THE SIDE

"If he listens to you, you have won over your brother." – Matthew 18:15

"You can always count on me to be the thorn on your side who gives you a reality check instead of telling you what you want to hear." I definitely can relate to this poster message. I have been branded countless times as a thorn for my attempts at fraternal correction.

People are typically non-confrontational. They'd rather not say anything than be told to mind their business. As a result, bad deeds persist. In the end, when damage has been inflicted, we regret not having done anything.

People are also typically defensive. "Sorry, I am only human and commit mistakes," would be their retort. Precisely why we should humbly welcome acts of fraternal correction. We are imperfect and the devil is preying on us 24/7. In the end, when the ill effects are irreversible, we regret not listening to good counsel.

We may be a thorn on someone's side in their eyes as we attempt to point out what is wrong, but to God, you are an angel. Let us watch for each other's welfare and salvation. *Marie Franco (mariefranco_pie@yahoo.com)*

Reflection: Have you thanked your mother, father, siblings, and well-meaning friends who were bold enough to point out your misdeeds? After all, they love you and are after your welfare.

In the name of Jesus, by the power of Jesus, for the love of Jesus, I forgive you. And in the name of Jesus, by the power of Jesus, for the love of Jesus, I forgive myself.

Joshua 3:7-10, 11, 13-17
Psalm 114:1-2, 3-4, 5-6
Matthew 18:21-19:1

70 X 7 TIMES

Jesus answered, "I say to you, not seven times but seventy-seven times."
— Matthew 18:22

Forgive seventy times seven times.

In the Bible, it means "infinity." It means you have to forgive every slight, every insult, every injury at every moment, every hour of every day, because God has already forgiven us for the things we did and the things we will do.

So it's just right that we extend the same mercy to others.

I used to think that I've covered "seventy times seven times," because there was a time when each time I remembered my father, I had to forgive him. Each time I got angry, I had to forgive him. I had to ask God for forgiveness, because no person should ever carry that much anger in their heart.

I used to forgive because I had to, because God said so, but not because I wanted to. But one time during worship, I felt it — God's boundless grace. His relentless love. And when you are swimming in such overwhelming love, you can't not overflow.

God died, so we could be free — from death. From sin. From hate. From anger.

Let us extend the same grace to others. *Karren Renz Seña (karren.s@ shepherdsvoice.com.ph)*

Reflection: Is there someone you need to forgive today? Think about God's love… and then overflow.

Dear Lord, Your grace and love are relentless. May we overflow this love to others, no matter how difficult. Teach us how to forgive. Amen.

St. Joan of the Cross, pray for us.

GOD OF THE IMPOSSIBLE

Joshua 24:1-13
Psalm 136:1-3, 16-18, 21-22, 24
Matthew 19:3-12

"Because they cried out to the Lord, he put darkness between your people and the Egyptians, upon whom he brought the sea so that it engulfed them." – Joshua 24:7

When the animated movie *Inside Out* became a hit, a friend would usually ask me, "Who are you in the movie? Are you Joy, Sadness, Fear, Anger or Disgust?"

If a close friend answers for me, he would probably say Joy. But I disagree. I'm not a positive person most of the time. In fact, deep inside, I'm the opposite!

Then it hit me. I was Fear.

I tend to plan way ahead of situations because I fear that it might not work out. I stress out on things that are not yet happening because I fear that it won't come out right. It takes me a long time to make major decisions because I fear that when I decide, I will mess up.

Then I'm reminded that the God I worship is the same God who delivered Israel from slavery and the same God who also brought them to the Promised Land — even at seemingly impossible costs.

So who am I to worry about tomorrow? If God can divide an ocean to let me pass through, I have nothing to fear. *Tintin Mutuc (kristinemutuc@shepherdsvoice.com.ph)*

Reflection: There are three things essential in your faith: trust, trust and trust.

Jesus, I trust and love You.

St. Louis of Toulouse, pray for us.

AUGUST 19
SATURDAY

Joshua 24:14-29
Psalm 16:1-2, 5, 7-8, 11
Matthew 19:13-15

ASK THE CHILDREN

"Let the children come to me... for the Kingdom of heaven belongs to such as these." – Matthew 19:14

There's a classic song by the legendary Pinoy folk band, Asin, titled, *"Itanong Mo sa Mga Bata"* (Ask the Children).

We, of course, believe it's poetic. Because we think it's us adults who know the answer.

Yet, see how adults solve, or are not solving, the problems of the world today. See how the problems may have even aggravated because we think as adults and not as children.

Because the solution to war, caused by discrimination, prejudice and inequality are tolerance, mutual respect and forgiveness, which children quickly give to one another.

Because the solution to hunger and poverty is less greed and more sharing, which children easily learn.

Because the solution to depression and hopelessness is a little more joy and laughter, hope, faith and trust, which children naturally manifest.

And because the solution to most, if not all, problems is more love, which children purely personify.

No wonder our Lord Jesus said, "The kingdom of heaven belongs to them." Alvin Barcelona (apb_ayo@yahoo.com)

Reflection: Check your actions if they are more childlike or childish – if it is God's Kingdom you are propagating, or just yourself.

Dear God, may the true child in me continue to live, that I may belong to Your kingdom forever. Amen.

St. John Eudes, priest, pray for us.

AUGUST 20
SUNDAY

Isaiah 56:1, 6-7
Psalm 67:2-3, 5, 6, 8
Romans 11:13-15, 29-32
Matthew 15:21-28

NOT JUST SCRAPS

"O woman, great is your faith!
– Matthew 15:28

I'd often tell myself, "O you of little faith." Faced with problems, I'd easily get discouraged and lose hope. Eventually, the problem would be solved. Thanking God, I'd think, "Why do I thank God only when things work out well? Why can't I thank God even in the midst of a difficulty trusting that He will take care of everything?" My faith was weak. Again and again, I would ask God to increase my faith.

I have come to realize that faith is a gift to be received and not something to be obtained. When I come to God with the faith of a little child, it is then that I release God to work miracles for me.

Little by little, my faith has increased over the years. I now have a quiet assurance that God doesn't just want to give me "scraps from the table," but He wants to spread a banquet before me. Jesus said, "Until now you have not asked anything in my name; ask and you will receive, so that your joy may be complete" (John 16:24). *Beth Melchor (epmelchor6@gmail.com)*

Reflection: The Canaanite woman in the Gospel knew her desperate need for God and knew that even if He would give the scraps from the table, it would be enough. Is God enough for you?

Lord, help my unbelief. Increase my faith.

Judges 2:11-19
Psalm 106:34-35,
36-37, 39-40, 43, 44
Matthew 19:16-22

"What would I do if I knew that I could not fail?"

This line is from Jana Stanfield's song "If I Were Brave." She sang it during her talk "The Launch Pad: Rock Star Strategies to Rocket Your Business." That was the highlight of my Kerygma Conference 2015 experience. It made me think about the things I could still do to reenergize my life and my career.

Jana said something else that made taking those steps less scary. She advised us to write down three things we can't possibly fail at in a week. Her example was about her dream of becoming a singer. Her baby step was: Call a voice coach. She didn't say take voice lessons from a professional coach; her goal was to just call. Things snowballed from that baby step, and she is now a rock star who has composed songs for and performed with big-name artists. All these things happened because she bravely took that baby step.

But more than taking those baby steps, the failsafe way is to follow Jesus. Discern and pray what His will is for your life.
Lella Santiago (mirellasantiago@yahoo.com)

Reflection: Have you decided to follow Jesus in all areas of your life?

Jesus, here I am, ready to follow You. There's no turning back. Give me a heart that is committed to You. Amen.

AUGUST 22
TUESDAY

Isaiah 9:1-6
(or Judges 6:11-24)
Psalm 113:1-2, 3-4, 5-6,
7-8
Luke 1:26-38
(or Matthew 19:23-30)

Memorial of the Queenship
of the Blessed Virgin Mary

MY ANGEL

"I shall be with you," the Lord said to
him. – Judges 6:16

Years back, I was a lost sheep. I found myself feeling alone even though I had many friends. I was in deep depression. It was so deep that I couldn't do any of my usual routines.

I had to drag myself to school and didn't care about my grades. Nobody took notice of the gravity of my situation. To them, I was just trying to get attention.

But then, Angel, an old high school classmate whom I hadn't seen in a long time, suddenly reached out to me. She asked about my feelings. Apparently, she noticed that I was posting negative stuff on my social accounts.

I poured out my heart to her. She listened. She never judged me. She just made herself available. She even informed my cousins about my situation. Her action enabled my family to better understand me, and eventually, I was able to meet people who led me to a relationship with the Lord. Such experience healed me and helped me move forward with my life.

I never forgot what my friend Angel did. She was literally my angel. I truly believe that God used her to be the portal of His promise: I will be with you. Thank you, Angel. Thank you, Father God. *Erika Mendoza (epaulmendoza@gmail.com)*

Reflection: Always pursue opportunities to be God's portal of love.

Lord, use me as a channel of Your love to others.

AUGUST 23
WEDNESDAY

Judges 9:6-15
Psalm 21:2-3, 4-5, 6-7
Matthew 20:1-16

ENTITLEMENT

"Are you envious because I am generous?"
– Matthew 20:15

We miss out on blessings because we feel we are entitled to privileges.

When I was still employed, there was a time when my salary rose higher than my coworkers in similar positions and who had worked in the company much longer than me. I attributed it to my work beliefs. I did my best in fulfilling my duties and responsibilities and did not focus on the compensation. I didn't allow envy to affect my work ethic.

Jesus' story about the workers in the vineyard teaches us about this. Many were called at different hours but received the same compensation. It talks of Jesus' generosity, calling workers who are willing to respond and who feel privileged just to be asked to work for Him.

If we focus on the rewards and feel we are "entitled," we will never be satisfied. When we work and feel grateful that God has called us to the task at hand, when we work excellently for Him and not for earthly rewards, our entitlement is to be with Him for all eternity. *Donna España (donna.espana@yahoo.com)*

Reflection: God's generous love is a reminder of His faithfulness to us.

O Holy Spirit, continue to inspire me to serve freely and generously without counting the cost.

St. Rose of Lima, virgin, pray for us.

AUGUST 24
THURSDAY

Revelation 21:9-14
Psalm 145:10-11, 12-13, 17-18
John 1:45-51

Feast of St. Bartholomew, Apostle

BLESSINGS IN SUFFERINGS

"Can anything good come from Nazareth?" – John 1:46

I was browsing the Internet when I read a letter of a nun who was raped by Serbian soldiers in Yugoslavia in 1995. She got pregnant and had to painfully leave the convent. When this happened, she was still grieving over the death of her two brothers who were killed by the Serbian soldiers. She was in "internal darkness," as she described in her letter.

From this devastating experience, we would expect a woman filled with much anguish, hatred and revenge. But she held on to God and saw it as sharing in Jesus' shame in Calvary and the shame of many women violated by evil deeds of men. In spite of her woundedness, she even thanked God for letting her join in the torment of thousands of her countrymen who experienced abuse and tragedy because of the war.

When her mother superior asked what she would do with the baby in her womb, she said that she would raise him in love and be a mother to him.

In our sufferings, blessings blossom if we have the faith to trust in God. *Ma. Luisa Dela Cruz (theessence_byluisa@yahoo.com)*

Reflection: Do you praise and thank God during moments of grief?

Beloved Jesus, in my painful moments, help me remember You in Calvary. Make me grateful and honored in sharing Your suffering. Amen.

St. Bartholomew, Apostle, pray for us.

Ruth 1:1, 3-6, 14-16, 22
Psalm 146:5-6, 6-7, 8-9,
9-10
Matthew 22:34-40

SELFLESS LOVE

"You shall love the Lord, your God, with all your heart, with all your soul, and with all your mind." – Matthew 22:37

One day, as I was browsing my Facebook account, I saw a pretty girl who sent me a private message. I do not know her personally.

When I replied to her message, she started a conversation with me. I wanted to find out how she came to know me, but as we went on, I noticed that her messages were turning malicious and titillating.

I was shocked when she asked me if I wanted to see her sexy photos. I immediately stopped our conversation, blocked her from my Facebook page and prayed.

I prayed for that girl that God would show her His light. I also prayed for myself that God keep me away from temptation and sin. I was on the brink of falling into temptation but I had to remind myself that I love God more than anything else in this world. I love Him more than what gives me pleasure. *Monty Mendigoria (montymendigoria@yahoo.com)*

Reflection: Love God with all your heart and with all your mind, period. There will be times when our love for God will be tested. Stand firm and don't give in. Our love for God should always prevail. Let nothing in this world ever replace that love.

Jesus, fill us with Your grace to love. Teach us to love You more and more so we can also share that love to people who are in dire need of You.

Ruth 2:1-3, 8-11; 4:13-17
Psalm 128:1-2, 3, 4, 5
Matthew 23:1-12

OUT OF SYNC

"... for they preach but they do not practice." – Matthew 23:3

I often watch dubbed TV shows and find the messed-up audio synchronization quite funny. Sometimes, the actor speaks only a syllable but the dubber blurts out a long sentence.

These dubbers are like us Christians. Many of us are experts at blurting out religious principles but our actions are out of sync. There's a great disharmony about the way we preach God's message from the way we practice it. This is hypocrisy. It speaks volumes on why a lot of nonbelievers say Christianity is shallow. Our "audience" doesn't take us seriously. What's worse, we fail to be accountable to God.

Working out this concern must come from within. Let's "remove the dubbing" and apply the actor's language genuinely. Jesus prompts us to heed, share and live out the Truth — humbly and wholeheartedly.

As American religious leader Hyrum Smith puts it, "Character, simply stated, is doing what you say you're going to do." When our lips and our deeds are synchronized, only then shall His Word be fully realized. *Ithan Jessemar Dollente (tanji6@gmail.com)*

Reflection: Take an honest assessment of the areas in your life where your walk doesn't match your talk.

Father, renew in me the heart to walk with You. May I genuinely live and breathe Your word for the rest of my life. Amen.

St. Joseph Calasanz, pray for us.

AUGUST 27
SUNDAY

Isaiah 22:15, 19-23
Psalm 138:1-2, 2-3, 6, 8
Romans 11:33-36
Matthew 16:13-20

PURPOSEFUL TWISTS AND TURNS

How inscrutable are his judgments and how unsearchable his ways! – Romans 11:33

Who would have thought I would be living in Manila when I am from the Visayas and I didn't want to go to "imperial Manila" and speak Tagalog? But despite the pain and challenges, it's where I got to know the Lord more intimately and grew in following Him.

Who would have thought that Ignatius of Loyola would become a saint? After all, he was a knight from a noble family, used to the good life. But he was wounded in battle and had nothing to read except his sister's pious books while convalescing. His heart was moved and he soon trekked the way of the Spirit.

You, too, have probably had your own twists and turns that you didn't expect in your life. You don't understand why things happened to you as they have. You may feel insignificant and trivial. But the things that happened to you were there for a purpose. The God of Wisdom has been orchestrating things for your good, if you will let Him. His judgments and His ways may be inscrutable, but His motive is not hidden. For He is Love Himself. So just trust. He knows what He's doing. *Joy Sosoban-Roa (jsosoban@gmail.com)*

Reflection: "We know that all things work for good for those who love God, who are called according to his purpose." (Romans 8:28)

Dear Jesus, I hold on to You in this adventure called life. My life is in Your hands. May Your Name be glorified in me.

IN WHATEVER WAY

Knowing, brothers and sisters loved by
God, how you were chosen...
– 1 Thessalonians 1:4

1 Thessalonians 1:1-5,
8-10
Psalm 149:1-2, 3-4, 5-6, 9
Matthew 23:13-22

In high school, I entered the *aspirantate* (minor seminary). I ended up staying for two years. That experience helped develop some of my personal and religious habits. Waking up at 5 a.m., daily Mass, morning and evening prayers, study time and love for sports. But why was I there? I was attracted to the Salesian way of life — how they interacted with us kids as they set up a religious yet happy environment. There I developed a mentality that I should take my faith seriously.

But it was on December 4, 1988, many years later, when I gave my heart to Jesus and found God my Father. My life was never the same again. I devoured the Bible like never before, spent quality time in prayer, and desired to serve the Lord in whatever way.

Why did I receive Him in the first place? I was tired of my sin. I wanted to be right with God and experience His salvation.

Jesus from my youth had been pursuing me. He wants to save me and get to know me intimately. He chose me.

We are all chosen. And God is committed to let us know in whatever way. *Ariel Driz (adriz77@yahoo.com)*

Reflection: God has chosen you. Have you chosen Him?

Father, thank You for choosing me. Thank You for pursuing me. I surrender all that I am to You.

AUGUST 29
TUESDAY

Jeremiah 1:17-19
(or 1 Thessalonians 2:1-8)
Psalm 71:1-2, 3-4, 5-6,
15, 17
Mark 6:17-29

Martyrdom of John the Baptist

YOUR WORD, YOUR VALUE

"He did not wish to break his word…"
– Mark 6:26

In one leadership seminar that I conduct, I would say to the audience, "Remember, promises are made..." Then almost everytime, the crowd would say with certainty, "to be broken." To which I would quip, "to be fulfilled! No wonder our world is in chaos!" The audience roars in laughter, then…silence.

How many relationships have suffered because of broken agreements? How much pain, suffering and evil happen when we don't fulfill our promises? But our word should be aligned to our true value.

Herod seemed to have fulfilled his promise. But to whom and with what intent? It was for the pleasure of others, in the service of self, a consequencial decision based on fear and cowardice. No wonder today we have unreliable and ineffective leaders. John the Baptist also fulfilled his promise. To whom and with what intent? To God, a true commitment based on faith and courage. No wonder he was the forerunner of the Messiah.

What kind of leader will you be — a Herod or a John the Baptist? Perhaps someday we will have true leaders. Then we will have peace. *Jonathan Yogawin (jyogawin@gmail.com)*

Reflection: How much is your word? Resolve today to commit to the value it intends.

Lord Jesus, thank You for being faithful to Your promises. May I fulfill mine. Amen.

St. Sabina, pray for us.

1 Thessalonians 2:9-13
Psalm 139:7-8, 9-10,
11-12
Matthew 23:27-32

DESPICABLE ME

"You are like whitewashed tombs, which appear beautiful on the outside but inside are full of dead men's bones and every kind of filth." – Matthew 23:27

I was so upset! I requested the dental lab to do a simple denture repair and they bungled it up. It was such a stressful situation since the patient was leaving for abroad and this was her last appointment. I lashed out at the one in charge in the lab for the unacceptable error and I hung up in a huff. As soon as I fixed the problem and the patient left satisfied, I quickly called the lab. I spoke to the person I almost crucified earlier with my words and I profusely apologized. She readily accepted. Their mistake was inexcusable but my reaction was unforgivable, inexpiable and downright despicable.

Even if I go faithfully to Mass every day and pray the rosary every night, that doesn't guarantee me a place in heaven if I do not act with love towards erring people. When I stand before the gates of heaven, I don't think I will be asked how many prayer meetings I have attended or how devoted I was to my prayer time. I guess I will only be asked one thing: How much did you love your brother?

I pray that I will not bow my head sadly and walk away in shame. *Ronna Singson Ledesma (ronna_ledesma@yahoo.com.ph)*

Reflection: It is better to love than to be right.

Lord, give me a heart like Yours that loves unconditionally.

AUGUST 31
THURSDAY

1 Thessalonians 3:7-13
Psalm 90:3-4, 12-13,
14, 17
Matthew 24:42-51

ONE WAY

*Now may God himself, our Father, and our
Lord Jesus direct our way to you…*
– 1 Thessalonians 3:11

There was once a seaman who walked aimlessly in the mall, devastated because his agency did not renew his contract. At that point, nothing seemed to work in his life. He had a wife and kids to support, plus his aging parents and younger sister depended on him. He was losing all hope. He wanted to jump from the escalator he was about to step out on. Then suddenly, a lighted sign caught his attention: The Feast. There were music, smiles and dancing. He opened the door. He entered and found the answers he was desperately looking for.

Then there was the husband — a drug addict, jobless, branded useless by his wife and in-laws, separated from his children. He could not live another day. But a priest took him in and brought him to a family. This family trusted him enough to let him stay, and even hired him as a driver. In that home, he found acceptance. Soon, while still residing in that house, he began to court his wife and earn her trust. He saw his kids once more. Much later, they reconciled and more kids followed.

These men were so lost, they couldn't find their way. But God found them. Because there's no place that God cannot reach if only we let Him in. *Lallaine Gogna (lallygogna@yahoo.com)*

Reflection: What is the distance between you and God right now?

Dear Jesus, You are the Way. May I never wander far from You. Draw me closer to Yourself every day. Amen.

Sts. Joseph of Arimathea and Nicodemus, pray for us.

1 Thessalonians 4:1-8
Psalm 97:1, 2, 5-6, 10, 11-12
Matthew 25:1-13

OUR AVENGER

For the Lord is an avenger in all these things…– 1 Thessalonians 4:6

My friend Mark lent P1 million to his business partner. It was a huge amount for my friend. But his partner ran away. This devastated Mark. It wasn't only the money but the betrayal. But instead of being bitter or thinking of ways to get back at him, Mark decided to expand his small business. Instead of spending his time cursing his enemy, he spent his time blessing his business.

Today, Mark earns P1 million every month. And what happened to the man who stole his money? Through the grapevine, Mark learned that the guy was still financially hard up.

Friend, God saw you when you were offended, hurt or abandoned. Let Him handle your case. Put the situation in His hands. He'll see to it that you'll receive double of what you've lost.

As long as you let go and forgive, God will be your vindicator.

He'll make your wrongs right.

He'll even the score.

And if you forgive and pray for your enemies, get ready to be very blessed! *Bo Sanchez (bosanchez@kerygmafamily.com)*

Reflection: Do you still keep a record of the offenses done against you? Put them now in God's hands.

Dearest Lord, I surrender to You my desire to take revenge against those who have wronged me. I forgive them now and pray that You bless them. Amen.

SEPTEMBER 2
SATURDAY

1 Thessalonians 4:9-11
Psalm 98:1, 7-8, 9
Matthew 25:14-30

RESPONSIBILITIES AND BLESSINGS

"Since you were faithful in small matters, I will give you great responsibilities. Come, share your master's joy." – Matthew 25:23

I belong to two Feasts (the weekly prayer meeting of the Light of Jesus Family) in Marikina and Cainta. I was their go-to guy whenever there was heavy lifting or manual labor. I accepted all invitations for help as long as it had nothing to do with going on stage, especially holding a microphone.

But the unthinkable happened. They asked me to lead worship and give a talk. I initially declined but I remember making a covenant with God: to serve Him in any way I can. So I half-heartedly accepted the task. It was the lousiest talk and worship leading ever. I never thought that one day, the man opening the doors will be the same man opening the hearts of people to Jesus. That the man arranging chairs will be the same man helping arrange people's lives. That the man lifting heavy speakers will be the main speaker himself. Today, I'm the Feast builder in Marikina and Cainta.

P.S. Before and after I give a talk, I still do all those tasks — and I love it! When you are faithful and grateful in small things, God will prosper you and entrust you with greater things.

Monching Bueno (ramon_bueno@yahoo.com)

Reflection: Do the smallest of tasks with love and gratefulness.

Lord God, teach us to be faithful in small things and help us prepare for the greater things You have in store for us.

Jeremiah 20:7-9
Psalm 63:2, 3-4, 5-6, 8-9
Romans 12:1-2
Matthew 16:21-27

WHAT'S YOUR AQ?

Then Peter took Jesus aside and began to rebuke him, "God forbid, Lord! No such thing shall ever happen to you."
– Matthew 16:22

For 37 years, Paul Stoltz studied about adversity. He surveyed half a million people all over the world and discovered that each person faces an average of 23 adversities each day. This only shows that hardship and difficulty is part and parcel of life. That's why it's important that we know how to face the challenges that come our way daily.

He calls this skill in facing our problems "adversity quotient" or AQ. There are people who quickly lose steam at the slightest of difficulties and give up. These people have low AQ. There are those who have gone through hell and back but are still standing. These are those with high AQ.

I learned these facts from Rosanne Romero, one of *Kerygma's* columnists who has been battling the crippling effects of multiple sclerosis for 30 years. When it comes to AQ, she must be a genius.

God has armed us with weapons to overcome our problems. In Jesus, we are more than conquerors. God has given us treasure in earthen vessels to show that our power comes from Him, not from us. *Rissa Singson Kawpeng (justbreatherissa@gmail.com)*

Reflection: "We are afflicted in every way, but not constrained; perplexed, but not driven to despair; persecuted, but not abandoned; struck down, but not destroyed." (2 Corinthians 4:8-9)

Lord, I am weak and broken, but let Your power shine through me.

St. Gregory the Great, pope and doctor of the Church, pray for us.

SEPTEMBER 4
MONDAY

WITH THE LORD

Thus we shall always be with the Lord.
– 1 Thessalonians 4:17

1 Thessalonians 4:13-18
Psalm 96:1, 3, 4-5,
11-12, 13
Luke 4:16-30

Moses had an issue with his self-worth. He was full of doubts. He didn't think he could make any difference in leading the Israelites to the Promised Land. But he remained faithful to God and the Lord used him to lead His people out of slavery.

Joshua had just crossed the Jordan River into the Promised Land. They were invaders facing the impregnable city of Jericho. It would take weeks and months of battle to break down their high, thick walls. But Joshua obeyed God's command to the letter and the walls came tumbling down.

Gideon was scared when he learned that their enemy had 135,000 men and he only had 32,000. Despite their inadequacy in number, God lessened their troops even more. Why? So that they would all know that a large army wasn't important. It was God who would give them victory.

Though these men of the Old Testament had their shortcomings, God still used them to fulfill His promises. Our great God can instantly turn our weakness into strength. When we are with the Lord, we need not be overwhelmed by the strength of our enemies, the size of our problems, or the gravity of our weaknesses. *Sem. Kein Harvey P. Chito (kein.chito@gmail.com)*

Reflection: Turn to God and He will equip you. He will never leave you.

Father, I thank Your Holy Name for all the blessings in my life. You are always there to fill me. I desire to always be with You.

St. Rose of Viterbo, pray for us.

1 Thessalonians 5:1-6, 9-11
Psalm 27:1, 4, 13-14
Luke 4:31-37

NEED TO BE RIGHT

Therefore, encourage one another and build one another up, as indeed you do.
– 1 Thessalonians 5:11

Have you ever had an "I told you so" phase? I had one in grade school. In my immaturity, I felt a deep need to prove that I was right. And every time I was, the phrase would slip off my tongue, "See? I told you so." I did it with everyone, disregarding how the person on the receiving end must have felt.

During a school project, one of my friends and I debated on the best method to make our science exhibit work. I finally gave in after arguing. But as we worked on it, I secretly wished that it would fail just to prove that I had been right all along.

When it did, I came home and snidely told my mom, "I told her so." My mom asked me one question, "Did being right feel good?" I paused. Actually, not really.

"It failed because one person on your team was trying to fail. But in the end, you were still wrong because you all failed together. If you didn't have so much foolish pride, you would have succeeded by working well together," she said. I learned from then on that letting others win doesn't make you a loser. It makes you part of the solution instead of the problem. *Eleanore Teo (elyo.lee@gmail.com)*

Reflection: Have you ever felt the need to be right at the expense of others?

Father, remind me that my service is not to stand on a higher pedestal but to lift others up and above my own intentions.

St. Teresa of Calcutta, pray for us.

SEPTEMBER 6
WEDNESDAY

Colossians 1:1-8
Psalm 52:10, 11
Luke 4:38-44

TGFY (THANK GOD FOR YOU)

We always give thanks to God, the Father of our Lord Jesus Christ, when we pray for you. – Colossians 1:3

Can I brag? Not about me or my achievements. I'd like to brag about the media ministers I have had the privilege to serve with.

One of my dreams in my *Novena to God's Love* booklet is to be surrounded by supportive, easy-to-work-with people who will help me achieve our ministry's mission.

God has blessed this dream and is continuing to do so. It's a blessing to lead talented, creative, selfless and tireless writers, photographers and layout/graphic artists. It's a blessing to be loved and cared for by the team heads in our Editorial Board Light Group. Every time the weekly bulletins and *Light Magazine,* Feast Alabang's evangelization tool, come out, I am bowled over by their talent and heart for service.

In my prayer, I cannot help but thank God for these people who serve off-site, invisible to the eyes of the attendees. They spend sleepless nights to beat the printer's deadline. I am grateful for the media ministry members who bring inspiration and hope with the service they do. *Lella M. Santiago (lellams88@gmail.com)*

Reflection: There are people who make your load lighter. Do you make the effort to affirm them?

Lord, I am eternally blessed by the people You have sent to assist me. Pour Your graces upon them today.

SEPTEMBER 7
THURSDAY

Colossians 1:9-14
Psalm 98:2-3, 3-4, 5-6
Luke 5:1-11

BIRDS OF A FEATHER
*"Put out into deep water and lower your
nets for a catch." – Luke 5:4*

I once gave a recollection to school teachers and I used the saying, "Birds of the same feather flock together." After the culminating prayer, people went around hugging each other, some even crying.

An English teacher hugged me and said she was so blessed. Still in tears, she whispered, "With all due respect, brother, the right phrase should have been, 'Birds of a feather, flock together.'"

OMG! What a learning experience! Well, nobody's perfect.

My dear friends, we belong to a big family called the Church. But the question is, "Are we of a feather?" Church is never just a shared activity. The spiritual community is about sharing our life in Jesus together.

Community comes from *commo,* meaning "shared or common"; and *uno,* meaning "one." So let us be one and share a common life in Christ. He is the Head and we are His Body. Let's grow deeply in sharing the same principles, purpose, parameters and persistence.

In Christ, let's grow deeper, so we can soar higher! Because we are of a feather. *Obet Cabrillas (obetcab@yahoo.com /twitter: @daddyobet)*

Reflection: The most natural thing to happen to a healthy body is to grow. Let's help build a healthy Church and growth will be automatic.

Lord, I want to help build community. Use me, Jesus.

Blessed Frederick Ozanam, pray for us.

SEPTEMBER 8
FRIDAY

Micah 5:1-4
(or Romans 8:28-30)
Psalm 13:6, 6
Matthew 1:1-16, 18-23

Nativity of the Blessed Virgin Mary

SWEETER THAN CHOCOLATES

All things work for good for those who love God, who are called according to his purpose. – Romans 8:28

When Michele Ferrero died in 2015, he was Italy's wealthiest man. His family business created Ferrero Rocher chocolates, Tic Tac mints and Nutella chocolate spreads. He was humble, working hard and committed to the welfare of his employees. More importantly, Ferrero said that he owed his success to Our Lady of Lourdes: "Without her, we can do little." Such was his devotion and faith.

I'm always reminded of Ferrero's story whenever I spot a jar of Nutella in a store, or see it included on a dessert menu. While we can't all be inspirational business tycoons, we can, however, try our best to live for God's glory as we go about our day — making an honest living and interacting positively with people.

Blessings come when we place the Lord at the front and center of our lives. Just as God is the source of love and all that is good, we can be a source of benevolence and love for others.

Imagine if we can liken ourselves to a jar of chocolate spread, oozing goodness with every spoonful. As the song goes, what a wonderful world it would be. *Gina J. Verdolaga (mgjver@yahoo.com)*

Reflection: "Love the Lord, all you who are faithful to him. The Lord protects the loyal, but repays the arrogant in full." (Psalms 31:24)

Lord, thank You for all You have bestowed upon me. Help me become a force of goodness in Your name.

St. Adrian, pray for us.

SEPTEMBER 9
SATURDAY

Colossians 1:21-23
Psalm 54:3-4, 6, 8
Luke 6:1-5

THE FACE OF HUNGER

"Have you not read what David did when he and those who were with him were hungry?" – Luke 6:3

On the mountaintop of Digos, Davao Oriental, Fr. Mario Quejadas watched with dread as the storm raged through the night. As expected, the morning trek to the tribal literacy school was fraught with danger. He grumbled to God as he struggled with slippery slopes and thick mud.

While visiting the classrooms, a fifth-grader asked, "Father, can you help us? We go to school hungry all the time." He stopped short, then asked the class, "How many here go to school with an empty stomach?" Most of the students raised their hands. "How many eat once a day?" About two-thirds raised their hands. "How many eat three times a day?" Nobody raised a hand. With tears in his eyes, he realized, "Here I am grumbling about mud on my feet when these children are starving!"

Sometimes, we are so focused on our own problems that we fail to see how others are faring. Look around. Is there a hunger for attention from your loved one? Is there a hunger for help from someone in need? Make it a point to respond. *Cecil Lim (cez_lim@yahoo.com)*

Reflection: "Sometimes, I want to ask God why He allows poverty, famine and injustice in the world when He could do something about it… but I'm afraid He might ask me the same question." (Anonymous)

Lord Jesus, give me the hunger to be part of the feeding and the healing of this world.

St. Peter Claver, priest, pray for us.

SEPTEMBER 10
SUNDAY

Ezekiel 33:7-9
Psalm 95:1-2, 6-7, 8-9
Romans 13:8-10
Matthew 18:15-20

ISN'T HE AMAZING?

"For where two or three are gathered together in my name, there am I in the midst of them." – Matthew 18:20

I looked out the window and saw a big storm coming. My heart skipped a beat because I knew we must hurry home. Otherwise, we would surely be stranded.

We were a group of four coming from an appointment in Manila on our way home to Quezon City where we live. We were riding a rundown car and I was afraid that if we would have to pass through flooded streets, we could get stuck in the middle of a raging storm.

Then God showed us a miracle.

As we plowed through a flooded street, the four of us prayed fervently using the gift of tongues. Our car was almost floating and water was entering the car, but we kept on. We trusted that God would see us through.

And He did. We reached dry land and got home safely. *Marisa Aguas (jojangaguas@yahoo.com)*

Reflection: Do you have a need that is aching in your heart right now? Pray with a friend or group of friends. Together, storm heaven with prayers. If it will be good for you, and it is in accordance with God's will, He will grant your prayer request.

Dear God, You said that if two or three are gathered in Your name, You dwell in the midst of them. Along with my friends and my community, I lift up to You the concern in my heart. If it is in accordance with Your will, please grant my prayer. In Jesus' name. Amen.

St. Thomas of Villanova, pray for us.

Colossians 1:24-2:3
Psalm 62:6-7, 9
Luke 6:6-11

"I ask you, is it lawful to do good on the Sabbath rather than to do evil, to save life rather than to destroy it?" – Luke 6:9

An ex-mayor from my hometown used to deal with insurgents by throwing them in jail, visiting them regularly, giving their mothers a livelihood, and putting their children to school. Nobody expected such things and he ended up being a true untouchable, respected and feared by both sides.

Jesus was the best in changing our perspective in doing good because He always emphasized that love and mercy are greater than the Law and the prophets. They asked Him which of the more than 600 Jewish laws was the most important and instead of picking one, He summarized them into two. Society expected Him to stay away from sinners and criminals, but instead, He befriended them and eventually changed their lives.

Love and mercy can be creative. Many Christians practice different ways of showing these. Some do tutorials for street children. Others give away food and clothes around the city. And still others just sit with patients to talk with them.

Whatever we choose, let us never tire of being creative in doing good, being merciful, and showing love. Let us always see others through Jesus' eyes. *Rod Velez (rod.velez@gmail.com)*

Reflection: Love and mercy begin at home. Before practicing it with others, how do you regularly show love and mercy in your family?

Grant me the grace, Lord, to do the good I need to do now. Let me not wait, but spur me to action and change my life in the process.

Colossians 2:6-15
Psalm 145:1-2, 8-9, 10-11
Luke 6:12-19

AWAKE, MY SOUL

"You were also raised with him through faith in the power of God, who raised him from the dead." – Colossians 2:12

There was a time in my life that I was asleep more than I was awake. When I woke up, I would sleep again until late afternoon. I was trying to escape my emotional pain. I was like a walking dead — alive but not really living.

Thanks be to God who saved me from such a wretched existence. He brought me to life again. First, He renewed my mind through reading the Bible. He led me to The Feast, a healing place where I felt accepted and loved unconditionally. He entrusted me to Mama Mary who accompanied me through the rosary. At The Feast and through the Blessed Sacrament, I sought to touch Jesus and He healed me.

I thought that my life was bleak, dark and hopeless. But God's mercy proved me wrong. His light shone through. He can bring dead things back to life with His Word and healing love.

If you are like me, believe me when I say that God is able to raise you up through the power of His Spirit. Reach out to Jesus, He will bring you back to life. *Marjorie Ann Duterte (marjorie.travels@gmail.com)*

Reflection: "Our daily problems and worries can wrap us up in ourselves, in sadness and bitterness... and that is where death is. That is not the place to look for the One who is alive! Let the risen Jesus enter your life, welcome Him as a friend, with trust: He is life!" (Pope Francis)

Lord, I want to be well. Please bring me back to life again. Mama Mary, pray for me.

St. Ailbhe, pray for us.

SEPTEMBER 13
WEDNESDAY

Colossians 3:1-11
Psalm 145:2-3, 10-11,
12-13
Luke 6:20-26

DEATH GIVES LIFE

Put to death, then, the parts of you that are earthly: immorality, impurity, passion, evil desire, and the greed that is idolatry.
– Colossians 3:5

I love eating fruits. I eat grapes the same way some people eat potato chips. And when I eat mangoes, I don't use a spoon. I eat them with my bare hands and it gets messy all over.

After eating a fruit, nothing is left of it except for its seeds. We usually throw it away because it doesn't have any more use.

But there are a few people who don't throw away the seed but instead bury it in the ground. After a few days, something sprouts. In a few months, it becomes a plant. And after a few years, that seed will bear fruit again that we can enjoy.

We are like a seed that needs to die so we can be reborn beautifully. We need to die to ourself, to our pride and to our sins for the good things in our life to blossom.

Let God plant, sow and prune us, trusting that He has a good plan for our life. Let's believe in His purpose for us. He has gifted us to become the most beautiful tree that will bear the greatest fruits the world will ever see. *JPaul Hernandez (Jpaulmh@yahoo.com)*

Reflection: What habitual sins do you need to surrender to God?

Father, I surrender to Your pruning. I believe that You will not cause me harm but I know You want to mold me to be a better Jesus-follower in this world. Amen.

St. John Chrysostom, bishop and doctor of the Church, pray for us.

SEPTEMBER 14
THURSDAY

Numbers 21:4-9
Psalm 78:1-2, 34-35,
36-37, 38
Philippians 2:6-11
John 3:13-17

Feast of the Exaltation of the Holy Cross

FRECKLES

*"For God did not send his Son into the world
to condemn the world..." – John 3:17*

Jenna, an elderly lady, was walking in the park with her grandson Elson. There happened to be a kids' party and a long line of children waiting for their cheeks to get worked on by the face paint artist. Elson excitedly joined the line but was stopped by an innocent young girl who said, "Your freckles are too many, there's no more space for the paint!"

Elson ran back to his grandma, hanging his head in embarrassment. Jenna witnessed everything, and she knelt down in front of him, "I've always wanted freckles when I was a little girl. I see stars in your freckles. They brighten up your face!" "Really?" Elson asked.

"Definitely!" says the grandma. "Tell me, is there anything you know that's prettier than freckles?"

Elson had a deep thought for a while and took a glued stare at Jenna's face. He leaned over to her ear and whispered, "Your wrinkles!"

"Really?" it was Jenna's turn to ask. "Definitely!" Elson explained, "They brighten up your face. I see love. I see Jesus!"

Jon Escoto (jonmaris@yahoo.com)

Reflection: What "freckles" do you see in the people you bump into today? Do you condemn their "freckles" or do you choose to see their stars?

Father, let me see the people around me through the eyes of Your mercy. Then they will see Jesus in me, even in my "wrinkles." Amen.

St. Notburga, pray for us.

Hebrew 5:7-9
(or 1 Timothy 1:1-2, 12-14)
Psalm 31:2, 3, 3-4, 5-6,
15-16, 20
John 19:25-27
(or Luke 2:33-35)

Feast of Our Lady of Sorrows

FROM PERSECUTOR TO PROMOTER

"I was once a blasphemer and a persecutor and an arrogant man" – 1 Timothy 1:13

Bro. Noe Dora was a radical Protestant preacher. He was determined to convert as many people as possible to his religion, especially Catholics. He hated the Catholic Church and believed that it was teaching evil, not good. He would visit the houses of his members to destroy the images and materials related to the Catholic Church.

One day, he was in the house of a newly converted follower doing his usual practice of destroying Catholic images. He picked up a statue of Mama Mary and stared at it. He felt something strange and heard these words in his mind: "What did My mother do, for her image to be destroyed this way?"

That odd event led him to study the Catholic faith. He secretly read about the faith, met up with a priest, and attended Mass. His six-year study led him to receive the sacrament of baptism and later he became a Catholic. Bro. Noe now travels around the Philippines and nearby countries to share his testimony. His personal goal is to bring back as many people as possible to the Catholic Church.

It's never too late for anyone to repent and change. *Alvin Fabella* (alvinfabella@yahoo.com)

Reflection: Your parish needs all the help it can get from you. Volunteer and be part of any service in your parish today.

Lord, help me to be a credible Catholic witness so that others may return to our Mother Church.

Our Lady of Sorrows, pray for us.

BEAR FRUIT

"A good tree does not bear rotten fruit, nor does a rotten tree bear good fruit. For every tree is known by its own fruit."
– Luke 6:43-44

My wife used to be insecure. She told me so. She didn't believe in herself and had low self-esteem.

But one day, she attended a retreat. And her life turned rightside up. She received affirmation that she was special and that she was wonderfully made.

She encountered the immense, unconditional, extravagant love of God.

From then on, she became a woman of Christ. She just knew that she had to share God's love and grace to everyone. And she did exactly that.

Once you feel the love of the Lord, it's not enough to just keep it to yourself. It's meant to be shared and to be experienced by others as well.

Jesus said, "The good person out of the good treasure of his heart produces good... for out of the abundance of the heart his mouth speaks" (Luke 6:45).

So, friend, grab every opportunity to feel the love of God. And surely, it will bear fruit. *Paolo Galia (pgalia@gmail.com)*

Reflection: What is God's story in your life that you can share to others?

Dear Lord, open my heart to receive Your love each day so that I may speak of Your goodness and grace forever.

SEPTEMBER 17

SUNDAY

Sirach 27:30-28:7
Psalm 103:1-2, 3-4, 9-10, 11-12
Romans 14:7-9
Matthew 18:21-35

CHOOSE LOVE

Wrath and anger are hateful things, yet the sinner hugs them tight. – Sirach 27:30

I am God's soldier. I'm His champion. I am His fire. I am firm in my identity in Christ. I know what I am called to do — to use the power of words to evangelize the world. Because of this, I'm constantly under attack.

The devil knows my weaknesses and he is vicious in using them against me. Often, when I am all fired up for God, the devil would use cheap but effective tactics to distract me from my mission. (Hello, Facebook.) He would use my emotions against me and he would plant seeds of sloth in my heart. But what I hate the most is when he would create strife within my family.

When the devil attacks my loved ones, my first reaction is to hate him. I would get the instinctive desire to address him directly and tell him that he can't win against me. But whenever this happens, I would always turn back to God and pray, because I know that lashing out — even against the devil himself — would be my downfall.

Where there is hate, where there is strife, where there is war, choose love. Let us not let the devil win. *Karren Renz Seña (karren.s@ shepherdsvoice.com.ph)*

Reflection: When you are pressed and attacked on all sides, do you choose to lash out, or do you choose to surrender the fight to God?

Lord, whenever I am under attack, let love still reign in my heart. Deliver me from hate, from pride, and from evil. Amen.

St. Robert Bellarmine, bishop and doctor of the Church, pray for us.

SEPTEMBER 18
MONDAY

PURE LOVE

... lifting up holy hands without anger or argument... – 1 Timothy 2:8

1 Timothy 2:1-8
Psalm 28:2, 7, 8-9
Luke 7:1-10

In his deathbed, the man raised his arms to his son, and slowly but clearly said, "I forgive you. Because I love you." Tears flowed from the father, the son, and everyone in the room. The father kept repeating, "I love you. I love you," until slowly, his arms went limp, he closed his eyes, breathed deeply and was gone.

It was five years to the day when the son ransacked his father's room, carted all his jewels, paintings and all the money in the sealed cabinet. The son disappeared but stories that would reach the family said he was into drugs and was caught. Because he was only a minor, he was sent to a drug rehab center.

After five years of good behavior and clean living, he sent a message to his sister and was told about their dying father. He was hesitant and afraid, but because he wanted to see his father, he went.

No matter how grave the sin of the son, or how contemptible he was because of what he did to his father, he received love and forgiveness. There was no anger at all, only pure love. *Chelle Crisanto (ellehcmaria@gmail.com)*

Reflection: "There is no pit so deep, that God's love is not deeper still." (Corrie Ten Boom)

Lord, I cannot forgive the person who betrayed me, but because You are always ready to forgive me for my sins, teach me please to forgive everyone who has hurt me. Amen.

SEPTEMBER 19
TUESDAY

1 Timothy 3:1-13
Psalm 101:1-2, 2-3, 5, 6
Luke 7:11-17

ARISE

He stepped forward and touched the coffin… and he said, "Young man, I tell you, arise!" – Luke 7:14

Jesus raised at least three dead people back to life: Jairus' daughter who just died, the widow's son at Nain in today's reading who was about to be buried, and Lazarus who was already dead for four days. All of them lived again!

I've had my own experiences of being "dead," on my way to "getting buried," or being "long dead." I died emotionally when my parents separated, socially when I lived in poverty, physically when I was dying of a fatal illness, financially when I got buried in debt, and spiritually when I committed grave sins. These "deaths" should have sealed me in a coffin, but I'm still alive! Because again and again, I hear Jesus telling me, "Arise!"

Is there anything in you that has just died? A relationship? A business venture? A dream? Are they on their way to get buried? Or have they been dead for some time now?

Know that any kind of death is never the end for God — not even physical death. Our departed loved ones are very much alive forever with God.

Hear Jesus today saying, "Arise!" By God's mercy and miracle, you will live! *Alvin Barcelona (apb_ayo@yahoo.com)*

Reflection: Nothing remains dead in God's hand. Whatever you think may be dying, have died, or even buried in your life, will rise again.

Dear God, by Your mercy and love, I am alive! And whatever is dying, dead, or buried in me will rise again. In Jesus' name. Amen.

St. Januarius, bishop and martyr, pray for us.

SEPTEMBER 20
WEDNESDAY

1 Timothy 3:14-16
Psalm 111:1-2, 3-4, 5-6
Luke 7:31-35

RULES ARE IMPORTANT

Beloved: I am writing you, although I hope to visit you soon. But if I should be delayed, you should know how to behave in the household of God. – 1 Timothy 3:14-15

No matter what stage in life we might be in, there is always a set of rules we need to adhere to.

As a child, our parents set rules that we had to follow. Be respectful when talking to your elders. Wash your hands before eating. Say sorry if you offended someone.

As teenagers, we had to be home by a certain time. No television during school days.

As adults, we have to abide by rules in the office or organizations we belong to. Come on time. Obey the dress code. Observe proper decorum during meetings.

I am a stickler for rules. For me, rules are to be followed no matter what. I am happy that God has given us His commandments that we may know and live according to His ways. It may not be easy to tow the path at all times. There are times that I trip and fall. But just as in a loving family, I am assured that my Father will always be there to guide me and pick me up when I go astray. *Reng Morelos (norinamorelos@gmail.com)*

Reflection: "Obeying God is listening to God, having an open heart to follow the path that God points out to us." (Pope Francis)

Lord, continue to guide me that I may live according to Your ways.

Ephesians 4:1-7, 11-13
Psalm 19:2-3, 4-5
Matthew 9:9-13

Feast of St. Matthew, Apostle

BEHIND THE SCENES

With patience, bearing with one another through love. – Ephesians 4:2

September is always a red month for the production team of Shepherd's Voice Publications. We have five devotional sets (like this *Didache* that you're holding now) and three to four new books to produce in time for the Manila International Book Fair that happens every September. That's, of course, aside from our normal load of four monthly magazines and book reprints.

The pressure of finishing everything in time for the book fair causes so much fatigue and stress that friction becomes inevitable. And because the "enemy" doesn't like what we are doing — proclaiming God's Word to the ends of the earth through print media — it also creates additional stress for us. Laptop crashes. Printer malfunctions. Lost files. Staff getting sick. Pest infestation in the office. And so on.

The year 2016 wasn't any different, and I know that trials will continue to come our way. But I thank God that our team has remained tight — loving and understanding, supporting and affirming one another despite weaknesses and failures. We bear with one another through love — the same love that God planted in our hearts that led us to this mission. *Tess V. Atienza (theresa.a@ shepherdsvoice.com.ph)*

Reflection: How do you handle day-to-day stress?

Dearest Lord, grant me the grace to be patient and loving amidst difficulties and stresses.

St. Matthew, apostle, pray for us.

GOD'S PROVISION

Many others who provided for them out of their resources. – Luke 8:3

1 Timothy 6:2-12
Psalm 49:6-7, 8-10,
17-18, 19-20
Luke 8:1-3

"Foundations of Leadership Excellence" was a seminar I wanted to experience, but I had no budget for it.

I told God that I'd use whatever I'd learn from it to help not just myself but also the brothers who would ask to have one-on-one talks with me.

In my community, the Light of Jesus Family, we're encouraged to have coffee dates or one-on-one sessions to help build relationships centered on God, to breathe out issues without judgment, and for life coaching. I surrendered this dream to God. If I receive funding, thank God; if I don't, thank God. As the Bible says, thank God in all circumstances (1 Thessalonians 5:18).

When people found out about my desire, they provided the funds out of their resources. They told me how God has been using me, and this time, they want to be God's instruments to help me financially. Just like that, God made a way for it to happen.

In a few days, as of this writing, I will be attending the seminar. I'm so excited to use it for my improvement and for the people that God sends me to help. *Carlo Lorenzo (carloflorenzo@yahoo.com)*

Reflection: Do you lack funds for something you want to do? Search your heart for your intentions and surrender it to God.

You are our generous Provider, Lord God. Search our truest intentions and if they please You, send us instruments to fund our dreams.

St. Lawrence Ruiz and Companions, pray for us.

THE LIVING WORD

1 Timothy 6:13-16
Psalm 100:1-2, 3, 4, 5
Luke 8:4-15

"But as for the seed that fell on rich soil, they are the ones who, when they have heard the word, embrace it with a generous and good heart, and bear fruit through perseverance." – Luke 8:15

At different stages in my life, my heart has been like the different kinds of ground described in the parable today — sometimes hardened and unbelieving, sometimes excited but non-committal, and sometimes too occupied with worrying.

When I allow my heart to become like this, there is no room for God's Word to take root and to grow. So no matter how many Bible studies I attend, or how often I read the Bible in the privacy of my room, I do not bear fruit. But when I take the time to truly meditate and allow God's Word to sink deep into my heart, I become like a "tree planted by streams of water, which yields its fruit in season and whose leaf does not wither..." (Psalm 1:3).

When I allow God's Word to affect me, disturb me, and move me, I find myself making good decisions, counseling others with wisdom, prospering in my work, and behaving how I should. I am amazed at the wonders He does through me and in me when His Word is alive in my life. I invite you to discover it, too! *Geraldine G. Catral (catral.geegee@beaconschool.ph)*

Reflection: "All Scripture is God-breathed and is useful for teaching, rebuking, correcting and training in righteousness, so that the servant of God may be thoroughly equipped for every good work." (2 Timothy 3:16-17)

Dear Lord, thank You for making Your Word available to me. May I treasure this gift and allow it to bear fruit in my life. Amen.

St. Padre Pio de Pietrelcina, pray for us.

GOD'S LITTLE MIRACLES

Seek the Lord… – Isaiah 55:6

Isaiah 55:6-9
Psalm 145:2-3, 8-9, 17-18
Philippians 1:20-24, 27
Matthew 20:1-16

"Is that sauteed mongo? Wow, Lord!" Yes, it was mongo! One day, I was craving to eat this, the next day it was on our table. Another time, I got sick and thought of my mom's congee. Again the next day, without having to ask, my sister brought Mom's congee for me. Months later, I wanted to eat mocha roll from a certain bakeshop. The next day, someone brought two cakes at work and one of them was the very cake I wanted.

These are just three of the many little miracles that God surprises me with. In all of them, I truly thank Him.

Often, we seek God in big miracles that wow us. But if we just look intently at the ordinary things in our daily lives, we will discover that we are surrounded with His loving presence and blessings. The wind's caressing touch, an enjoyable breakfast, a restful sleep, a child's smile, the janitor's greeting, and so on.

Let's seek the Lord not only in big miracles, but most especially in the little miracles which He sends us each day. *Ma. Luisa Dela Cruz (theessence_byluisa@yahoo.com)*

Reflection: When was the last time you sought the Lord? How can you develop the habit of looking for Him more in the ordinary events of daily life?

Beloved Lord, grant that I may have a heart that misses You. May I seek You and be grateful always when I find You. Amen.

Ezra 1:1-6
Psalm 126:1-2, 2-3, 4-5, 6
Luke 8:16-18

GOD'S GENEROSITY

"To anyone who has, more will be given, and from the one who has not, even what he seems to have will be taken away"
– Luke 8:18

"We cannot outdo God's generosity." I've heard this many times from people getting more than what they give.

Meet *"Kuya* T." He always gives in generous amounts at every opportunity to help the parish. He used to live in a modest house in a small village. He now owns a big house in a nice village, bought an adjacent lot, and owns a few cars.

Meet "Family K." This family is a big-time benefactor of parishes. This family funded a substantial portion of the new church building requiring over P15 million. The Lord continues to prosper their family business even more.

I have my own little story, too. My family helped a rural village build their own modest chapel. At that time, we were still praying for our own house. I claimed God's word in Luke 6:38: "Give, and it will be given to you. Good measure, pressed down, shaken together, running over, will be put into your lap...." I know God would fulfill His promise. Three years later, we moved in our own house in a quiet neighborhood in the metro!

Yes, we receive in the measure we give. *Danny Tariman (dtariman.loj@gmail.com)*

Reflection: "Whoever sows sparingly will also reap sparingly, and whoever sows bountifully will also reap bountifully." (2 Corinthians 9:6)

Lord Jesus, please forgive me for being stingy. Grant me the grace to be generous, as You are.

SEPTEMBER 26
TUESDAY

Ezra 6:7-8, 12, 14-20
Psalm 122:1-2, 3-4, 4-5
Luke 8:19-21

THE CROWD

But were unable to join him because of the crowd. – Luke 8:19

The crowd. Sometimes, it veers us away from Jesus.

One of my favorite scenes in *Forrest Gump* (Tom Hanks, 1994) was when he suddenly decided to run across America for no reason at all! Out of depression, he wore his running shoes, and just ran, and ran, and ran! He crossed borders, traversed highways, visited beaches, navigated historical sites, and just ran.

A crowd started to follow him, and it grew in number each day. They kept running alongside Forrest, but never really knew why he was running. But they kept running just the same.

Then one day, Forrest decided to stop. His reason? "I'm tired. I want to go home now." Can you imagine the reaction of the people who ran with him for countless days and thousands of miles, thinking that he was running for a great cause?

Friend, you are part of the crowd. Your crowd is going somewhere. At some point, your leader will stop. And when he stops, will you find yourself closer to Jesus?

Get closer to Jesus. Follow the Christian crowd. *Boggs Burbos (boggsburbos@yahoo.com)*

Reflection: Will my current "crowd" bring me closer to Jesus? If not, follow the Christian crowd.

Lord, continuously lead us to the right people who will bring us closer to You. And use us to do the same with others.

Sts. Cosmas and Damian, martyrs, pray for us.

TRAVEL LIGHT

"Take nothing for the journey." – Luke 9:3

Ezra 9:5-9
Tobit 13:2, 3-4, 4, 7-8
Luke 9:1-6

Years ago, our family served as lay missionaries in Timor Leste. We only had two kids at the time. We were based in Dili, the capital of Timor, but would sometimes go on mission trips to other places.

During one such trip, our local full-time missionary joined us, and brought along his little girl. I remember asking him where their bags were, and he pointed to the small messenger bag he was carrying. I felt ashamed upon seeing it, because I had packed so many things for our kids, including food and drinking water. The rear seat of the pick-up we brought was almost half-full with just our stuff!

Needless to say, after that mission trip, I learned to travel light and to trust that God would provide for whatever we would need.

Similarly, God calls you to do the same, dear friend. Our life here on earth can be considered one long journey, and just as the Twelve in today's Gospel took "nothing for the journey," He wants you to surrender your needs to Him.

Don't worry. He will provide! *Tina Santiago Rodriguez (trulyrichandblessed@ gmail.com)*

Reflection: "Seek first the kingdom of God and his righteousness, and all these things will be given you besides." (Matthew 6:33)

Lord, You are Jehovah Jireh, our Great Provider. Thank You for meeting my needs every day.

St. Vincent de Paul, priest, pray for us.

Haggai 1:1-8
Psalm 149:1-2, 3-4, 5-6, 9
Luke 9:7-9

JESUS WHO?

"Who then is this about whom I hear such things?" – Luke 9:9

Medical researchers Barry Marshall and Robin Warren made this surprising discovery: Ulcers are caused by bacteria (later to be named Helicobacter pylori or H. pylori). Prior to their discovery, the cause of ulcer was a mystery so its painful symptoms were just managed. Now that the cause was known, it could be cured. But since they didn't have credibility in the medical world, no one believed them.

To prove their discovery, Marshall skipped breakfast and in the presence of his colleagues, gulped a glass filled with about a billion H. pylori. Within a few days, he already had the symptoms of gastritis (early stage of ulcer). He cured himself with antibiotics and bismuth. Despite the evidence, other scientists raised their objections. Years later, their efforts were recognized and they received the Nobel Prize in medicine for their work.

In today's Gospel, Herod wondered who Jesus was. Some were saying He was John the Baptist or Elijah or some other prophet who came back to life. Even though Jesus performed miracles, it was not enough for them to believe that He was God's Son, the promised Messiah.

For someone who has true faith, no evidence is necessary. But for one who refuses to believe, no evidence is enough to bring him to faith. *Judith Concepcion (svp_jmc@yahoo.com)*

Reflection: Who is Jesus to you? Does He need to prove Himself?

Increase my faith, Lord. Help my unbelief.

St. Wenceslaus, martyr, pray for us.

DON'T KEEP YOUR DISTANCE

Daniel 7:9-10, 13-14
(or Revelation 12:7-12)
Psalm 138:1-2, 2-3, 4-5
John 1:47-51

Feast of Sts. Michael, Gabriel and
Raphael, Archangels

Jesus answered and said to him, "Do you believe because I told you that I saw you under the fig tree? You will see greater things than this." – John 1:50

I wasted many years by living a life of complacency — of just being a good citizen and living a simple life. Never did I realize the urgency of following Jesus.

For some time, I kept my distance from Jesus, just like Nathaniel who just stood under a fig tree. My tree was filled with anger and hatred, instead of the fruits of love and peace. This was rooted in the pain I experienced early in my life. The physical and emotional abuse I received as a child broke my heart and pulled me away. I wanted to see miracles before I started believing.

Then I got tired of my adversities and surrendered myself to God. It was then that I realized that Jesus had been watching over me all my life. He had seen me long before I sought Him.

Many times we keep our distance from Jesus because of our shame, resentment and pain.

But He sees you. He knows who you are and what you're going through. Come to Jesus now. Life in Him is the "greater thing!" *Shari Anas (sharianas26@gmail.com)*

Reflection: Do you have to wait for miracles before you believe and follow Jesus?

Lord, there are times when we keep our distance from You. But thank You for never giving up on us and calling us to follow You.

Sts. Michael, Gabriel and Raphael, archangels, pray for us.

SEPTEMBER 30
SATURDAY

Zechariah 2:5-9, 14-15
Jeremiah 31:10, 11-12, 13
Luke 9:43-45

Memorial of St. Jerome, priest and
Doctor of the Church

GLORY IN PAIN

*"I will be for her an encircling wall of fire,
says the Lord, and I will be the glory in her
midst." – Zechariah 2:9*

I was happy to see old-time friends, Rocky and Agnes Bacani, attend The Feast Alabang one Sunday in 2014. They attended weekly despite Agnes's battle with cancer. They even served with us in our ministry in spite of what they're going through.

Amidst massive challenges, Rocky and Agnes remained strong and faithful to God. When they discovered that God's love is far more valuable than worldly matters, they became even more loving and generous people.

Sadly, months later, Agnes's father was also diagnosed with cancer. Not minding her own pain, Agnes lovingly took care of her Papa. She prepared him for the inevitable. In August 2015, her father joined our Creator with peace in his heart.

Faithfully, Agnes made every pain count as a sacred sacrifice. Cancer led her to seek God more. She transformed such tragedy into a gift to her family, friends and, most especially, to God.

On December 29, 2015, Agnes passed away peacefully in her sleep. God's promise of glorious victory through her pain and suffering was fulfilled. *Mary Jo Ann Catapusan-Fauni (joann_fauni@yahoo.com.ph)*

Reflection: Have you been struggling for a long time? Believe that our faithful God is encircling you now with His wall of fire and victory will soon come.

Lord God, we pray for wisdom and strength to carry on in our journey. Help us to be steadfast as we await Your glorious victory. Amen.

St. Jerome, priest and Doctor of the Church, pray for us.

OCTOBER 1
SUNDAY

Ezekiel 18:25-28
Psalm 25:4-5, 6-7, 8-9
Philippians 2:1-11
Matthew 21:28-32

Memorial of St. Therese of
Lisieux, virgin and Doctor of
the Church

IS IT TIME TO QUIT?

Do nothing out of selfishness or out of vainglory. – Philippians 2:3

I have a friend who wanted to be a dentist. After four years in college, he took the board exam. The first time, he failed. He took it three more times, and still he failed.

He talked to me after that and it was clear to me that his dream was killing him. He couldn't think straight anymore. I felt he was on the verge of a nervous breakdown.

I told him, "I think if you persist in this dream, it will kill you. I believe God is not rejecting you; He is redirecting you. God is telling you that your success and happiness and mission may be found elsewhere."

He told me the age-old reason for not quitting: "But if I quit, people will say I'm a quitter." I told him, "That's pride talking. Your decisions should never be based on what other people will say, but on what God is telling you."

Today, my friend is working as a well-paid manager, happy with his life and family, and serving God in The Feast.

Friend, do you feel frustrated at not getting what you want in life? Maybe it's time to quit and see if God's leading you somewhere else. *Bo Sanchez (bosanchez@kerygmafamily.com)*

Reflection: What is God telling you through your failures?

Dearest Lord, open my eyes and my heart to receive Your wisdom and light for my life. Amen.

St. Therese of the Child Jesus, virgin, Patroness of Missions, pray for us.

OCTOBER 2
MONDAY

Exodus 23:20-23
Psalm 91:1-2, 3-4, 4-6,
10-11
Matthew 18:1-5, 10
(or Luke 9:46-50)

Memorial of the Guardian
Angels

SUCCESS WITHIN YOU!

"Whoever humbles himself like this child, is the greatest in the Kingdom of heaven."
– Matthew 18:4

Name some characteristics of a successful person.

Committed, responsible, creative, wise, honest, generous, loving – among many others.

Do you have all these characteristics all the time? You might scratch your head and say, "I'm committed, but not all the time." "I'm loving, but not all the time."

Well, think again. There's actually a group of people alive today who possess all these characteristics all the time. Who are they?

Children. All children are already successful! They are committed to play. They're responsible in sleeping. Creative in drawing on walls. Wise in their example. Honest in their opinions. Generous in their cuteness. Loving in all their ways. So if all children are successful, what happened to you?

Because of problems, traumas, lies and bullies, we forget that we are already successful all the time. All we need for success is already within us. And that's all that matters.

Embrace the child within you. And this world will be a more beautiful place. *Migs Ramirez (migsramirez.seminars@gmail.com)*

Reflection: What lies do you tell yourself that are preventing you from believing in your God-given greatness?

Mary, Queen of Angels, please whisper to your Son Jesus to protect me from all lies, so that only in Him may I find my true meaning.

OCTOBER 3
TUESDAY

Zechariah 8:20-23
Psalm 87:1-3, 4-5, 6-7
Luke 9:51-56

GOOD COMPANY

"Let us go with you, for we have heard that God is with you." – Zechariah 8:23

There are people who just have all the right connections. They can get you into the exclusive clubs and seem to know the right people to call when you need to expedite something. It's a treat to be in their company because you benefit from their privileges.

Then there are people who are like accidents waiting to happen. It's just a matter of time before misfortune comes their way. Like this friend of mine from my younger days. He was attacked in a public toilet at the mall. Once, he was abducted and beaten. Another time, he was arrested by the police and spent a night in jail.

People like him are the kind you want to avoid because being in his company could get you embroiled in his troubles. His presence makes me nervous because I never know when a pleasant conversation would turn into a volatile situation.

But the best kind of company are those people who are like a breath of fresh air after you've been trapped in a smoke-filled room. Their presence lifts you up. They bring laughter to your day and their concern for your problems is like a soothing balm to a wound. They pray for you and inspire you to draw closer to Jesus. *Rissa Singson Kawpeng (justbreatherissa@gmail.com)*

Reflection: "Some friends bring ruin on us, but a true friend is more loyal than a brother." (Proverbs 18:24)

Jesus, let me be the kind of company that brings people closer to You.

St. Theodora Guérin, pray for us.

Nehemiah 2:1-8
Psalm 137:1-2, 3, 4-5, 6
Luke 9:57-62

Feast of St. Francis of Assisi,
religious

CONDITIONAL OBEDIENCE

"I will follow you, Lord, but first let me say farewell to my family at home." – Luke 9:61

"I will forgive, but he has to apologize first."

"I will tithe, but God has to fix my finances first."

"I will serve, but God has to heal me first."

Have you heard or used these lines before? Has Jesus called you to follow Him, but you found yourself giving an excuse, or giving conditional obedience?

I've met many people who followed Jesus without conditions. After 20 years, Ana (not her real name) decided to forgive her father who molested her, even if he never apologized. Today, their relationship is restored. She even found real peace and joy in taking care of him despite his critical illness.

Dexter continued to give generously to God despite being buried in debt. Today, he is debt-free, his businesses flourishing.

Gladys, another friend, never stopped serving despite being diagnosed with a rare brain disease. Today, she is not yet completely healed, but she has a newfound purpose in giving hope to people like her who want to give up on themselves.

Friend, don't delay. It's time to follow Jesus radically. Let go of your conditions. *Velden Lim (veldenlim@gmail.com)*

Reflection: Are you following Christ 100 percent? Or is there still an untouchable area in your life that you don't want to involve God in?

Jesus, I fix my eyes on You. I'm not turning back.

St. Francis of Assisi, pray for us.

OCTOBER 5
THURSDAY

Nehemiah 8:1-4, 5-6, 7-12
Psalm 19:8, 9, 10, 11
Luke 10:1-12

REST, RELAX AND REJOICE

"Rejoicing in the Lord must be your strength!" – Nehemiah 8:10

A few years ago, I went through burnout several times. I would be OK for a season, then I would fall into it again (repeat 10 times). I constantly felt depleted. I found myself irritated over the littlest things and had no drive to work. I possibly had undiagnosed bouts of depression also.

During that season of my life, I had several impressions from the Lord telling me to rest, slow down and be intimate with Him, and to have fun. I didn't heed His advice right away. But after the nth burnout, I said to myself, "This has to stop!"

I had to intentionally take time off for myself to regain my joy for living. After some time, I felt the passion, joy and inspiration come back. Now, I deliberately structure my schedule to make sure I don't fall into the burnout pit again.

My greatest lesson from this experience? When you rest, relax and rejoice with Jesus, you are sharpening the saw. You're making yourself better, sharper and more creative. Don't think that having fun is unproductive or a waste of time. It helps you regain your strength. *Mike Viñas (mikemichaelfcv@yahoo.com)*

Reflection: Refuel before the needle points to empty.

Jesus, let's hang out for a while. Let's rest, relax, rejoice and have some fun!

OCTOBER 6
FRIDAY

Baruch 1:15-22
Psalm 79:1-2, 3-5, 8, 9
Luke 10:13-16

WHITE LIES AND ANSWERED PRAYERS

We have sinned in the Lord's sight and disobeyed him. We have neither heeded the voice of the Lord, our God.
– Baruch 1:17-18

"If people call, tell them I'm not here," I told my secretary. I had tons of paperwork to attend to, so I didn't want to be disturbed with phone calls. But I seemed to hear my conscience saying, "You're teaching your secretary to lie."

So I called back my secretary and told her, "Don't lie. If people call, tell them, 'She can't come to the phone right now. May I take a message?'"

Small lies, or white lies as we call them, may seem harmless. But my experience is that little sins are the root of bigger sins.

I've had a number of answered prayers and people ask me why I receive so much blessings. The secret, I tell them, is the gist in today's readings: Obey God.

Disobeying God — like lying and cheating — means sinning against Him. God and sin cannot coexist. So when we sin, we disconnect from Him. If we are disconnected from Him, we do not hear His answers to our prayers, and we do not see the blessings He wants to give us.

The second secret is to accept His answer. Even if it's not what we really want, trust that it's the best answer ever. Again, that means obey Him. *Chay Santiago (cusantiago@gmail.com)*

Reflection: How often do you say, "Yes, Lord!"?

Lord, humbly, I will follow You.

St. Bruno, priest, pray for us.

Baruch 4:5-12, 27-29
Psalm 69:33-35, 36-37
Luke 10:17-24

Feast of Our Lady of the Rosary

FOR CHILDREN ONLY

*"For although you have hidden these
things from the wise and the learned, you
have revealed them to the childlike."*
– Luke 10:21

After a big prayer rally, a man stayed to savor the wonderful things that transpired. Just then, the guest evangelist passed by. The man was star-struck. "Brother, what a powerful talk you gave! I'm a baby Christian for only a month now."

The evangelist replied, "Oh, it's not really me but God at work, thanks to all the formation and training in ministry, worship, spiritual warfare, and many more. What about you, what's happening in your spiritual life?

The man felt a bit ashamed for his lack of experience and training in the spiritual life. "Oh, I used to be an alcoholic, a heavy smoker and an unfaithful husband. But now I'm clean and striving hard to love and serve my family. I'm young in the faith and every moment, I have to repent of my sin and would burst into tears of joy out of gratitude for God's faithful love!

End of story.

Never mistake religiosity for spirituality, childlikeness for childishness. God intended to "have hidden these things from the wise and the learned and revealed them to the childlike."

Obet Cabrillas (obetcab@yahoo.com)

Reflection: In heaven there's a big sign that says, "For children only; adults not allowed!"

Our Father, help us to behave as sons of God.

OCTOBER 8
SUNDAY

Isaiah 5:1-7
Psalm 80:9, 12, 13-14, 15-16, 19-20
Philippians 4:6-9
Matthew 21:33-43

FULL HEALING

Make your requests known to God. Then the peace of God that surpasses all understanding will guard your hearts and minds in Christ Jesus. – Philippians 4:6-7

I saw in my Facebook newsfeed an unusual family picture with two daughters, a dad, and a coffin at the back with a photo of a mom. What made it more unusual was they were all smiling and greeting everyone a happy new year.

Rocky lost his wife, Agnes, to cancer at the age of 39. For the last two years of her life, he had prayed for her full healing. But she passed on, leaving her family behind.

It would have been natural for Rocky to doubt if God even heard his prayers. But because he prayed unceasingly, he grew intimate with Him. Peace guarded his heart and mind. He knew that even though his wife didn't receive physical healing, she was completely healed and no longer in pain. In his own words, "Our Father has answered our prayers and has given Agnes the peace and eternal life that only Jesus can give."

Let today's reading and the story of Rocky inspire us to pray in all circumstances so that, in the face of tribulations, the peace of God that surpasses all understanding will guard our hearts and minds. *Veia Lim (veiallim@gmail.com)*

Reflection: Prayer doesn't change the mind of God; it changes our hearts.

Heavenly Father, reveal Your face to me as I pray. May I find peace in the truth that You are always with me.

OCTOBER 9
MONDAY

Jonah 1:1-2:1-2, 11
Jonah 2:3, 4, 5, 8
Luke 10:25-37

COMPASSION AT WORK

A Samaritan traveler who came upon him was moved with compassion at the sight.
– Luke 10:33

Aylan Kurdi's photo was all over the Internet. The three-year-old kid was wearing a red shirt, blue shorts and black shoes. He lay face down on the beach, lifeless. The caption read, "Humanity washed ashore." It brought to stark reality the desperate plight of the Syrian refugees.

Cristal Munoz-Logothetis was horrified by the picture and decided to find a way to help. The Californian mom saw in the news haggard refugees with babies in their arms. She then remembered her baby carrier collecting dust in the garage. Thus Carry the Future was born. Its mission is simple: collect baby carriers and distribute them to refugee families arriving in Greece. They have helped thousands of grateful families to date.

How many pictures and stories have we "liked" and "shared" in social media to let others know we care? How many times have you commented "Amen!" to show your support and prayer? In real life, how many have you actually helped?

True compassion means not only feeling another's pain but also taking action to help relieve it. May our compassion move us into concrete action. *Cecil Lim (cez_lim@yahoo.com)*

Reflection: "The proof of love is in the works. Where love exists, it works great things. But when it ceases to act, it ceases to exist." (Saint Gregory the Great)

Lord, break my heart with the things that break Yours.

OCTOBER 10
TUESDAY

Jonah 3:1-10
Psalm 130:1-2, 3-4, 7-8
Luke 10:38-42

WORSHIP!

"You are anxious and worried about many things." – Luke 10:41

Kerygma Conference 2015 had to be cut short to two days from the original four because of the unexpected road closures during the APEC State Leaders' Gathering held in Manila. As part of the working committee, the sudden changes hit me hard. I had to inform our sponsors about the two-day cut on the night before the event was supposed to start. I was prepared for angry remarks. Yes, there were a few who expressed disappointment. But what surprised me was the overflow of understanding from other partners who assured me of their continuous support and prayers.

Come conference day, I didn't feel like worshiping but I did anyway. That decision brought me to a moment of total surrender to God. I knew I still had so many things to do, but my heart was at peace.

When you find yourself in a situation that's beyond your control, the battle is no longer yours. It is the Lord's. When you know you've done everything, let go and allow God to steer your plans into His. Continue to worship in the midst of your worries, and God will come to your rescue. *Ruby Albino (r_jean07@yahoo.com)*

Reflection: When we worship God in song or in deep prayer, we acknowledge that He is greater than any situation we find ourselves in. When we choose to worship, we choose to trust.

Lord, many things in my life will worry me, but I surrender my plans to You for I know I will only be at peace with Your grace.

St. Francis Borgia, pray for us.

OUR FATHER

"…Lord, teach us to pray…" – Luke 11:1

Jonah 4:1-11
Psalm 86:3-4, 5-6, 9-10
Luke 11:1-4

Sometimes, repeating prayers often blur their value. But pausing for a while and thinking about the "Lord's Prayer," we can actually pick out things that we can incorporate in our own prayers.

Jesus always emphasized the two greatest commandments: love of God and neighbor. The Lord's Prayer incorporates these in the right priority.

It is communal. You cannot pray it without including others. When we say "Our," it means we think of others in our prayer.

It is personal. When we say, "As we forgive those who sin against us," this includes us. We need to forgive ourselves too.

It is ecumenical. Read through it. There is nothing specifically Christian about it. Any religion can pray it without offending their own beliefs.

It's a family thing. When we say "Father," we declare what God has often emphasized to us — that we are God's children.

So in our own prayer lives, let's remember the lessons Jesus taught us and let God draw near to us. *Rod Velez (rod.velez@gmail.com)*

Reflection: Think about the most stressful person you met this week. Can you pray with sincerity the parts that say, "Forgive us our sins" and "forgive those who sinned against us"?

Lord, as we learn to pray from You, grant us the grace to celebrate our growth and also accept in humility the things we do not like about ourselves.

St. John XXIII, pray for us.

OCTOBER 12
THURSDAY

Malachi 3:13-20
Psalm 1:1-2, 3, 4, 6
Luke 11:5-13

A RECORD OF BLESSINGS

"For everyone who asks, receives."
– Luke 11:10

Today's Gospel made me read my old gratitude journals. I thank the Lord for His faithfulness as documented in those pages — for the gift of family and home, healing and wholeness, good friends and good food, for financial blessings in times of need, for rest and travels, for tasks accomplished and dreams fulfilled. Indeed, if you ask, you will receive.

Consider today's reading: "A record book was written before him of those who fear the Lord and esteem his name" (Malachi 3:16). God wants to remember. Maybe He also reads our journals when we are sleeping.

If you haven't been recording your blessings, try it. Write down your prayers and how God has answered them. You will be amazed. It will give you hope and increase your faith. Your prayers will turn to praise. It's like having your own Facebook Memories, where you will be reminded of what God has done in your life.

I believe God wants to bless us — we only need to ask. And when we have received, to give thanks! *Marjorie Ann Duterte (marjorie. travels@gmail.com)*

Reflection: "Gratitude is a flower that blooms in noble souls." (Pope Francis)

Dearest Father, thank You for all our answered prayers. Thank You for blessing us with every good and perfect gift. Amen.

Joel 1:13-15; 2:1-2
Psalm 9:2-3, 6, 16, 8-9
Luke 11:15-26

PRIZED POSSESSION

When a strong man fully armed guards his palace, his possessions are safe.
– Luke 11:21

I felt my heart drop when I saw a lump of oily food land on my brand-new signature bag that was sitting next to me over lunch. It was a gift given by our daughter, Trina, from her honeymoon trip and it was my precious possession.

Google became my faithful guide in a desperate effort to restore the soiled spot on the leather. I dedicated many long hours trying out various methods from talcum power, to liquid detergent, to a homemade baking soda solution, and more.

I was pleased with the outcome. My unprofessional hard work paid off and I gently put the purse back in its original dust bag, promising myself to be more careful.

And then I realized that this *is* just a bag that I am overly protective of. It led me to imagine how God cares for me. "He chose to give birth to us by giving us his true word. And we, out of all creation, became his prized possession" (James 1:18).

You and I are the Lord's prized possession. How do we protect what's precious to Him? *Mari Sison-Garcia (mari_sison_garcia@yahoo.com)*

Reflection: How do you think God feels when we damage His treasures?

Lord, give us the grace to realize how precious we are in Your eyes.

OCTOBER 14
SATURDAY

Joel 4:12-21
Psalm 97:1-2, 5-6, 11-12
Luke 11:27-28

DISTURBED TO OBSERVE

He replied, "Rather, blessed are those who hear the word of God and observe it."
– Luke 11:28

Some words are difficult to listen to because they disturb us and pierce our hearts.

I just came from Mass and the priest said words in his homily that disturbed my heart. A part of me knew that God was speaking to me. But the words that I heard were not easy to live out. I needed a major change of heart. I need a lot of grace to observe the words Jesus preached tonight through the priest celebrant.

It's so easy to ignore words that are not aligned with our way of thinking or with the way we do things. When someone starts talking about something we do not like or agree with, we tend to tune out. And in case we hear that person out, a lot of times we just let that person's words slip away as if we didn't hear anything from him.

But will it benefit us if we do not let Jesus' words take root in our hearts? No. If we want to be blessed, we need to listen and let His word transform us. *Teresa Gumap-as Dumadag (teresa@fulllifecube.com)*

Reflection: What keeps you from applying the lessons you've learned from God? Why are you struggling to live them out?

Lord, grant me the grace to not just listen to Your words but to also live them out.

OCTOBER 15
SUNDAY

Isaiah 25:6-10
Psalm 23:1-3, 3-4, 5, 6
**Philippians 4:12-14,
19-20**
Matthew 22:1-14

FREE HUG

It was kind of you to share in my distress.
– Philippians 4:14

Kaye was a fresh grad who joined our team at work. At the time, I was her trainer so we often spent time together and grew close. She was a hardworking kid, intelligent and jolly. Her laugh was contagious.

One morning, I noticed that she wasn't her usual self. She went straight to her seat and started work, instead of the usual morning pleasantries.

I asked her how she was doing. She stood, tears flowing, and said, "I need a hug." Immediately, I embraced her. She just learned that her dad was having an affair. Her mom didn't know.

They say a 20-second hug provides comfort. I think we did longer than that. Other colleagues took notice, obviously intrigued. But I ignored them. Here was a distressed spirit in need of comfort.

In life, we all have crosses to carry, and it can be easy to focus only on ourselves. But God calls us to help one another and share in each other's sufferings. When we do, we'll realize that our personal burdens become lighter. *Osy Erica (osy.erica@gmail.com)*

Reflection: Do you know someone who needs your help? Don't hesitate to offer a hand, an embrace, a prayer.

Father, You have sacrificed Your Son for us. Teach us to follow Your example as we sacrifice for others and share in their sufferings. Amen.

St. Teresa of Avila, virgin, pray for us.

OCTOBER 16
MONDAY

Romans 1:1-7
Psalm 98:1, 2-3, 3-4
Luke 11:29-32

WISHY-WASHY

While still more people gathered in the crowd, Jesus said to them, "This generation is an evil generation; it seeks a sign, but no sign will be given it, except the sign of Jonah." – Luke 11:29

"Lord, please give me a sign if 'this' is really for me."

How many of us have prayed a similar prayer?

It may be a new job for a person seeking a better opportunity.

It may be a new love for a person seeking a better love life.

It may be anything that we think can make our life better.

But what have we really done to make things better?

Do we find ways to solve our problems, or do we just wait and see what happens?

Do we focus and never quit, or do we give up the first time we encounter challenges?

Do we persevere and endure, or do we end up cutting corners?

If we want a better life, then do not leave it to chance. Be committed instead. *Orange Garcia (orange.garcia@outlook.com)*

Reflection: A goal without a plan is just a wish.

Lord, please strengthen my will to do whatever it takes to fully realize my dreams.

OCTOBER 17
TUESDAY

Romans 1:16-25
Psalm 19:2-3, 4-5
Luke 11:37-41

POWER OF THE WORD

I am not ashamed of the Gospel. It is the power of God for the salvation of everyone who believes… – Romans 1:16

As I write this, I just finished reading news about the Orlando shooting, where more than 50 people were brutally killed in a gay nightclub.

Last year, our country was divided by the national elections. So many people had "unfriended" each other on social media because they couldn't support each other's political bets. Before that, there were bombings in some major cities in the world.

In a world divided by strife, anger, greed, politics and pride, can we still find hope? Yes, we can.

I'm always blessed by the posts, articles and reflections of the people in my newsfeed. While many share negative things, there are a lot more who are committed to sharing testimonies to God's love: an answered prayer, a much-awaited reconciliation, meaningful bonding session, precious moments with loved ones. They might not have worldwide impact, but these are enough to uplift one's day.

Everything we need has already been given us through the Scriptures. Let us not be afraid to proclaim God's Word to bless the world today. *Karren Renz Seña (karren.s@shepherdsvoice.com.ph)*

Reflection: Share a testimony of God's love in social media today.

Dear Lord, Your Word helps me make sense of this mad, mad world. Help me to hold on to Scripture. Help me hold on to Your love. Amen.

St. Ignatius of Antioch, bishop and martyr, pray for us.

2 Timothy 4:10-17
Psalm 145:10-11, 12-13,
17-18
Luke 10:1-9

Feast of St. Luke, evangelist

MAKE A DIFFERENCE

*"The harvest is abundant but the laborers
are few." – Luke 10:2*

His story became viral a year ago. Carlo Diaz was a Grab Car driver who pulled over to give food to a homeless woman on the street. It was later discovered that Carlo, his girlfriend and his friends have been doing this regularly. It was such a simple yet inspiring story that shows that an act of kindness doesn't have to be a grand thing. I hope this story wasn't just "liked" or "shared" by netizens; rather, I hope that it actually propelled people to act and make a difference in their own ways.

This is what Jesus calls us to do — to be His hands and feet here on earth. But how can we be that if we are too consumed with our own interests? It takes a conscious effort to shift our focus away from ourselves to other people. American pastor Rick Warren once said, "You'll find happiness in serving God through serving others."

To those of us who say we love God, let us accept our role as "laborers." Let's spread the love and change the world one person at a time. *Lala Dela Cruz (bella.delacruz@gmail.com)*

Reflection: How can you serve someone today? Let this be your guiding thought every day.

Help me to see You in others, Lord. Let my love for You be evident in the way I treat other people.

Romans 3:21-30
Psalm 130:1-2, 3-4, 5-6
Luke 11:47-54

NITPICKER

For they were plotting to catch him at something he might say. – Luke 11:54

After hearing Mass, we went to dine at a nearby restaurant. We talked about how we were blessed by the priest's homily, until we started talking about the "wrong points" in his sermon. "How could the priest forget how many days the flood was in the story of Noah?" "How could he say he ate meat on a Lenten Friday?" "And did you notice how his tummy bulged? Not a good model of discipline!"

Nitpickers! Yes, that's what we were. We dwelt on the faults and mistakes instead of the benefit we received. By God's grace, we quickly realized our fault and immediately repented. We at once focused on how the priest had blessed us not just by his wonderful sermon but by his humble attitude as a servant of God.

Jesus was the perfect Priest, the perfect Preacher, the perfect God-Man. Yet, He too had nitpickers who were "plotting to catch Him at something he might say."

Ahh, may we not be like the scribes or Pharisees who only wait, talk or feast on others' faults and mistakes.

May we see that good and great things still happen to more people, to the world, and from a good and great God! *Alvin Barcelona (apb_ayo@yahoo.com)*

Reflection: Today, focus more on the good in others. And see how you'll be happier.

Dear God, may I be more generous in appreciating You and others, and be less critical, through Your grace and love. Amen.

OCTOBER 20
FRIDAY

Romans 4:1-8
Psalm 32:1-2, 5, 11
Luke 12:1-7

HAIRS OF YOUR HEAD

"Even the hairs of your head have all been counted. Do not be afraid." – Luke 12:7

Falling hair is a daily occurrence for many of us. When I brush my hair, numerous strands fall to the ground only to be thrown away without much thought. Yet God knows every hair on our head.

If God pays attention to that tiny detail of our life, how much more is He aware of the bigger concerns we have — in our family, at work, with our health. Not one of them escapes the attention of God.

I once left my bag with my passport, mobile phone and money in an airport shuttle van while traveling. Immediately, I turned to God for help while thinking of what to do. God led me to approach the airport hotel reservation desk where I contacted my hotel and asked if they could contact the shuttle driver and ask him to return to the airport. I anxiously waited for more than an hour and finally caught sight of the shuttle van. Despite the unexpected delay, I was able to catch my flight and make it home safely.

Indeed, we need not fear. God cares for us and knows every detail of our life. *Beth Melchor (epmelchor6@gmail.com)*

Reflection: "Every detail of our life has been an object of a divine thought, and that thought has always been one of love." (St. Marie Eugenie of Jesus)

Jesus, open my eyes to see You in the details of my life. Jesus, I trust in You. I will not be afraid.

MOTHER HEN
"Thus shall your descendants be."
– Romans 4:18

Romans 4:13, 16-18
Psalm 105:6-7, 8-9,
42-43
Luke 12:8-12

Many moons ago, when I was discerning my state of life, this passage spoke to me. As a baby Christian back then, I thought it meant I was for married life. But years passed and no marriage came. (Well, it almost did come!) Instead of being an "impatient bride," I continued doing what I discerned to be my life's work and became happy with it.

Next month, I will be a senior citizen — and a happy single. But really, God has a sense of humor. Last year, when I did one-to-one performance evaluation discussions with my staff, some of them told me that I have become like a mother to them. Maybe it's in how I've been patient with their shortcomings, or in the way I listen to them, or in the wisdom I impart to them. Whatever. But let me share with you another story.

I have a close friend who calls me "Mother Hen." The monicker started when a common friend of ours was preparing for his ordination to the priesthood. We were both so serious in helping him in the preparations that my friend's brother said I was like a mother hen.

Well, maybe, I am meant to be a "mother hen" to many, just as God said. His words remain true through the years. *Tess V. Atienza (theresa.a@shepherdsvoice.com.ph)*

Reflection: Is there a word that God has spoken to you that hasn't come to pass yet? Hold on to it.

Dearest Lord, Your word is my hope and my strength. Amen.

Isaiah 45:1, 4-6
Psalm 96:1, 3, 4-5, 7-8,
9-10
1 Thessalonians 1:1-5
Matthew 22:15-21

EXPENSE OR GAIN?

"Then repay to Caesar what belongs to Caesar and to God what belongs to God."
– Matthew 22:21

I used to be stingy in giving money to God. I thought that giving my time and talents to serve Him in work and ministry was already enough to cover what was due.

When I got married, one best thing I learned from my wife was to put tithing first. When we got financial gifts from our wedding, we made sure that our first expense was our tithe. It was our act of putting God first in our marriage, especially in our finances.

Amazingly, God cannot be outgiven. He provides more than what we need.

We are blessed not just through monetary means; we are blessed with good health, breakthroughs in our careers, and business opportunities. We are surrounded with empowering mentors as well as loving and supportive friends and community.

When we give to God, it's not an expense but a gain. Giving to God leads us to the path of abundance. *Didoy Lubaton (didoymd@gmail.com)*

Reflection: Tithing unlocks blessings we would not have received if we hadn't obeyed.

Dear Lord, I put You first in all things. It's in giving that we receive. Thank You for all the blessings.

OCTOBER 23
MONDAY

Romans 4:20-25
Luke 1:68-69, 70-72,
73-75
Luke 12:13-21

WHEELS OF FORTUNE

"Take care to guard against all greed, for though one may be rich, one's life does not consist of possessions." – Luke 12:15

At the height of my business, I was given an opportunity to earn more. The banks had processed a huge loan so that I would have a larger stake in the business. This business had grown and given us windfalls for many years. It was easy for me to think that money would continue to flow. The business was anchored on the premise that oil prices would continue to remain at high levels because our competitors were oil-based products.

Today, oil prices have plunged more than 70 percent and our competitor products are back dominating the market, principally due to their lower costs. Had I taken the loan then and pursued more profits, I will be deep in financial debt today. And as fuel prices continue to go down, I cannot help but sigh a prayer of gratitude that I decided to entrust my financial future to God.

Money and wealth give false hopes and false insurance. My financial insurance and fortune is God Himself and His promises. Faith is a deep belief that to the faithful, He is always faithful.

Rolly España (rollyespana53@gmail.com)

Reflection: Money and wealth leave us with a false sense of self-sufficiency and may cause spiritual arrogance.

Father in heaven, I acknowledge You as the source of all wealth. I pray that I will be a faithful steward of Your blessings and gifts.

OCTOBER 24
TUESDAY

Romans 5:12, 15, 17-19, 20-21
Psalm 40:7-8, 8-9, 10, 17
Luke 12:35-38

DAMAGED BUT RESTORED

Where sin increased, grace overflowed all the more. – Romans 5:20

I am scared of the dark. But what's even more frightening for me is the thought of being trapped in that darkness, not knowing how to get out to see light again.

This is exactly what happens when we allow sin to paralyze us. When we let our guilt reign over our faith. When we give in to temptations because we think there's no way out, and we feel unworthy of God's forgiveness and love.

But God's love is far beyond our guilt and weaknesses. God has given us the gift of Himself — the gift of grace. It's a pure gift, an undeserved yet overflowing favor from the Lord not to justify our sinful behavior and encourage us to keep on sinning many times over, but rather, to give us hope for our salvation. It's God's assurance that no matter what, His love and forgiveness will always be far greater than our worst offense.

Sin may ruin us but with faith, God's grace can mend our brokenness and put us back together again — reformed, renewed, restored — even better than before. *Jane Gonzales-Rauch (mgr516@gmail.com)*

Reflection: Are you drifting away from God because of sin? Do not be overcome by guilt. No sin is so great that it cannot be conquered by God's grace.

Lord, I need You now more than ever. I ask that You cleanse and protect me. Help me to fight the things that pull me away from You and grant me the strength that I may live by Your grace each day. Amen.

St. Anthony Mary Claret, bishop, pray for us.

OCTOBER 25
WEDNESDAY

Romans 6:12-18
**Psalm 124:1-3, 4-6,
7-8**
Luke 12:39-48

GOD IS ON OUR SIDE

Had not the Lord been with us...
– Psalm 124:1

I was afraid of our dentist. So when Mom was scheduled to take me, I hid under her sewing machine. She searched for me but left the house when she couldn't find me. I stayed out of her sight by hiding outside our store.

Suddenly, a car coming down the bridge lost its brakes and rammed into our jeep parked in front of our store. Our jeep jumped up the sidewalk in my direction. It missed me by a few inches. If God hadn't been on my side, I could have been pinned to the wall.

One night, my brother Richard was coming home from a ball game. His team was walking along a street that was pitch-black. He walked right into an uncovered manhole. His teammates helped him out. He suffered body pains and some bruises. If God had not been on my brother's side, he could have been badly hurt.

My friend's mom wanted to abort the child in her womb. Her mother tried all possible means to get rid of the pregnancy but the fetus held on and was born full-term. If God hadn't been on the child's side, I wouldn't have my good friend. *Meann Tee (meanntytee@yahoo.com)*

Reflection: Do you feel alone? Abandoned? Defeated? Lost? Confused? Ordinary? Insignificant? God is always on your side. You are a champion! You are special!

Father, thank You for being with me always and not leaving me, especially in the most difficult times of my life. With You by my side, I will overcome.

St. Antonio de Sant'Anna Galvao, pray for us.

Romans 6:19-23
Psalm 1:1-2, 3, 4, 6
Luke 12:49-53

ETERNAL LIFE ON EARTH

For the wages of sin is death, but the gift of God is eternal life in Christ Jesus our Lord. – Romans 6:23

I like giveaways and freebies, who doesn't? These include leaflets and brochures being left at the gate of our house, being given to me while I'm walking along the streets, or even by some strangers in the jeepney or bus. Usually, these materials have catchy titles like "Do you want to be saved?" or Bible verses that pertain to helping solve the problem of everyday life. I've noticed that they have a common message though: to receive and accept Jesus as the Lord and one's Savior.

I believe that one doesn't need to die in order to have eternal life. We can have eternal life on earth by seeking God's forgiveness for our sins and believing that God sent His only Son, Jesus Christ, to die on the cross to pay for our sins. We need to firmly believe and trust in Jesus as our Lord and Savior. As stated in 1 John 5:11: "God gave us eternal life, and this life is in His Son." *Gracious B. Romero (graciousromero@gmail.com)*

Reflection: "But now that you have been freed from sin and have become slaves of God, the benefit that you have leads to sanctification, and its end is eternal life." (Romans 6:22)

Father God, I cannot thank You enough for sending Your only Son Jesus Christ to save us. I humbly ask You to forgive my daily sins. I proclaim Your glory, O Lord, as my Savior. Be the Lord of my life. Help me to attain eternal life here on earth. Amen.

OCTOBER 27
FRIDAY

Romans 7:18-25
Psalm 119:66, 68, 76, 77, 93, 94
Luke 12:54-59

EVIL AND GOOD

I know that good does not dwell in me, that is, in my flesh. – Romans 7:18

There's this TV show where they dramatize real stories of evil women. One woman read an article of a man who wanted a wife. So she sent her half-nude pictures to the man who was a doctor. Soon enough, she moved in with him. She was able to convince him to change his will and make her his heir. Not long after, he was dead.

Oswald Chambers wrote, "The reason we see hypocrisy and fraud and unreality in others is because they are all in our own hearts… Yes, all those things and other evils would have been manifested in me but for the grace of God, therefore I have no right to judge."

Yes, we are proud, greedy, jealous, ambitious and many of the evil that we hate in others. Because we live uneventful, everyday lives, we forget those tendencies. But when we look honestly at ourselves in prayer, we know that it is true.

Though evil may be in us, let us never forget that we are made in the image and likeness of God. We are fallen, but He came to redeem us. So let's live in humility and gratitude. For as the saying goes: "If not for the grace of God, there go I." *Joy Sosoban-Roa (jsosoban@gmail.com)*

Reflection: "More tortuous than anything is the human heart, beyond remedy; who can understand it?" (Jeremiah 17:9)

Dear Lord, sustain me by Your grace to do good, inspire me by Your grace to plan good, and bring me home by Your grace to be with You.

OCTOBER 28
SATURDAY

Ephesians 2:19-22
Psalm 19:2-3, 4-5
Luke 6:12-16

Feast of Sts. Simon and Jude,
Apostles

SOAKED

*Jesus went up to the mountain to pray,
and he spent the night in prayer to God.*
– Luke 6:12

As a young guy serving in ministry, I had the notion that serving Christ was about preaching, singing, teaching and just being busy with the "visible" work for God. Then I joined the intercessory ministry, where we were assigned to pray an hour a day for God's work in community as well as for participants during spiritual seminars and activities. My biggest realization is that the ministry of prayer is as important as the visible execution of the work. Things go smoother and participants experience a more powerful outpouring when the affair is soaked in prayer.

Sometime ago, my wife and I were undergoing a big crisis. A number of times, I would wake up at 3 a.m. and "accidentally" watch the Divine Mercy chaplet sang in prayer on TV. It was a time that we were literally soaked in tears because desperation was starting to set in. I realized that when I go before God with a broken heart and a crushed spirit, He heals, mends and restores.

Jesus soaked Himself with the Father's presence all night before He made one of the most important decisions in His life here on earth.

Let's soak it up. *Ariel Driz (adriz77@yahoo.com)*

Reflection: Have you bathed in the Lord's presence lately?

Father, grant me the grace to constantly bask in Your presence. Before You, I am made whole, in Jesus' name.

OCTOBER 29
SUNDAY

Exodus 22:20-26
Psalm 18:2-3, 3-4, 47, 51
1 Thessalonians 1:5-10
Matthew 22:34-40

THE GREATEST COMMANDMENT

"Love the Lord… love your neighbor as yourself." – Matthew 22:37,39

Lord: Love comes from and is sustained and modeled by God. Let us be grateful for the love in our lives, no matter how difficult or seemingly limited. By God's grace, let us love more and let our love mirror Jesus: unconditional, self-sacrificing, enduring till the end. God is love.

Others: Love of God is eventually measured by love of neighbor. I do not believe in a spirituality that does not take relationships seriously. Our relationships should reflect and even indicate the quality of our relationship with God. The way we love one another is a measure of true discipleship.

Voluntary: Love is a choice. It is not forced, not required, not manipulated. Love is freely given and is freely received. But as God chose to love us, He leaves it to us to choose to love Him.

Encompassing: God's love should be in all areas of our lives — our purpose (heart), our emotions (soul), and our thoughts (mind). It also includes loving one's self, or one cannot love another. Finally, loving God is giving our all, as God gave His all to us in Jesus. *Jonathan Yogawin (jyogawin@gmail.com)*

Reflection: Choose to love. It's the most powerful choice you can ever make.

Lord Jesus, teach me to love just like You.

Romans 8:12-17
Psalm 68:2, 4, 6-7,
20-21
Luke 13:10-17

RELINQUISHED

For if you live according to the flesh, you will die, but if by the Spirit you put to death the deeds of the body, you will live.
– Romans 8:13

I was struggling with my feelings. I wanted so much to go to Singapore for a business meeting. But I knew it wasn't God's will for me.

Inside my head was where the fiercest battle on earth was taking place. One voice was saying, "Everybody's going there anyway and there's nothing wrong with it," while the other voice was saying, "You're not like everybody else."

In the end, I abandoned all to God knowing He knows what's best for me.

Decades ago when I completely surrendered my life to the Lord, I decided that I will only be accountable to Him. I have had many opportunities to lie, steal or cheat without anybody ever finding out. It didn't even have to involve sin. I could do whatever I wanted since I was old enough anyway. But I knew that my life was not my own anymore. I had already relinquished it to the One who had given up His life for me. There was no turning back. And there has never been any regrets.

God can always give the best. Why settle for second best?
Ronna Singson Ledesma (ronna_ledesma@yahoo.com.ph)

Reflection: Did you surrender with your heart or just with your lips?

Abba, I am Yours and Yours alone. May nothing ever compete with my love for You.

St. Alphonsus Rodriguez, pray for us.

OCTOBER 31
TUESDAY

CRISIS

I consider that the sufferings of this present time are nothing compared with the glory to be revealed for us. – Romans 8:18

Romans 8:18-25
Psalm 126:1-2, 2-3, 4-5, 6
Luke 13:18-21

A few years ago, I watched my husband undergo what others said was mid-life crisis. He became weak and fearful. Most days, he was depressed. He suffered from chronic tiredness that he could not get out of bed. He lost his appetite, lost weight, and worst of all, he lost passion for life itself.

We went to all kinds of doctors, tried different treatment modalities, and even tried all sorts of medicines and herbs in the house. Thankfully, all his test results came out normal. So on paper, there was nothing wrong with him. But his body told him otherwise. His condition dragged on for many months, trying and testing us. It pained me to watch him suffer like that.

When any form of illness comes to us, we are confronted with two choices: to see what is happening presently or to see what is beyond all the suffering. We are reminded today that all sufferings cannot compare to the glory that is to come. I held on to these words when we were going through that crisis.

Today, the Lord's purposes for that crisis are still not fully revealed to us. But I do not wait for God to explain. His love was enough to see us through. And God's glory shines brightly through all that has happened. *Lallaine Gogna (lallygogna@yahoo.com)*

Reflection: Are you in a crisis? Know that Christ *Is*.

May the sufferings I undergo still speak about Your providence and mercy, Jesus.

St. Wolfgang of Regensburg, pray for us.

NOVEMBER 1
WEDNESDAY

Revelation 7:2-4, 9-14
Psalm 24:1-2, 3-4, 5-6
1 John 3:1-3
Matthew 5:1-12

Solemnity of All Saints

PRAISE ALL THE TIME

All the angels stood around the throne and around the elders and the four living creatures. They prostrated themselves before the throne, worshipped God.
– Revelation 7:11

When I was 15 years old, I competed in a Bible Quiz that was televised nationwide. I held a thick, fat pen and a long cardboard in front of me — and I was nervous.

Ronald Remy, the quiz master, said, "And now, a fill-in-the-blank question. In Luke 1:48, it says, 'And the Lord's _____ fell upon Mary.' Your seven seconds start now…"

I was stumped. I didn't know the answer. So I put my pen down on the table and did what I always do when I don't know what to do — I started praising God.

When I'm at a loss, I praise God. When I'm confused, I praise God. When I'm down and out, I praise God. Beneath my breath, I said, "Thank You, Jesus. Thank You, Jesus…"

But on the sixth second, I heard a loud voice inside me, saying, "Power!" The force was so strong, so spontaneous. I grabbed my pen and wrote "Power" on my cardboard.

Ronald Remy then said, "And the answer is 'And the Lord's power fell upon Mary.'"

Friends, when you can't answer a question that life is asking you, it's time to worship. Because when you worship, you'll feel His power flow out to you! *Bo Sanchez (bosanchez@kerygmafamily.com)*

Reflection: How have you availed of the power of worship?

I praise You, Lord, and ask for Your holy indwelling in me. Amen.

Wisdom 3:1-9
Psalm 23:1-3, 3-4, 5, 6
Romans 5:5-11
(or Romans 6:3-9)
John 6:37-40

All Souls Day

A RAINBOW AFTER THE STORM

Those who trust in him shall understand truth, and the faithful shall abide with him in love. – Wisdom 3:9

Being human, we tend to question God and find reasons when faced with extreme trial. I have a friend named Lerwin. He and his family were happy and devout Catholics. They gave their all to God.

One day, while they were capping off a Life in the Spirit Seminar, someone approached him while he was singing at Mass. Apparently, there was an accident a few meters from their church. It was their car, and in it was his family. Unfortunately, his parents and his brother died on the spot. His grandfather also passed away on that same day.

Did Lerwin question God? Yes! Where's he now? Faithfully serving God at The Feast, singing songs of praise and leading people to worship every week. Did anything change in him after the incident? Yes, he loved God even more!

Whenever I look at Lerwin, I see strength. It's impossible for anyone to fully understand God's wisdom. All we can do is trust Him and be faithful in all circumstances, knowing that there's always a rainbow after every storm. *Monching Bueno (ramon_bueno@yahoo.com)*

Reflection: What are you grieving for today? Don't blame God. It's not His fault. Put your whole trust in the Lord.

Father God, thank You even for the difficult storms in my life. Help me to be faithful in all circumstances. Show me Your rainbow of blessings!

All Souls, pray for us.

Romans 9:1-5
Psalm 147:12-13, 14-15, 19-20
Luke 14:1-6

RHETORICAL QUESTION

But they were unable to answer his question.
– Luke 14:6

I was at the Hillsong Conference in Sydney, Australia a few years ago. When I set my budget for pocket money, I didn't know they would ask for love offerings every night of the five-day event. By the third night, I was hesitant to give because my dollars were dwindling. But grace prevailed and I gave anyway.

Later that evening, someone came up to me and said he would reimburse my plane ticket. I was delighted and shamed at the same time. Even though I had hesitated to give, the Lord returned to me forty-fold of what I had dropped in the offertory just a couple of hours ago. God cannot be outdone in His generosity! He spoke in my heart and asked me a question that needed no answer: When did you ever choose Me and it didn't pay off?

Whenever we decide on God's way, when we follow Him even when we think it'll be to our disadvantage, or when we give in faith even if it's beyond our capacity, we will discover that He wants to give us more all along. He expands our vision so that we see His infinite resources and not just our limited supplies. He teaches us that He is more than willing and able to repay us when we walk in His ways. *Rissa Singson Kawpeng (justbreatherissa@gmail.com)*

Reflection: Lord, help us to live the virtue of generosity, to love without limits.

Jesus, let Your rhetorical questions find their answers in my obedience.

St. Martin de Porres, religious, pray for us.

Romans 11:1-2, 11-12,
25-29
Psalm 94:12-13, 14-15,
17-18
Luke 14:1, 7-11

INVISIBLE

"For everyone who exalts himself will be humbled, but the one who humbles himself will be exalted." – Luke 14:11

When I was young, I always experienced being bullied and humiliated. My heart cried out for attention. Won't somebody treat me with respect?

I felt like the wind, so alone in this world.

Even now, I still experience moments like these. I would turn to God and tell Him, "Lord, I don't even feel You. You are also ignoring me. I feel so unimportant."

Then one day, I was on a jeep praying the rosary when I saw a handsome man get into the vehicle and sat in front of me.

He looked straight into my eyes, His gaze penetrating my being.

With my spiritual eyes, I saw Jesus motioning to me with His hands, "I see you!"

I couldn't help but smile.

Jesus delights in me after all. I'm visible to my invisible God! *Banjoy Santillan (pasantillan58@yahoo.com)*

Reflection: A regular prayer connection with God is all we need to see Him and be invisible no more.

Open the eyes of my heart, Lord, I want to see You.

NOVEMBER 5
SUNDAY

Malachi 1:14-2:2, 8-10
Psalm 131:1, 2, 3
1 Thessalonians 2:7-9, 13
Matthew 23:1-12

LIKE A CAN

"Whoever exalts himself will be humbled; but whoever humbles himself will be exalted." – Matthew 23:12

My parents are quite balanced. My dad likes to sing our praises constantly (sometimes with bias) and then there's my mom who isn't as generous with compliments. When I was younger, I came home bragging about how I had been awarded Best Public Speaker in my class and that no one could deliver speeches better than I could because my fluency in English was impeccable. My mom flatly responded, *"Sige, salita ka nang salita. Parang lata."* (Ok, keep talking. You're like a tin can.)

I was confused. "Why am I like a can?" She was never one to mince words. "You make a lot of noise but your words are empty. You have no substance. You sound good but do you know what you are talking about? *Lata nga.* (Like a tin can.) Clang, clang, clang!" I learned my lesson that day. From then on, I promised myself not to pretend to know what I didn't. I began to speak only about what I understood or to listen intently to what others had to say.

I'm so grateful for a mother who isn't afraid to teach me the value of humility. She lives by example, too. Except when I hear her bragging to her relatives about how amazing her kids are when she thinks we're not listening. *Eleanore Teo (elyo.lee@gmail.com)*

Reflection: Is it easy for you to admit to others what you do not know?

Holy Father, remind me that I am but flesh and blood so that I do not take for granted Your eternal, immortal spirit burning inside me.

Venerable Solanus Casey, pray for us.

NOVEMBER 6
MONDAY

Romans 11:29-36
Psalm 69:30-31, 33-34, 36-37
Luke 14:12-14

FOCUS, FOCUS, FOCUS
The gifts and the call of God are irrevocable. – Romans 11:29

Since Feast Alabang started, I have served with and headed a couple of ministries: Secretariat, Music, Creatives, Media and Events. After several years, I was burnt out because I served in at least two ministries at the same time. Halfway through my journey, God impressed upon me the service He wanted me to perform. I was called to serve as His spotlight — one who will shine the light on Him by writing about His Word.

But as Events head of one of our sessions, I could not leave that ministry without finding a capable and willing replacement. I plodded on for three years while concurrently serving as Media head. The teachings at The Feast reinforced the call to focus on Media. I felt God's leading to concentrate on writing.

It was a wrench to leave the session I was serving with and my co-servants there, but the call of God was strong. He even arranged things and moved people to make this possible. This new focus made me realize we are happiest and most useful when we follow God's irrevocable call. *Lella M. Santiago (lellams88@gmail.com)*

Reflection: What is your special calling? Use the gifts God has given you to make this world a better place.

Use my gifts, O Lord, for that special mission You designed me to accomplish.

WE'VE GOT THE FIRE

"Go out quickly into the streets and alleys of the town and bring in here the poor and the crippled, the blind and the lame."
– Luke 14:21

Romans 12:5-16
Psalm 131:1, 2, 3
Luke 14:15-24

The matchsticks in a matchbox were worried. "Each time the box opens, one of us is taken away. A few more days and we'll all be gone! What will we do?" they said among themselves.

As they spoke, the box opened again and a big hand took another matchstick. But a second stick fell with it. It went on a long fall and hit the floor. Dazed, he looked up and saw what happened to the other matchstick. The big hand struck the stick's head on the side of the matchbox — and lo and behold — it burst into a beautiful flame!

The stick that fell exclaimed, "Whoa! So that's what we are! We are light! I wish I could go back to the darkness of the matchbox and announce to everyone that we have fire!"

Friends, we are like the matchstick. We can go into the darkness of people's hopelessness and be Jesus to them!

Bring back to God the poor in self-worth, the crippled in life balance, the blind with selfishnessness, and the lame with idleness. Announce to them, "We've got Jesus' spark of hope! We've got the Holy Spirit's fire!" *Obet Cabrillas (obetcab@yahoo.com)*

Reflection: Let us live out what St. Vincent de Paul proclaimed: "Love itself is fire…we are called to bear the love of God, this Divine Fire everywhere."

Lord, let me always burn with Your love so that no one will die in the darkness of never having known You.

St. Didacus, pray for us.

NOVEMBER 8
WEDNESDAY

Romans 13:8-10
Psalm 112:1-2, 4-5, 9
Luke 14:25-33

NOT STUFF

"Everyone of you who does not renounce all his possessions cannot be my disciple."
– Luke 14:33

I often wear a small hair comb to keep my hair neat. It's not commonly available in stores, so I hoard several pieces. One morning, I was standing on a downward escalator in a mall. My comb fell from my hair. I bent to grab it when suddenly, I lost my balance. My feet flew up in the air as the steps moved toward the ground floor.

Two guys ran down and lifted me up in time for us to get off safely. I managed to say thank you to my saviors before they quickly disappeared. I couldn't believe I stupidly risked my life just for a hair accessory.

We're aware that possessions don't provide real meaning to our existence. But media heavily influences us into acquiring more material things. Sometimes, our possessions own us and we forget that God is our ultimate provider.

My guardian angels worked hard that day to dramatically remind me to rearrange my priorities. What really brings joy and contentment to my soul? Not my stuff but my love for God, love for my family, friends and my brethren. *Gina J. Verdolaga (mgjver@yahoo.com)*

Reflection: The best things in life are intangible. Simplify and let go to create space for God to come in.

Oh, Lord, enrich my life with Your spiritual blessings. Only Your love sustains me.

Ezekiel 47:1-2, 8-9, 12
Psalm 46:2-3, 5-6, 8-9
1 Corinthians 3:9-11, 16-17
John 2:13-22

Feast of the Dedication of
the Lateran Basilica in Rome

BROKEN TEMPLE

Do you not know that you are the temple of God? – 1 Corinthians 3:16

I live with a chronic illness. I tried to find meaning for the pain and found none. Instead, I found meaning for life.

I learned broken bodies can carry beautiful souls and beautiful bodies can mask broken souls. I learned life is not about suffering. It's about finding God even in our pains, hardships and sacrifices. And finding God gives nothing but true joy. I learned that self-care is not selfishness. It is impossible to give without taking care of yourself first. I learned that there is nothing more healing than self-forgiveness. I learned to believe in purpose; that I wasn't randomly chosen to suffer or had the worst luck. I am alive because I am part of God's plan. The fact that I exist means I am playing out my part in His grand scheme.

I learned that tears are such great blessings. It's right up there with hugs, kisses, and sincere words of love and care.

I learned to see the God who dwells in me, that I am indeed His temple, and there is no such thing as broken for He makes all things beautiful. *Cecil Lim (cez_lim@yahoo.com)*

Reflection: "Our Lord does not come down from heaven every day to lie in a golden ciborium. He comes to find another heaven which is infinitely dearer to him — the heaven of our souls, created in His Image, the living temples of the Adorable Trinity." (St. Therese of Lisieux)

Grant me, O Lord my God, a mind to know You, a heart to seek You, wisdom to find You, conduct pleasing to You, faithful perseverance in waiting for You, and a hope of finally embracing You. (Saint Thomas Aquinas)

St. Benignus, pray for us.

FINAL GRADE

"Prepare a full account of your stewardship." – Luke 16:2

Romans 15:14-21
Psalm 98:1, 2-3, 3-4
Luke 16:1-8

Memorial of St. Leo the Great,
pope and Doctor of the Church

When I was in college, I devoted less time on a major subject, thinking that I could pass it without much effort. I spent more time in other "pursuits." At the end of the semester, I got a final grade of 5.0 — a failing mark for the mediocre effort I put in. It was a good thing I was given the chance to retake and pass the subject.

Many of us approach our spiritual life this way. We know it is the most important subject, requiring much effort, but we put it aside in favor of enjoyment, pleasure or comfort.

We live as lukewarm Christians, living our faith only when it suits us, pray only when we "have time," and continue with our gossiping, lying, cheating and other sinful ways. We convince ourselves that we can repent later and still make it to heaven.

The reality is that our final exams may come without warning. Unlike college, there is no retake once God gives the final judgment.

If God will ask you to account for your life today, what grade will you get? *Jun Asis (mabuting.balita@gmail.com)*

Reflection: Live life for God's eternity and not for the worldly comfort of the temporary.

Lord, grant me the grace to live my faith with a heavenly perspective, every time, all the time.

St. Leo the Great, pope and doctor of the Church, pray for us.

1 WALKER

Greet one another with a holy kiss. All the churches of Christ greet you.
– Romans 16:16

Romans 16:3-9, 16, 22-27
Psalm 145:2-3, 4-5, 10-11
Luke 16:9-15

Once upon a time, God chose a random place to gather His children. There, a group of married couples and a few "singles" met once a week to discuss a passage in the Bible and its impact on their lives.

They would share testimonies and sing worship songs *a cappella* to their hearts' delight.

Not long after, the worship singing grew and required a guitar, keyboard, drums, bass and purcussions, and so a set of musicians joined in. A Christian worship group inevitably formed. It's composed of singers and musicians who are Catholics and Born Again, united in Christ.

1 Walker became the name of the group composed of showbiz talents including big-name singers like Ogie Alcasid, Regine Velasquez and Jaya. Together, we've had the privilege of singing worship songs for the Lord in big concerts and events.

Great things are born when brethren dwell as one. *Eugene Cailao (eugenecailao@gmail.com)*

Reflection: Have you found that special place to commune with God and share the Word with your brothers and sisters?

Father, lead me to that place where I can get to know You more through community with Your children and co-believers in Christ.

Wisdom 6:12-16
Psalm 63:2, 3-4, 5-6, 7-8
**1 Thessalonians
4:13-18**
Matthew 25:1-13

BEST BIRTHDAY GIFT

…so that you may not grieve like the rest, who have no hope. – 1 Thessalonians 4:13

I wondered why God took my father away on my birthday two years ago today. But then I realized that God, in fact, had given me the most perfect gift — eternal life for my dad. In His perfect wisdom, God had given my father a far better healing, something that will last forever.

My father had been far from the Lord when I was growing up. But towards the end of his life, the Lord used cancer to heal him. It was not a physical healing but a spiritual one. In those few months, I saw him humbly receive Communion from the minister who would visit him. He also received the sacrament of anointing of the sick. All my life, it seemed I have prayed for the healing of our relationship. Before he died, the Lord healed us.

I am reminded of the repentant thief at the time of Jesus' crucifixion. He had been far away from the Lord all his life, but God saved him up to the last moment. As I prayed the Divine Mercy prayer at the morgue, I asked Jesus to have mercy on my father's soul. It was my birthday wish. When I saw his face, I found a peaceful, contented smile. I know God has forgiven my dad completely, totally and perfectly. *Marjorie Ann Duterte (marjorie. travels@gmail.com)*

Reflection: Love doesn't end in death. Someday, you and your loved one will meet again.

Thank You, Father, for the gift of Christian hope. Thank You, Jesus, for Your Divine Mercy. Because of Your love for us, we are saved.

St. Josaphat, bishop and martyr, pray for us.

NOVEMBER 13
MONDAY

Wisdom 1:1-7
Psalm 139:1-3, 4-6, 7-8, 9-10
Luke 17:1-6

DEPRESSION
"Increase our faith." – Luke 17:5

I've noticed that more counselees referred to me are suffering from depression. Causes vary: brokenheartedness, career stifled by family demands and sickness.

I journey with them as a professional but I can't resist passing on the need for prayer and faith.

I have no doubt in my heart that an "increase in faith" — having complete trust in the Lord — solves half of the problem.

In my own life, I've carried on with a low-grade depression for several years after my father died. But work, prayers and complete trust in the Lord helped me through it.

Listening to God and obeying His direction can weather any human condition. *Cristy Galang (cristy_cc@yahoo.com)*

Reflection: Are you satisfied with the amount of faith you already have? Do you have a need to pray for more? Do you have to build your spiritual life in the direction of increasing your faith in the Lord?

Lord of mercy and compassion, You have done everything in Your power to bring me closer to You, to save me, to help me — all because You know what is best for me. Thank You, Jesus! Please remind me You're always there for me, especially in times when I forget You. Jesus, I trust in You.

St. Frances Xavier Cabrini, virgin, pray for us.

NOVEMBER 14
TUESDAY

Wisdom 2:23-3:9
Psalm 34:2-3, 16-17, 18-19
Luke 17:7-10

ENTITLEMENT

"We are unprofitable servants; we have done what we were obliged to do."
– Luke 17:10

Service is not our job. It's our calling. It's not a transaction that ends after 5 p.m., then we demand to be immediately paid, insist to be recognized, shove to switch places with the customer, and then become the boss. Having a sense of entitlement is a sure success killer when you talk about service.

Here's a simple business wisdom from Jesus: Serve genuinely and you'll get rewarded. Always! Maria got promoted recently. Why? The boss required submissions only once a week, and she submits twice a week. My brother-in-law runs a successful physical therapy clinic in New York. Why? Pinoy as he is, he finds time to listen and make friends with patients, not minding the excess minutes. Robert, my former officemate, started as an entry-level technician servicing our machines. He is now the service manager. Why? You call him to fix the monitor gauge, he goes further and lubricates all the gears, aligns all four machine legs, and even brings you this quarter's issue of *Didache!*

Serving genuinely shouldn't be too hard for us simply because our identity is that we are servants of the Most High God! Jon Escoto (faithatworkjon@gmail.com)

Reflection: Do you want to have an extraordinary day today? Serve with a little more extra.

Lord, teach me how to serve like You do — in my family, and in the place where I work.

DECLARE GOD'S GOODNESS

Desire therefore my words; long for them and you will be instructed. – Wisdom 6:11

Wisdom 6:1-11
Psalm 82:3-4, 6-7
Luke 17:11-19

Riza was working in Singapore when she learned that her mother was sick and needed money for medication. Her salary was already allotted for monthly financial obligations. She had limited options on who to approach for assistance. The only person she thought of was her cousin who was also her housemate.

But this presented another dilemma. She already owed this cousin a lot of favors, so she wasn't comfortable to ask again. But left with no choice, she prayed about it. She asked God to give her the right words to say. Too shy to approach her personally, she shared with her all the details of her mom's condition via text. Then, she closed the conversation with her need for financial assistance. Riza got an immediate reply from her: "hm."

What could "hm" mean? Was it "hmm," or was she mad as in "hmmph!"? Then, she realized that "hm" was for "how much?" Riza thanked her cousin profusely. When she texted the amount needed, her cousin replied with a screenshot of the online bank transfer she did to her account. Riza was desperate for help but she knew who could teach her the right words. Jesus is the Way and He showed Riza how to do it. *Alvin Fabella (alvinfabella@yahoo.com)*

Reflection: Are you facing an obstacle in your life and you don't know what to do? Pray to Jesus for guidance and expect that He will give you the right words and actions to do.

Lead and guide me, Jesus.

Wisdom 7:22-8:1
Psalm 119:89, 90, 91, 130,
135, 175
Luke 17:20-25

REQUIRED CHANGE

And she, who is one, can do all things, and renews everything while herself perduring.
– Wisdom 7:27

It took a health scare for me to realize I had to make changes in my life and reevaluate my priorities.

I had been taking my health for granted by not being conscious of the food I eat. I figured I could eat anything since I don't gain much weight anyway. I also didn't exercise regularly. I didn't think that I was doing myself physical harm since I wasn't feeling anything abnormal or having any kind of intolerable pain.

I now realize that taking care of myself is not being self-centered. I need to be healthy physically and spiritually for the people I love, most especially for my kids.

I know it will take some sacrifice — not to mention discipline — to nurse myself back to health. But I believe I can do it hand in hand with taking care of my spiritual health.

When my relationship with God is in the right place, l feel more relaxed, confident in the activities that I do, and I'm able to set my priorities right.

I believe that keeping my spiritual life strong will renew me, not only in soul but in body as well. *Mae Ignacio (maemi04@aim.com)*

Reflection: Are you healthy physically and spiritually?

Lord, I pray that You continue to provide us with spiritual nourishment that we may be healthy in body and soul.

NOVEMBER 17
FRIDAY

A BETTER PLAN

Let them know how far more excellent is the Lord than these. – Wisdom 13:3

Wisdom 13:1-9
Psalm 19:2-3, 4-5
Luke 17:26-37

Have you ever planned something so well that you were sure it was the best plan ever? I remember when we were planning for our wedding 11 years ago. Since we were based abroad doing mission work, we left instructions with family and close friends on what to do. Six weeks before our wedding date, we went back to the Philippines to be hands-on with the final preparations.

But to our surprise, nothing had been done. The church and the reception venue that we originally wanted had not been booked, on top of everything else that needed to be arranged for. It was panic time.

But lo and behold, the Lord had better plans than ours. My aunt who lived in Valle Verde called and offered their village clubhouse at a discounted resident's rate. One of our wedding sponsors recommended the church where they renewed their wedding vows. By God's grace, it was available and located near our new reception venue — and newly renovated, too! Everything else also fell into place, and we ended up with a beautiful, memorable wedding. All because God's plan was better than ours. *Anthony Rodriguez (anthony.r@svrtv.com)*

Reflection: Do you have big plans for your life? Offer everything up to the Lord. He knows what's best for you.

Lord, teach me to let go and let God in everything that I do.

Wisdom 18:14-16; 19:6-9
Psalm 105:2-3, 36-37, 42-43
Luke 18:1-8

Dedication of the Churches of
Sts. Peter and Paul, Apostles

JUSTICE DELIVERED

"I tell you, he will see to it that justice is done for them speedily." – Luke 18:8

My IT company has been servicing a big US grocery chain since 2004. We deploy IT consultants and programmers to support the client's applications and infrastructure network. Because of their merger with another grocery chain, management had to expand their own HR team to build capacity.

I felt that the new person assigned to us had a preference for another vendor and that most of our endorsements had been declined and marked "invalid." Although we didn't have new contracts and knowing that some injustice was happening, I kept my faith in their management and most especially in God. My prayers for justice were answered when we learned that the new HR person was caught on CCTV stealing credit cards from wallets of her colleagues. She was terminated and replaced with a very professional staff.

No matter what your circumstances are, turn your troubles to God and allow Him to guard your heart with peace. Faith will not eliminate your problems but will keep you trusting in the midst of those troubles. With faith, justice is served in God's time. *Dean Pax Lapid (happyretiree40@gmail.com)*

Reflection: Seeking justice from someone? God's got your back.

Father, thank You for supplying every resource that is available to us who believe. Strengthen our minds and hearts as we continue to put our trust in You.

St. Rose Philippine Duchesne, pray for us.

GIVE BIG, GAIN BIG

"Since you were faithful in small matters, I will give you great responsibilities."
– Matthew 25:21

Proverbs 31:10-13,
19-20, 30-31
Psalm 128:1-2, 3, 4-5
1 Thessalonians 5:1-6
Matthew 25:14-30

"If only they would give me a bigger salary, they'll see how I could perform better!"

"Why don't they try promoting me and give me that leadership position? They'll see how I could really make things right."

I hear these very often — in the workplace, in public service, even in community life. People rant that they only do little because they are given little – little pay, little position, little recognition, etc. They justify that if given more, they could do more. Ah, but to me, that's putting the cart before the horse.

Because the reason why you will have more is because you are giving more!

Try giving more to your job, to your service, to your ministry, to your family life, to your health life, to your spiritual life – and see how you will gain more!

It's a solidly tested principle: The more you give, the more you receive. Because you will remain small if you give small.

Watch how you gain big, but only after you give big. *Alvin Barcelona (apb_ayo@yahoo.com)*

Reflection: In the areas of your life that you think are "small," decide today to give more. Watch how big it will grow!

Dear God, let me realize that there are no small things from You. Everything you give are big opportunities for me to live more, love more and serve more. Amen.

St. Agnes of Assisi, pray for us.

NOVEMBER 20
MONDAY

BFF

1 Maccabees 1:10-15, 41-43, 54-57, 62-63
Psalm 119:53, 61, 134, 150, 155, 158
Luke 18:35-43

Jesus asked him, "What do you want me to do for you?" – Luke 18:40-41

During conferences or seminars, we have people in the audience who ask the speaker questions during the open forum, just as there are those who prefer to stay in the background, who are timid and shy to ask. Maybe they're afraid that people will find their questions silly or ridiculous.

Jesus already knows what's in our minds even if we don't say it, but still He asks, "What do you want Me to do for you?" He wants to make sure that we are with Him, that we believe in Him and that we trust Him all the way.

True prayer is talking to God as if we're talking to a friend. It's being at home and at ease with that friend. We can be who we really are, warts and all, knowing He will always accept us no matter what.

Jesus is our BFF (Best Friend Forever). So go ahead and ask Him anything and believe that you have received it. *Dr. Henry L. Yu (henrio_md@yahoo.com)*

Reflections: What are your heart's desires? What do you want to ask Jesus? "Ask and you shall receive."

Thank You so much, Lord, for listening. You are indeed one of a kind — my Best Friend Forever.

NOVEMBER 21
TUESDAY

2 Maccabees 6:18-31
Psalm 3:2-3, 4-5, 6-7
Luke 19:1-10

Memorial of the Presentation
of the Blessed Virgin Mary

AMIDST WORLDLY PRESSURES

"I am not only enduring terrible pain in my body from this scourging, but also suffering it with joy in my soul because of my devotion to him."– 2 Maccabees 6:30

I knew in my heart that I was fighting for the right thing. But when my colleagues kept their distance to maintain their peaceful career, I began to wonder if I was really doing it the right way. Why were most of them against me when I was setting things aright? Many people questioned my credibility, knowledge and purpose in pursuing my cause. My mind was confused, my body was weakening, and my heart was broken.

The burden became heavier when nobody dared to speak honestly. I cried often and dreaded going to work. As days become longer, I held my ground and stood by what was true. I surpassed that challenging phase of my career and I was happy to know that a positive change ensued because of my persistence.

People may say negative things about you or the present condition may seem to torment you, but in the end, it will always be just between you and God.

Many people choose to abide with the majority's preference even if it's wrong because they don't want to rock the boat. Don't let that influence you. If you have God on your side, you're the majority. *Sarrah Cea (sjbcea@gmail.com)*

Reflection: Will God applaud your actions and decisions for today?

Lord, open my eyes and strengthen my heart as I respond and guide others according to Your will. Amen.

St. Gelasius, pray for us.

2 Maccabees 7:1, 20-31
Psalm 17:1, 5-6, 8, 15
Luke 19:11-28

HIGHLY REGARDED

"Then the other servant came and said, 'Sir, here is your gold coin; I kept it stored away in a handkerchief, for I was afraid of you, because you are a demanding man; you take up what you did not lay down and you harvest what you did not plant.'"
– Luke 19:20-21

"God saw all that he had made and it was very good" (Genesis 1:31). God saw all creation, including us, and He was happy. He regarded us as good — absolutely positive.

Unfortunately, we cannot say the same of our regard for God.

Why do we worry so much? Why do we acquire too much? Why do we do the many things we do to protect our own interest, safeguard our future and establish ourselves?

If we will be honest, more often than not, all our frantic efforts are because we don't regard the Lord as highly as He regards us. We don't believe that He is as good as He says He is.

What utter foolishness on our part. For if we just sit for one hour at the foot of the Cross, beholding that great Sacrifice, we surely will come out with a different perspective.

But then again, one hour? That would be too much. There again is the definition of regard. *Joy Sosoban-Roa (jsosoban@gmail.com)*

Reflection: "I do believe, help my unbelief." (Mark 9:24)

Dear Lord, I'm so sorry for disbelieving You — for doubting Your goodness, Your kindness, Your love for me. Help me, O Lord. Amen.

NOVEMBER 23
THURSDAY

1 Maccabees 2:15-29
Psalm 50:1-2, 5-6, 14-15
Luke 19:41-44

UNCOMPROMISING CHARACTER

"We will not obey the words of the king nor depart from our religion in the slightest degree." – 1 Maccabees 2:22

I recently saw *Unbroken,* the life story of American Olympian Louis Zamperini who's also a war hero and a spiritual giant.

His war plane crashed and he spent 47 days at sea. He was saved by the Japanese navy only to be violently tortured at a prison camp to break his "American" spirit. At the end of the war, he went back to Japan as a Christian missionary, sought out his torturers and forgave them. He believed that God allowed him to survive for a divine purpose. His story is inspiring.

Even animated movies like *The Lorax* propped my belief to be relentless in the fight for what's right and the greater good.

Despite all the negative and worldly values media portrays, there are still good movies that inspire us to be resolute in our faith walk. So let's be discerning with the things we watch. Even in our entertainment, let's choose things that strengthen our faith. So that when faced with sin and temptations, we will be uncompromising and like St. Peter, declare: "We would rather obey God than men." *Donna España (donna.espana@yahoo.com)*

Reflection: "I ask the risen Jesus who turns death into life, to change hatred into love, vengeance into forgiveness and war into peace." (Pope Francis)

Jesus, teach me to stand up for You with all courage and firmness.

NOVEMBER 24
FRIDAY

1 Maccabees 4:36-37,
52-59
1 Chronicles 29:10, 11,
11-12, 12
Luke 19:45-48

PILLARS OR TERMITES
"My house shall be a house of prayer..."
– Luke 19:46

It might have started as a simple dislike of the choir, or the pastor who is not good at giving homilies, or maybe a minister living a double life, or the stifling regulations of the church.

The simple dislike eventually led to a full-blown disgust. Now, going to church has become a burdensome obligation. It's not how it used to be. And whenever you hear a scandal about the Church, judgment and criticism easily come forth from you. What used to be pillars in your life have now become termites.

The Church is not made up of building materials; it's a congregation of people who believe in Christ. And Christ dwells within us; therefore, we are the very foundation of the Church.

So before we criticize the Church, maybe it would help if we ask ourselves first, "Have I been an inspiration or a cause of destruction?" It's always easy to find fault and criticize, but as Jesus has said, His house should be a house of prayer, not a house of complaints; a place of hope and comfort, not a turf of enmity and despair. *Jane Gonzales-Rauch (mgr516@gmail.com)*

Reflection: We can never have peace and contentment if the reason we go to church is anything other than to be with Christ.

Heavenly Father, forgive me for the times I have caused disservice to the Church. May the Holy Spirit guide me that I may reach out only to Christ. Amen.

NEW LIFE

"… for to him all are alive." – Luke 20:38

1 Maccabees 6:1-13
Psalm 9:2-3, 4, 6, 16, 19
Luke 20:27-40

I am overwhelmed by this verse. In another version, this is rendered as, "He considers all people to be alive to him" (ISV). We are all "dead to sin" (Romans 6:11). But the Lord has redeemed us to give us "new life" (Romans 6:4)! We received this new life when we were baptized in the Lord.

A dead person cannot eat. He cannot hug and experience love. He cannot walk and explore the beauty that surrounds him. He cannot hear and enjoy the harmony of music.

I thank the Lord for giving me this new life. I have a family who loves me and whom I can hug and laugh with anytime. We can go out for food trips and taste the feasts that the Lord abundantly provides. We can walk and explore mountains, rivers and seas together and enjoy the beauty of God's creation. We can go to theaters and concerts, and enjoy music symphonies.

This is life — the new life that the Lord had promised in John 10:10: "I came so that they might have life and have it more abundantly."

Thank You, Lord, for this new, abundant life! *Danny Tariman (dtariman.loj@gmail.com)*

Reflection: Are you still living in the dark, and not enjoying life? Be set free and let Jesus be the Lord of your life!

Lord Jesus, please forgive me for all my sins. Come into my life and be my Lord and King. Amen!

Ezekiel 34:11-12, 15-17
Psalm 23:1-2, 2-3, 5, 6
1 Corinthians 15:20-26, 28
Matthew 25:31-46

Solemnity of Christ the King

A WAKE-UP CALL

"Then the King will say to those on his right, 'Come, you who are blessed by my Father. Inherit the kingdom prepared for you…'" – Matthew 25:34

I had a smile on my face when I answered a call from Eliz. She is one of my closest friends. I was maid of honor during her wedding. I've transferred work, but we remained in close contact. I thought it was just one of those casual calls. But the smile on my face was later replaced by tears. She has cancer.

I was not prepared for the pain. All I could think of at that moment was death and hopelessness. It hit me that for us to appreciate how we live, we have to face the reality of death. We need to be reminded of the end to make us wonder if we're accomplishing our life's purpose.

When faced with a dark uncertainty, we need to go back to Who is in control. It reminds us that our God is king and that He has a kingdom prepared for us. We are heirs of that kingdom.

As for Eliz, she has been receiving an abundance of God's love. Her journey continually reminds me to live a life of purpose worthy of God's inheritance. *Jan Ada Gerangaya (email address@yahoo.com)*

Reflection: How do you live your life so you can be worthy of the Kingdom God has prepared for you?

My God, My King, grant me the grace to live my life worthy of the Kingdom You have promised as my inheritance.

GIVE YOUR ALL

"She, from her poverty, has offered her whole livelihood." – Luke 21:4

Daniel 1:1-6, 8-20
Daniel 3:52, 53, 54, 55, 56
Luke 21:1-4

Merriam-Webster.com has a simple definition of livelihood: "a way of earning money in order to live." Although simple, it can also be profound, especially in the context of today's Gospel reading.

The widow, though already poor, "offered her whole livelihood" to God. Thus, we could say she offered her job or occupation – whatever it might have been – to Him. Another way of looking at it is she offered all that she had to God, despite her poverty.

This is not an easy thing to do — to give our all to God, even if we are down to our last centavo. It's not easy to offer our livelihood — our source of income, and even our income itself — to Jesus. Yet He calls us to do so every day, along with the other aspects of our lives. He wants us to surrender everything to Him and trust that He will always provide.

Just like the poor widow, let's give God our all. Let's surrender not just our livelihood, but our whole lives to Him.

Tina Santiago Rodriguez (trulyrichandblessed@gmail.com)

Reflection: God gave Himself to you; give yourself to God. (Blessed Robert Southwell)

Dearest Lord, I surrender everything to You. May my life give glory to You and You alone.

NOVEMBER 28
TUESDAY

Daniel 2:31-45
Daniel 3:57, 58, 59, 60, 61
Luke 21:5-11

THE MACHINE THAT LIED

"See that you not be deceived…"
– Luke 21:8

The baby's color turned bluish black. The nurse in the neonatal intensive care unit suspected a pneumopericardium, a condition in which the air in the sac surrounding the heart prevents the heart from beating. But the medical team assumed that the baby's lung had collapsed and prepared to reinflate it. The nurse insisted that it was a heart problem but the monitor showed that the baby's heart was fine.

The insistent nurse placed a stethoscope on the baby's chest to check for a heartbeat. There was none. The heart monitor misled the medical team because it was designed to measure electrical activity, not actual heartbeats. The baby's life was spared because the nurse relied on her gut feel and focused on the physical manifestations (i.e., the baby's skin color) rather than on the machine.

Similarly, Jesus warned His disciples about false teachers preaching a different gospel and claiming to have revelations from God. We must be vigilant so we will not be deceived by them. We need to focus only on Christ and His words that lead us to the truth. *Judith Concepcion (svp_jmc@yahoo.com)*

Reflection: "Your Word is a lamp for my feet, a light for my path" (Psalm 119:105). Do we turn to Jesus and His Words to guide us in our faith walk so we won't stumble and fall?

Lord, grant me wisdom to apply Your Word in my day-to-day life so I may stay on the right path.

St. James of the Marches, pray for us.

DEFEND YOUR FAITH

By your perseverance you will secure your lives. – Luke 21:19

My father was a Black Nazarene devotee. A few months before he died at age 72, he still joined the procession in Quiapo and even figured in a stampede. My mother, on the other hand, prays the rosary anywhere. These are expressions of her deep faith and devotion. In the olden times, those who believe in God were persecuted. But God's loyal servants didn't mind losing their lives to uphold their faith.

In the Bible, I greatly admire the story of Daniel, who, despite a decree stating that no prayers were allowed for 30 days, continued to pray to the God of Israel and was thrown into a lion's den. But God proved that the loyalty of His servants weren't put to waste as God sent an angel to close the jaws of the lions and he remained unharmed.

Another inspiring story was that of the Shadrach, Meshach, and Abednego, who refused to worship a golden statue built by King Nebuchadnezzar. They were instead thrown into a blazing furnace but remained firm in their belief until the end. True enough, God saved them and the fire did not even touch them.

Such stories of people who didn't give up and stood by their faith are truly remarkable. Let us not be afraid to live up to our faith, as God is and will always be with us. *Gracious B. Romero (graciousromero@gmail.com)*

Reflection: How far would you stand up for your faith?

Father God, help us to stand up for what is right at all times. Amen.

St. Clement, pray for us.

NOVEMBER 30
THURSDAY

Romans 10:9-18
Psalm 19:8, 9, 10, 11
Matthew 4:18-22

Feast of St. Andrew, Apostle

NOT JUST LIP SERVICE

For one believes with the heart and so is justified, and one confesses with the mouth and so is saved. – Romans 10:10

During my younger years, I was a nominal Catholic. As a "single-day practitioner," I fulfilled my obligation by attending Mass every Sunday. I felt holy and content that I would be saved because I attended Mass while others didn't. At least I was better than others.

The problem was, I was on my own for the rest of the week. My faith was merely a blip on my life's radar.

Then I met Jesus. The real, personal, living, and death-conquering Jesus! I experienced His love and mercy in a gathering called The Feast. I fell in love with Him. The Mass was no longer an obligation, but a date where the One I love meets me, speaks to me and empowers me.

Jesus lives. He lives through my actions and my words. He now makes me walk the talk and talk the walk 24/7.

I'm not perfect, but He perfects me daily. Jesus is Lord and God has raised Him from the dead (Romans 10:9). That alone is enough assurance that I'll make it as He promised. *Rye Belen (rye.belen@gmail.com)*

Reflection: Is your faith just lip service? Grow in the Spirit!

Father God, help us to live out our faith not just on Sundays but every day of our lives.

DECEMBER 1
FRIDAY

Daniel 7:2-14
Daniel 3:75, 76, 77, 78,
79, 80, 81
Luke 21:29-33

REACH FOR YOUR DREAMS

"But my words will not pass away."
– Luke 21:33

You're in a party. It's noisy. But from the other side of the room, you hear someone whisper your name. Thank your reticular activating system (or RAS) for this phenomenon. It's a filtering mechanism at the base of your brain that sorts through the entire tidal wave of visual, sensory and auditory stimuli you receive.

It's the same thing when you write down your dreams. Your RAS zeroes in on the many things that will contribute to the fulfillment of that dream.

Someone asked me, "When I pray, can't I just say, 'Lord, just give me whatever You want to bless me with'? Why do we have to specify what we want?" Sure you can pray that way. But I think there should be times when we pray with more specificity. When I do, I see the ingredients that I need fall into place like a jigsaw puzzle right before my eyes.

So write down your dreams — those tiny whispers that God planted in your heart. As you prepare for Christmas, open your heart to listen more to God's dreams for your life. He will help you make them happen. His words will not pass away. *Bo Sanchez (bosanchez@kerygmafamily.com)*

Reflection: What dreams do you hear in your heart?

Dearest Lord, allow me to dream the dreams You have for me. Amen.

DECEMBER 2
SATURDAY

Daniel 7:15-27
Daniel 3:82, 83, 84, 85, 86, 87
Luke 21:34-36

JESUS IS COMING

"Beware that your hearts do not become drowsy from carousing and drunkenness and the anxieties of daily life..."
– Luke 21:34

Last year was the most "social media engaged" elections to date – 51 million users on the final weeks before May 9. That's close to half of the country's population. It was a free-for-all bashing, hating and unfriending spree that soon divided everyone. There was so much going on that we didn't know who to believe anymore. Each time we opened our accounts, we would be surprised at how stressful staring into a screen could be.

But right after election day, I admired how those same people who divided the country told everyone to unite and support the would-be leaders. Candidates started to concede, and soon, Facebook showed pictures of oneness and love.

This is much like what happens each day.

We look at the news, the traffic, our workplace, our families – aren't we all stressed just by being swallowed by all these worries? It feels like everything is just tangled together and we can't see the end.

But like the rainbow after the elections, we know that Jesus will put things aright. He reminds us not to be anxious about each day, but be vigilant, because hope is coming. Change is coming. Jesus is coming. *Migs Ramirez (migsramirez.seminars@gmail.com)*

Reflection: What are you anxious about today? Surrender it to Jesus.

Dear Mary, pray that I may have the gift of surrender. May I constantly trust in the love of Jesus who knows what is best for me at His perfect time.

Blessed Rafael Chylinski, pray for us.

DECEMBER 3
SUNDAY

Isaiah 63:16-17, 19;
64:2-7
Psalm 80:2-3, 15-16,
18-19
1 Corinthians 1:3-9
Mark 13:33-37

First Sunday of Advent

IN CALM WATERS
God is faithful… – 1 Corinthians 1:9

Two nights ago, we had a terribly rough day at sea. My husband and I woke up past midnight because it felt as if we were on a pendulum ride at a theme park. It didn't help that the cruise ship we were on creaked as it tossed and tipped with the swelling waves. We were in open seas.

Today, we sailed smoothly on an ocean of glass, thanks to the mountains on both sides that kept the waters calm. Strong and steady, the mountain range was like a bulwark that protected the waters from the volatile winds.

Our experience at sea is a reminder of how I should live my life. When I choose my own way and stray away from God, I open myself to the consequences that sin brings. But when I live according to His commands and choose His ways, I know that I remain in the protective scope of His will. Even if I experience tough trials, I'm assured of His presence and purpose that will turn all things unto good for me.

Christmas is the time when God reminds us of the Gift He lovingly gives us. He sent Jesus to be our bulwark from sin and darkness so that we will forever know that no matter how rough our sailing gets, Emmanuel is there to calm the waters.

Rissa Singson Kawpeng (rissa@shepherdsvoice.com.ph)

Reflection: "God never gives someone a gift they are not capable of receiving. If he gives us the gift of Christmas, it is because we all have the ability to understand and receive it." (Pope Francis)

Jesus, thank You for always being with me.

St. Francis Xavier, priest, pray for us.

DECEMBER 4
MONDAY

Isaiah 2:1-5
Psalm 122:1-2, 3-4, 4-5,
6-7, 8-9
Matthew 8:5-11

BECAUSE DAD SAID SO

The centurion said in reply, "Lord, I am not worthy to have you enter under my roof; only say the word and my servant will be healed." – Matthew 8:8

I was on my last year in high school when my parents had financial trouble. They couldn't pay the tuition of their five kids.

It was already the last week of the school year and my parents hadn't paid a single centavo for my schooling. What we had was a promissory note requesting the school to extend the deadline with a guarantee that we would pay as soon as we had the means to do so. I reminded Dad that we had to pay my tuition the following week or else I wouldn't march during graduation. All he said was, "Don't worry, I'll find a way."

I wondered where he'd get the money because I knew that he had no projects or clients at the time. But because Dad said so, it was enough assurance for me that it would happen. By God's grace, Daddy was able to pay the tuition in full the following week just as he had said. He kept his word.

Has God promised you anything? Trust His word. Just like the centurion who didn't need proof of God's power, let Jesus' word be enough for you. Because when Dad says so, consider it done. *Velden Lim (veldenlim@gmail.com)*

Reflection: God is always true to His Word. Keep believing even if your circumstances tell you otherwise.

Father in heaven, when the world tempts me to despair, teach me to put my hope in Your everlasting Word.

St. John Damascene, priest and doctor of the Church, pray for us.

CHILDLIKE FAITH

"… you have revealed them to the childlike…" – Luke 10:21

Isaiah 11:1-10
Psalm 72:1-2, 7-8, 12-13, 17
Luke 10:21-24

Vera, which means "faith" in Russian and "truth" in Latin, was six months in her mother's womb when she was diagnosed with a congenital heart defect. Seven days after her birth, the doctor said she had truncus arteriosus, a rare heart condition causing delayed growth, fatigue, and shortness of breath. She had several surgeries, the first one when she was only four months old. Today, she is seven and she continues to take heart tests and medication.

All her life, this girl has been fighting to survive, yet she is so full of life, hope and faith. "You are unstoppable, God," she would pray with passion. When asked about this difficult journey, her parents said, "We just continue to believe and speak God's promises concerning Vera until the facts align with the truth that she is healed by the Lord."

What childlike faith both Vera and her parents have. They have no ounce of doubt or skepticism. Despite everything they've been through, they continue to boldly believe in a God who is loving, faithful and can do the impossible. *Mike Viñas (mikemichaelfcv@yahoo.com)*

Reflection: Speak to your circumstances until the surrounding facts align with God's truth.

Jesus, teach me to have childlike faith in the midst of difficulties.

DECEMBER 6
WEDNESDAY

Isaiah 25:6-10
Psalm 23:1-3, 3-4, 5, 6
Matthew 15:29-37

CHRISTMAS LEFTOVERS

They all ate and were satisfied. They picked up the fragments left over — seven baskets full. – Matthew 15:37

During this most wonderful time of the year, I receive ham, cheese and pasta as Christmas gifts. I share the bounty with relatives and neighbors. But after the season, I still have leftovers. I hardly have time to cook, so here's my easiest recipe for leftover ham: Slice an apple into thin pieces and arrange alternately between ham slices on a flat plate. Sprinkle brown sugar on the arrangement. Garnish with slices of leftover cheese and voila! You have a new dish!

Tip: To prevent apples from turning brown, quickly coat the pieces with calamansi juice before arranging them with the ham slices.

Yes, as the parable in the Gospel today tells us, God is ready to give us food more than we can eat— or, for that matter, blessings we don't even expect to receive.

But what I like more about the parable is what the disciples did with the leftovers. They gathered the broken pieces.

My humble interpretation? When I am broken, God and His angels will pick me up. I won't be left over. *Chay Santiago (cusantiago@gmail.com)*

Reflection: God is not a wasteful God. He doesn't discard you when you're broken but picks you up and makes you whole.

I am precious in Your eyes, Lord. For that I'm forever grateful.

St. Nicholas, bishop, pray for us.

DECEMBER 7
THURSDAY

Isaiah 26:1-6
Psalm 118:1, 8-9, 19-21, 25-27
Matthew 7:21, 24-27

THE GREATEST CONTRIBUTION

"Everyone who listens to these words of mine and acts on them will be like a wise man who built his house on rock."
– Matthew 7:24

What do you think is a person's greatest contribution to the world? Is it wealth? Intellect? Entertainment? Pleasure? I believe that a person's greatest contribution is to hear God's Word and make the Word come alive in one's life (see John 1:14). This means impacting other people's lives for the better and bringing out the best in them for Jesus.

Nothing beats modeling good character. As the saying goes, "We teach much with what we say. We teach more with what we do. We teach most with how we live."

Evangelii Nuntiandi says that the world does not need more preachers; it needs more witnesses. I strongly agree. We need witnesses and models of Jesus' heart of servanthood. We need to proclaim His life of service by the way we live. Jesus said, "If I therefore, the Master and teacher have washed your feet, you ought to wash one another's feet. I have given you a Model to follow, so that what I have done for you, you should also do" (John 13:14-15).

People are looking for stability. Build your house on the Rock! *Obet Cabrillas (obetcab@yahoo.com)*

Reflection: One Word of God is enough to make a saint.

Lord, deliver us from the "sands" of sloth and apathy, and help us to stand on Your Word.

St. Ambrose, bishop and doctor of the Church, pray for us.

DECEMBER 8

FRIDAY

Genesis 3:9-15, 20
Psalm 98:1, 2-3, 3-4
Ephesians 1:3-6, 11-12
Luke 1:26-38

Solemnity of the Immaculate
Conception of the Blessed Virgin
Mary

PURPOSE

In him we were also chosen, destined in accord with the purpose of the One who accomplishes all things according to the intention of his will. – Ephesians 1:11

Tears fell as Lysa flipped the alphabet cue cards and asked herself, "Why did I ever want this again?" Lysa Terkeurst, an author and motivational speaker, left her preaching ministry to pursue a significant calling— to teach basic education to two orphans she adopted from a war-torn orphanage in Africa.

When the boys got tested for schooling, they found out that they would need to be in kindergarten. But there were no classes that accept students aged 13 and 14. Lysa put on hold all her speaking engagements and committed to daily sessions of teaching the alphabet and numbers to her teenage boys.

Many times she just wanted to return the boys and go back to preaching, but she knew in her heart she was destined for a special purpose designed by the One who accomplishes all things according to His will.

Now, the boys are in college and Lysa is back to preaching God's Word. And because people were inspired by her story, 44 other kids were adopted from the same orphanage.

When God calls us for a purpose, God honors our yes. He equips us to accomplish the mission He calls us to do. *Veia Lim (veiallim@gmail.com)*

Reflection: Where God guides, God provides.

Lord, I set my eyes on the prize until I see Your glory fulfilled.

Blessed Virgin Mary, pray for us.

DECEMBER 9
SATURDAY

Isaiah 30:19-21, 23-26
Psalm 147:1-2, 3-4, 5-6
Matthew 9:35-10:1, 5, 6-8

THE BREAK-UP HELP

He will be gracious to you when you cry out; as soon as he hears he will answer you. – Isaiah 30:19

I made a tough decision. My girlfriend and I broke up after five years of being together.

I initiated the break-up but I was still brokenhearted. I asked myself, *Was this the right decision? Why do I have to hurt a good person? Is this what God wants?*

Then rumors behind the reason for our break-up started to spread and my past mistakes resurfaced. Soon, some people left the ministry and friends unfriended me in social media. But the most heartbreaking part was knowing that my ex was having a hard time and I couldn't comfort her.

I cried to God for help, for strength, for good friends and for the fear in my heart to be removed. I prayed for love to overflow and for healing to come.

God answered my prayers, through loved ones and friends who stayed, listened and loved me through it all. They helped me overcome the situation and journeyed with me through my healing.

Friends, when you cry for help, know that God hears you. He has the solution and the healing at hand. He loves you! *Jan Carlo Silan (jcsilan@gmail.com)*

Reflection: Do you believe that God hears you when you cry out to Him? Do you believe His plans are better than your plans?

Lord, thank You for Your love. May we hear Your voice in times of need.

St. Juan Diego, pray for us.

DECEMBER 10
SUNDAY

Isaiah 40:1-5, 9-11
Psalm 85:9-10, 11-12,
13-14
2 Peter 3:8-14
Mark 1:1-8

Second Sunday of Advent

HIS PERFECT TIME

*The Lord does not delay His promise…
but He is patient with you… – 2 Peter 3:9*

When the Lord prematurely called my sister from this life at the age of 31, I asked Him, "Why her? Why not me? She has three daughters (aged four, one, and one and a half months) to raise. They need a mom. I don't have a family of my own yet. I'm single. I want to go to heaven now. Life is so unfair!"

My demanding questions, bargaining and anger fell on deaf ears. His only answer was a painful silence.

Good thing these were just some of the painful stages of my grief.

Achi (elder sister in Fookien) was Miss Congeniality. The funeral parlor along Araneta Avenue teemed with friends and loved ones day in and day out. It was like a reunion. We even had to extend her wake so that our other relatives and her friends could pay their last respects.

Then it dawned on me: I was not the one in that casket because I am still a work in progress. The Potter is still making a beautiful masterpiece out of this obstinate clay. *Ems Sy Chan* (leeannesy7@yahoo.com)

Reflection: Are you preparing every day for your reunion with your loved ones in heaven?

Thank You, Lord, for being a God of second, third and many other chances. Thank You for being patient with a sinner like me.

DECEMBER 11
MONDAY

Isaiah 35:1-10
Psalm 85:9, 10, 11-12,
13-14
Luke 5:17-26

GHOSTBUSTER

*"Say to those whose hearts are frightened:
Be strong, fear not! Here is your God,
he comes with vindication; with divine
recompense he comes to save you."*
– Isaiah 35:4

I'm afraid of ghosts.

That tingling feeling at the back of my neck as I enter a dim room or that whiff of a candle burning or the sweet scent of flowers as I step into the office elevator at 11 p.m. sends chills up my spine.

I am no ghost detector but the thought of encountering specters frightens me. But nothing is scarier to me than the ghosts of my past. Fear overcomes me when I realize how my past mistakes affect me at present. I get nauseous at the thought of how it will affect my future decisions. I'm terrified that it can define my character.

Thankfully, God is my stronghold. His Bible promises comfort and assure me. He is my Ghostbuster who wipes away my sins and transforms me into the person He wants me to be.

Eugene Cailao (eugenecailao@gmail.com)

Reflection: What is it that you fear most, that keeps you from trusting fully in God's Word?

Father, liberate me from my fears. Allow me to bask in Your presence and know You more through Your Word.

DECEMBER 12
TUESDAY

Zechariah 2:14-17
(or Revelation 11:19, 12:1-6, 10)
Judith 13:18-19
Luke 1:26-38

Feast of Our Lady of Guadalupe

YOUR MIRACLE IS COMING

"For nothing will be impossible for God."
– Luke 1:37

According to statistics, a woman who reaches the age of 40 and who's never been married, has a one in four chance of being married. As you get older, the chances of being able to conceive also decline. This gives many singles like me much pressure and anxiety. Though there are biological considerations, I am comforted by what God tells Mama Mary about Elizabeth who conceived a son in her old age. "For nothing will be impossible for God," says Gabriel.

I believe that God will make a way to fulfill His plan for your life. The partner in life you long for will come. The payment to your debt will arrive. The baby you've been waiting for will be conceived. It may take time but it will happen.

I'm inspired by Mary's trust in God's promise to her even if it seemed impossible: God becoming a child through the Holy Spirit. I also remember the elder Sarah, Abraham's wife, who laughed at the incredulous news that she would bear a son. Sarah did give birth to Isaac and Elizabeth to St. John.

And Mama Mary, because she believed in God's Word, paved the way for the birth of Jesus who is able to save us from our doubts and fears. *Marjorie Ann Duterte (marjorie.travels@gmail.com)*

Reflection: What impossible thing God is telling you, He will do. "Prayer works wonders, but we have to believe!" (Pope Francis)

Dear God of the impossible, I believe! Like what Mary said, "May it be done to me according to Your word." Amen.

Our Lady of Guadalupe, pray for us.

EXCESS BAGGAGE

"For my yoke is easy, and my burden light."
– Matthew 11:30

Isaiah 40:25-31
Psalm 103:1-2, 3-4, 8, 10
Matthew 11:28-30

My two-and-a-half-year-old toddler loves to do things on her own. Once, she insisted on wearing her backpack and carried another bag of toys, her "luggage" that's a small satchel with some diapers and a book. And this is just for a trip to the mall. Naturally, she struggled.

"You don't have to bring all that," I pointed out. "But I need it," she replied with conviction.

"Give it to Mommy. I'll help you."

"No, no, no. I do it!"

I watched her stumble out the doorway. Then, she finally turned around and said, "Mommy, can you help me with this?" as she dropped some of her things on the floor.

"Of course!" I said as I helped her.

As adults, we sometimes insist on our heavy baggage. We stuff our lives with burdens that cause us toxic stress and unhappiness. We forget that we have the Lord who offers and waits for us to let go of the load we cling to.

When we allow Him to help us, our burdens become bearable. *Kitty D. Ferreria (kittydulay@yahoo.com)*

Reflection: What is the Lord asking you to surrender?

Lord, help me learn to let go and trust in You.

DECEMBER 14
THURSDAY

Isaiah 41:13-20
Psalm 145:1, 9, 10-11,
12-13
Matthew 11:11-15

BEHIND THE SCENES

That all may see and know, observe and understand, that the hand of the Lord has done this… – Isaiah 41:20

I couldn't help but be grateful and amazed as I recalled how God orchestrated the events of my life to perfectly fall into place.

A week ago, I was reminded of this as I wrote about my transition from a career woman to a stay-at-home mom and from a stay-at-home mom to a work-at-home mom for my latest book. I just knew that it was God's hand at work behind the scenes — moving the right people, providing the right projects and opening doors of opportunities. Even the amounts that I earned when I started perfectly matched the bills I needed to pay. There's no denying that God made those things possible.

I mentioned this as I told my story because I want those who will read my book to know that God helped me during my transitions. He blessed the work of my hands beyond my expectations.

I don't want to take all the credit for what I have accomplished. Deep in my heart, I know that things happened as they did because I made room for God to work miracles in my life. *Teresa Gumap-as Dumadag (teresa@fulllifecube.com)*

Reflection: Recall the times when you recognized God's hand in your circumstances. Thank God for each one of them.

Lord, may my lips be ready at all times to proclaim Your goodness and faithfulness in my life.

St. John of the Cross, priest and doctor of the Church, pray for us.

LEAD THE WAY

I am the Lord, your God… leading you on the way you should go. – Isaiah 48:17

Isaiah 48:17-19
Psalm 1:1-2, 3, 4, 6
Matthew 11:16-19

It was 7:30 p.m. and I was nowhere near my hotel in Kyoto. I was still in Nara and needed to ride the correct train immediately. Otherwise, I'd have to go by bus, which I was less confident on taking.

It was my first trip to Japan and I was alone. I don't speak Nihonggo, and the train master in Nara knew no English. He couldn't answer my question on which train to ride. The desperate conversation was then interrupted by a teenage boy who offered to accompany me to the correct train. I was hesitant but I needed to leave that train station right away.

Taking a leap of faith, I rode the train with him. Instantly, he chatted with me, asking about the Philippines and sharing everything he learned from school about the 7,107 islands. He proved to be an angel. I was in bed at my hotel in no time.

Many times in our lives, we may feel lost and desperate to find our way. Know that God will never abandon us. He has gone before us and will lead us to where He wants us to be. *Osy Erica (osy.erica@gmail.com)*

Reflection: Are you feeling lost in life? God will clear the pathways to where you should be.

When I can't find my way, lead me, Lord. Your light I will seek and Your staff I will follow. Amen.

Blessed Mary Frances Schervier, pray for us.

DECEMBER 16
SATURDAY

Sirach 48:1-4, 9-11
Psalm 80:2, 3, 15-16,
18-19
Matthew 17:9, 10-13

BULLET OR GOD

"You should be the one to calm God's anger…" – Sirach 48:10

Action star Ramon Revilla was known in his movies for having an amulet. It supposedly protected him from harm.

My friend must have been his fan. He wore a bullet pendant as an amulet believing it was his protection. He never left the house without it nor would he allow anyone to remove it. One day, he came home from an out-of-town trip with his pendant missing. He was restless and irritable as he searched for it. He pestered me to go back to the province to retrieve it. He didn't know that he left it in the drawer but I brought it back to Manila and kept it. I wanted to wean him out of his false sense of security.

Our friendship led him back to his Catholic faith. Providentially, his bullet was confiscated at the airport but he was not detained. I gave him a crucifix pendant that he now wears and will not do away with. Once, during a terrifying circumstance, he held on to it as he fervently prayed to God.

Let us be instruments of God. As bearers of our faith, let us remind people that only God is our true protector. *Marie Franco (mariefranco_pie@yahoo.com)*

Reflection: Were there instances when you, as a Catholic, missed the chance to take a bold position to stand up for God?

Dear God, grant me wisdom and courage to be Your angel here on earth to "calm Your anger" for the misdeeds of my brothers. And send me Your angels to "calm Your anger" for my misdeeds.

Blessed Honoratus Kozminski, pray for us.

Isaiah 61:1-2, 10-11
Luke 1:46-48, 49-50,
53-54
1 Thessalonians 5:16-24
John 1:6-8, 19-28

Third Sunday of Advent

QUESTIONS TO THANKSGIVING

"I rejoice heartily in the Lord, in my God is the joy of my soul." – Isaiah 16:10

When my dad passed away four years ago, I had many questions for the Lord.

Why did he have to go through this? Why did the family have to experience this? Why does my mom have to be alone so early in life? Why do I have to lose my dad? Why our family?

I had so many why's. "Why, Lord? I have been serving You and offered You the prime years of my life and this is what I get," I complained.

Then it suddenly dawned on me that the Lord does not owe me anything but I owe everything to Him. My questions suddenly turned into thanksgiving. "Thank You, Lord, that my dad did not have to suffer so much. Thank You, Lord, for giving our family strength. Thank You, Lord, for giving my mom the will to carry on." *Anthony Rodriguez (anthony.r@svrtv.com)*

Reflection: Jesus' plan is far greater than ours. Thank God He turns our mourning into dancing.

Lord, instead of complaining, allow me to seize every chance to thank You at all times.

Jeremiah 23:5-8
Psalm 72:1-2, 12-13, 18-19
Matthew 1:18-25

JUST SAY YES!

*When Joseph awoke, he did as the angel
of the Lord had commanded him and took
his wife into his home.*
– Matthew 1:24

There was a time in my ministry life when I got appointed as a ministry head. I was dumbfounded. The responsibility was huge, and I thought I couldn't handle it. Ninety-nine percent of the ministry members then were older than me. Why would they listen to me? How could I lead them? What if I fail? What if the ministry fails?

Nevertheless, I said yes, worked as hard as I could, and surrendered to God. He didn't fail me. Opportunities opened, new members stepped up, and the ministry thrived.

God's ways are not our ways. I've learned that when God allows things to happen to you, even if you disagree with it, He intends it for a greater purpose. And all the hurt and sacrifices will be worth it.

St. Joseph was afraid at first when he found out that Mary was pregnant. But because he was obedient to the Lord, he said yes to the calling to be Jesus' earthly father. With his yes, Joseph played a key role in the salvation of mankind. *Tintin Mutuc (kristinemutuc@shepherdsvoice.com.ph)*

Reflection: Don't fear when God calls you to do something beyond what you think you're capable of. He is the God who enables and equips!

Jesus, use me. Use my gifts. Use my knowledge. Use my life.

Blessed Anthony Grassi, pray for us.

DECEMBER 19
TUESDAY

Judges 13:2-7, 24-25
Psalm 71:3-4, 5-6, 16-17
Luke 1:5-25

'I AM GABRIEL'

"I was sent to speak to you and to announce to you this good news." – Luke 1:19

It's Advent season and a few more days before Christmas, so today I declare by God's grace, "I am Gabriel."

"I am Gabriel." I am sent to speak to you.

"I am Gabriel." I speak of hope, faith and love.

"I am Gabriel." I speak of peace and joy, restoration and redemption.

"I am Gabriel." I uphold and uplift, encourage and empower.

"I am Gabriel." I tell you of the exciting and amazing plans God has for you.

"I am Gabriel." I proclaim the great and mighty things God will do to you and through you.

"I am Gabriel." I assure you, "With God nothing is impossible!"

"I am Gabriel." I announce to you the Good News!

This Christmas, and the coming New Year, hear and listen to Gabriel.

Better yet, be Gabriel. Be a bringer of the Good News.

God is with you! *Alvin Barcelona (apb_ayo@yahoo.com)*

Reflection: Today, decide to be a bringer of the Good News. Uplift, encourage, give hope and joy to someone. Be Gabriel!

Dear Lord, by Your pure grace and love, may my life be good news to others.

Blessed Pope Urban V, pray for us.

GODPOSSIBLE

"May it be done to me according to your word." – Luke 1:38

Isaiah 7:10-14
Psalm 24:1-2, 3-4, 5-6
Luke 1:26-38

She was way beyond child-bearing age. Besides, if she could have children, shouldn't she have gotten pregnant when she was much younger? But by now, Sarah's womb was practically dead.

Yet God promised she would bear a child.

In another time and another place, a woman was young and fertile. But she had no spouse, no contact with man. She was a virgin.

Yet God promised she would bear a child.

Two impossible situations. One God who promised the same thing. And in both situations, God made good on His word.

No matter how incredible or impossible things are, we have to obey and trust that God will always fulfill His promises, the ones that He has made yesterday, today and tomorrow. God never changes. His plans are always the best. When He says something, better believe it. Because it's Godpossible!

What a great God we have! *Dr. Henry L. Yu (henrio_md@yahoo.com)*

Reflections: Christmas is the season of fulfilled promises. What promise has God made to you? What promises have you made to Him?

Lord, my sins, mistakes and shortcomings will never thwart Your plan. Thank You, Lord, for being a faithful God.

Song of Songs 2:8-14
(or Zephaniah 3:14-18)
Psalm 33:2-3, 11-12,
20-21
Luke 1:39-45

MAGNIFY THE GOOD

Mary set out in those days and traveled to the hill country in haste to a town of Judah, where she entered the house of Zechariah and greeted Elizabeth. – Luke 1:39-40

"The great visitation that followed the great revelation." This is a line I remember from a recent reflection I read regarding Mary's visit to Elizabeth.

Today, of course, any great revelation will become a great declaration, which might be done through Facebook, Facetime, Skype or the myriad of other social media that abound in our life nowadays.

But we are tempted to make a great declaration not only of good news. Perhaps more often than not, and many times unmindfully, we magnify the bad news instead of the good.

If we are to become better children of Mary, we have to try to follow her example and magnify the good news in our life. A new job perhaps? An encouraging word received? A much-sought after parking? (Yes, even that.)

We each have our good news. Let us magnify Him who has done these great things for us—for everything is great, if only we realize how in need we are. *Joy Sosoban-Roa (jsosoban@gmail.com)*

Reflection: The world is weary of bad news. It's crying out to you, "Inspire me!" How can you uplift someone today?

Dear Lord, now I realize how great Mother Mary's humility was, for she never took any credit for herself. Help me to be like her, Lord. Amen.

St. Peter Canisius, priest and doctor of the Church, pray for us.

1 Samuel 1:24-28
1 Samuel 2:1, 4-5, 6-7, 8
Luke 1:46-56

SIMPLY FAITHFUL

"I prayed for this child and the Lord granted my request. Now, I in turn give him to the Lord as long as he lives, he shall be dedicated to the Lord." – 1 Samuel 1:27-28

Just last year, our family was having financial problems. As the breadwinner at the time, I felt that the entire burden was on me. I found myself in deep prayer pleading to God for assistance. I asked Him to guide me and lead me to where I should go.

God, the faithful Father that He is, heard my prayer and granted my plea. He helped me through the people I talked to, the situations that I found myself in, and through the loving kindness of my mentors and friends.

Eventually, a solution was presented to our family that is helping us until now to slowly eliminate our debts. God answered my prayer.

I found myself so grateful for His act of love that I wondered, "Lord, in what way do You want me to repay You?" He spoke to my heart as if He was right beside me. "My daughter, just remain in Me."

I realized that God does not ask that we repay Him with grand gestures. What He desires is that we simply remain faithful to Him. *Erika Mendoza (epaulmendoza@gmail.com)*

Reflection: God does not ask that we succeed in everything but that we remain faithful.

Lord, I want to remain in Your love — always.

Blessed Jacopone da Todi, pray for us.

Malachi 3:1-4, 23-24
Psalm 25:4-5, 8-9, 10, 14
Luke 1:57-66

MIREYA

All who heard these things took them to heart, saying, "What, then, will this child be?" – Luke 1:66

After consultations and check-ups, doctors told us it would be impossible to conceive naturally given our medical conditions. Even after work-ups to boost our fertility, our chances seemed nil. Our hearts were broken and we spent lonely nights, but we were not in despair. We chose to continue trying without artificial means. We asked friends and family to intercede for us. Long before we conceived, we listed down baby names, and we had my husband's old baby cabinet repaired and painted, awaiting our baby-to-be. We knew God would hear our prayers in His perfect time.

His answer came after six years. "Her name will be Mireya Isabella," we said. Mireya, meaning "miracle," and Isabella, "consecrated to God." When we announced the good news to family and friends, exclamations of thanksgiving and amazement at God's power poured in. She had not yet been born, and already people were praising God because of her. I could not help but wonder what God's marvelous plan for her life would be.

The Lord is the Giver of life who brings each child into this world. Let us pray that they may grow up to fulfill their life purpose and, just like John the Baptist, give glory to God and lead others to Jesus one day. Geraldine G. Catral (catral.geegee@beaconschool.ph)

Reflection: How are you leading the children in your life to Jesus?

Lord, we dedicate to You our children. May they grow to fulfill their life's purpose and one day bring others closer to You.

St. John of Kanty, priest, pray for us.

DECEMBER 24
SUNDAY

2 Samuel 7:1-5, 8-12, 14, 16
Psalm 89:2-3, 4-5, 27, 29
Romans 16:25-27
Luke 1:26-38

Fourth Sunday of Advent

MY GIFT TO CHRIST
"Thus says the Lord, should you build me a house to dwell in?" – 2 Samuel 7:5

Mr. Harry Wayne Huizenga is a wealthy American businessman who has several multimillion dollar mansions in South Florida, one of which he gave to his niece as a wedding gift. Can you imagine receiving a multimillion-dollar house as a gift?

Tomorrow is the Lord's birthday. How nice would it be to give Him a house as a present — not the structure, but our very own self. We're worth more than any mansion on earth and I am sure the Lord would be delighted with the gift that we bring. He knows that we are a work-in-progress, but we can at least prepare as we welcome Him into our hearts.

As we give Him this "house," maybe a little cleaning up by going to confession and receiving the Eucharist would be timely. And it would be nice to find ways to engage Him in a good conversation by reading Scriptures and spending more time in prayer and reflection.

There are many ways to prepare. It doesn't have to be big and extravagant. We can start with a clean and contrite heart.

Jane Gonzales-Rauch (mgr516@gmail.com)

Reflection: No matter how small, no matter how simple, the best gift of all is a life transformed.

Father in heaven, I offer myself to You today. In spite of my frailty, use me as You please. There is nothing more I desire today but to be in Your presence. Amen.

St. Adele, pray for us.

DECEMBER 25

MONDAY

Isaiah 52:7-10
Psalm 98:1, 2-3, 3-4, 5-6
Hebrews 1:1-6
John 1:1-18

Solemnity of the Nativity
of the Lord (Christmas)

GOD WITH US

And the Word became flesh and made his dwelling among us, and we saw his glory...
– John 1:14

I went to Divisoria to buy materials for Kerygma Conference. But I miscalculated my expenses and ran out of money. Good thing that I already bought the things I needed. My problem was I didn't have money left for gas. I was worried.

I drove back to Makati for The Feast where I volunteered to fix the stage. I talked to God in my car. I asked Him to give me a miracle immediately. I prayed, "Lord, I need money and I need at least P500 even just for my gas only."

Then I proceeded to The Feast venue when *Tita* Eva, our finance ministry head, came and handed me a small envelope. I opened it and saw a P500 bill. "What's this for, *Tita?*" She replied, "That's for your gas since you volunteered to dress up the stage. It's Feast Makati's way of helping our volunteers."

I was surprised when she told me that she felt that I needed money for gasoline. I told her about my prayer in my car. I felt God's love so much because He used *Tita* Eva to let me know that He is with us and He was born to save to us. *Monty Mendigoria (montymendigoria@yahoo.com)*

Reflection: This Christmas day, reflect on the power of the Most High. He sent His only begotten Son to be with us and to show His love and mercy to those who need Him.

Lord, thank You for giving us Your only Son, Jesus, to let us know — without a shadow of a doubt — that You are with us.

St. Eugenia, pray for us.

THE TRADE

"You will be hated by all because of my name, but whoever endures to the end will be saved." – Matthew 10:22

Acts 6:8-10; 7: 54-59
Psalm 31:3-4, 6, 8,
16, 17
Matthew 10:17-22

Feast of St. Stephen, protomartyr

When my wife needed to undergo a minor procedure, I had to drop everything. She needed me 24/7 so I wasn't able to work for two months. I even asked help from brothers for my ministry. I had to say no to some earning opportunities because I had to be there for her. I considered that I'd lose money or, worse, have debts because of my decision, but I couldn't afford to lose time being with her. Everything else I could get back after.

Family is our first ministry. Serving a loving God brought me back to love my family. I realized it's not what you lose, but what you gain. It's not who hates you but who loves you. When you follow Jesus, sin will hate you, your vices will hate you, but you will gain your life back. You will receive peace, love, hope, joy.

Choose to follow the One who loves you, the One who gave everything for you. His name is Jesus.

Following Jesus brings us closer to what we are really made of — love. *Dreus Cosio (andreus.cosio@gmail.com)*

Reflection: It is not who hates you but who loves you. God loves you. Choose to love someone today.

Lord, thank You for Your love, thank You for this life. I am Yours. Love me today, guide and guard me along the way.

COMPLETING OUR JOY

We are writing this so that our joy may be complete. – 1 John 1:4

1 John 1:1-4
Psalm 97:1-2, 5-6, 11-12
John 20:1, 2-8

Feast of St. John, Apostle,
Evangelist

Recently someone emailed me about my *Didache* reflection to say how blessed I am that even if I live abroad, I still get to share about the Gospel.

When I share about a good thing that has happened to me, I relive that experience all over again and become grateful. That's what happens to me when I write my reflections. I am ministered, humbled and made more grateful. Sometimes, I'm the first one to cry over them.

Not all of us can write or would want to, but everyone can share about the Gospel. Sharing person-to-person is a most powerful way of "completing your joy" over what God has done in your life.

How was God's Word handed down from generation to generation? It was through word of mouth — what we now call the Oral Tradition. So yes, you and I can always share the Gospel.

Just share your story. That may be what someone needs to do the next courageous act, to step out in faith, or to do a good deed. *Joy Sosoban-Roa (jsosoban@gmail.com)*

Reflection: You don't need to be an eloquent speaker to touch someone's life with God's Word. The first evangelists were uneducated men.

Thank You, Lord, for the privilege to share about how You move in my life. Grant me the opportunity and the grace to do so — written or otherwise.

DECEMBER 28
THURSDAY

1 John 1:5-2:2
Psalm 124:2-3, 4-5, 7-8
Matthew 2:13-18

Feast of Holy Innocents, martyrs

JESUS PRAYER

If we acknowledge our sins, he is faithful and just and will forgive our sins and cleanse us from every wrongdoing.
– 1 John 1:9

I start my day by uttering a simple prayer: "Lord Jesus Christ, Son of the Living God, have mercy on me a sinner." I find myself murmuring this at sporadic times of the day.

I learned this from a saintly priest who heard my confession. After reciting my litany of sins, I was expecting him to ask me to say the Act of Contrition and a long prayer for penance. Instead, he instructed me to repeat this short variant of the Jesus Prayer.

The origin of the Jesus Prayer is from our Eastern Catholic brothers and later on accepted in the Roman Catholic Catechism.

"The invocation of the holy name of Jesus is the simplest way of praying always…. This prayer is possible 'at all times' because it is not one occupation among others but the only occupation: that of loving God, which animates and transfigures every action in Christ Jesus" (CCC 2668).

This prayer was scripturally inspired by the parable of the publican and the Pharisee. There are many theological explanations on this prayer, whose profound beauty is in its simplicity when prayed wholeheartedly. It is short yet powerful.

It changed my life. *Ariel Driz (adriz77@yahoo.com)*

Reflection: Have you called out to Jesus lately?

Lord Jesus Christ, Son of the Living God, have mercy on me a sinner. Lord Jesus, my Savior, thank You for Your love.

DECEMBER 29
FRIDAY

1 John 2:3-11
Psalm 96:1-2, 2-3, 5-6
Luke 2:22-35

PRESENT

… to present him to the Lord…
– Luke 2:22

Have you ever really "stopped, looked and listened?"

In the hustle and bustle of the Christmas season, we experience a deluge of stimuli and a smorgasbord of tasks to do, so much so that Christmas could be described as the busiest of the seasons and the most stressful of occasions.

This reminds me of Christ's visit to Martha and Mary's home, with Martha attending to every manner of work, while Mary sits right in front of Jesus. In the end, the Lord emphasized that what was most important was being "present" to Him.

Friends, in the midst of family reunions and parties, the gift-giving and gatherings, let us make a choice to stop, look and listen… to *Jesus*.

What is He saying and showing you this Christmas? Are you looking? Are you listening? Let us be "present" to Him as He came as a baby just to be "present" to us.

As we do this, Jesus would indeed be born into our lives once again. Jonathan Yogawin (jyogawin@gmail.com)

Reflection: What gift will you give Jesus this Christmas season?

Lord Jesus, may I be present to You throughout the coming year.

WHEN WAITING HURTS

She never left the temple... awaiting the redemption of Jerusalem. – Luke 2:37-38

1 John 2:12-17
Psalm 96:7-8, 8-9, 10
Luke 2:36-40

My eldest brother abroad texted in the wee hours of the morning. Our other brother figured in a very bad biking accident. He was operated immediately but the trauma to the head was pretty bad. The doctor said we would know in three days if he will survive.

That must have been the longest three days of my life. I was constantly glued to my phone waiting for any message of good news while dreading to receive what seemed inevitable then. The three days stretched into a week, then to a month, and then to more tormenting months. The waiting was agonizing. During that time, our family lived to hear even one bit of good news every day as we prayed simultaneously in whatever part of the world we were in. After several months, my brother was declared out of the woods and was moved out of the ICU.

Waiting is never easy, especially when you're not sure of what you will receive at the end of all your waiting. If you are going through a period of uncertainty and sorrow and the night seems to last forever, know that daybreak is just around the corner. Just hold on a little more and hang on to Jesus. The sun is just about to rise again in the horizon! *Ronna Singson Ledesma (ronna_ledesma@yahoo.com.ph)*

Reflection: No matter how dark and long your night may be, know for sure that there's no stopping the sun from rising.

Jesus, You are my light in my darkest night. Thank You for always holding my hand in the dark.

St. Egwin, pray for us.

DECEMBER 31
SUNDAY

Genesis 15:1-6; 21:1-3
(or Sirach 3:2-6, 12-14)
Psalm 105:1-2, 3-4, 6-7, 8-9
Hebrews 11:8, 11-12, 17-19
(or Colossians 3:12-21)
Luke 2:22-40

Feast of the Holy Family of Jesus,
Mary and Joseph

HE KEEPS HIS PROMISES

The word of the Lord came to Abram in a vision: Fear not, Abram! I am your shield; I will make your reward very great.
– Genesis 15:1

One of the lessons my father taught me and my siblings is to be true to our word. Growing up, we knew that his yes meant yes and his no meant no.

Back then, my father was a supervisor in a sales department. He was usually out of town, but he always promised to be home on Sundays. I held on to his promise that our Sundays would be family day — to hear Mass, eat and spend the afternoon together. He has always fulfilled it. This habit inspires me to apply the same tradition when I have my own family someday.

Your 2017 might be full of fulfilled dreams, healing and financial success. Or it could have been a year of loss, broken dreams, sickness or of financial challenges. Know that regardless of your situation, God is always with you.

In the readings, God promised Abram an offspring. He also promised Simeon that he will see the Messiah. It took time, but He fulfilled His promise to them. In the same way, nothing will stop the Lord from fulfilling His promises to you. Keep the faith!

Jan Carlo Silan (jcsilan@gmail.com)

Reflection: God fulfills every promise He makes. Do you have enough faith to trust His plans?

Lord, thank You for keeping Your promises. I will wait and be open to the best version of Your promise for me. Amen.

St. Sylvester, pray for us.

MEET YOUR
DIDACHE WRITERS

Bo Sanchez
Catholic Lay Preacher / Author
bosanchez@kerygmafamily.com

Alvin Barcelona
Preacher-Educator / World Bank
Consultant
apb_ayo@yahoo.com

Rissa Singson Kawpeng
Author / Editor / Preacher
justbreatherissa@gmail.com

Jon Escoto
Corporate Training Consultant /
Preacher / Author
faithatworkjon@gmail.com

Obet Cabrillas
Preacher / Youth Missions &
Campus Life Director / Life Coach
kpreacherobet@gmail.com

George Gabriel
Writer / Director / Preacher
george.svp@gmail.com

Mike Viñas
Investment Trainer / Preacher
mikemichaelfcv@yahoo.com

Dean Pax Lapid
Negosyo Mentor, AIM Professor,
Business Consultant / Author
happyretiree40@gmail.com

Velden Lim
Preacher / Feast Builder of Feast
SM Bicutan
veldenlim@gmail.com

Migs Ramirez
Author / Creativity Trainer /
Lay Missionary
migsramirez.seminars@gmail.com

MEET YOUR DIDACHE WRITERS

Monching Bueno
Preacher / Businessman
ramon_bueno@yahoo.com

Jonathan M. Yogawin
Meta-Coach / Trainer /
Consultant
jyogawin@gmail.com

Didoy Lubaton
Medical Doctor / Preacher
didoymd@gmail.com

Jan Carlo Silan
Feast Builder for Makati
jcsilan@gmail.com

JPaul Hernandez
Preacher / Author
jpaulmh@yahoo.com
jpaulhernandez.com

Carlo F. Lorenzo
TV Host / Blogger
carloflorenzo@yahoo.com

Andreus Cosio
Preacher / Financial Advisor
andreus.cosio@gmail.com

Paolo Galia
LOJ Youth Missions Director
pgalia@gmail.com

Boggs Burbos
Corporate Inspirational Speaker
Preacher / Feast Builder - Cavite
boggsburbos@yahoo.com

JC Libiran
LOJ Campus Life Director /
Author
jclibiran@ymail.com

MEET YOUR
DIDACHE WRITERS

Aben Garlan
Feast Builder, Feast CDO /
Corporate Speaker and Trainer /
NLP Practitioner
mail@abengarlan.com

Stephen Nellas
Feast Builder / Entrepreneur
sinfts@live.com

Joel Saludares
Inspirational Speaker /
Corporate Trainer
joelsaludares@yahoo.com

Reng Morelos
Kerygma Writer / Wife and Mom
hermierengmorelos@yahoo.com

Tess V. Atienza
Production Mgr. / Managing Editor /
Writer
theresa.a@shepherdsvoice.com.ph

Chelle S. Crisanto
Principal Staff Officer
ellehcmaria@gmail.com

Dina Pecaña
Writer/ Managing Editor
dpecana@yahoo.com

Karren Renz Seña
Digital Department Manager/
Author/ Writing Coach
karren.s@shepherdsvoice.com.ph

Marjorie Ann Duterte
Author / Editor
marjorie.travels@gmail.com

Maymay Salvosa
Assistant Managing Editor /
Author
christiane.salvosa@gmail.com

MEET YOUR
DIDACHE WRITERS

Lallaine Gogna
Mom/Dentist
lallygogna@yahoo.com

Meann Tee
Freelance Sales and
Marketing Agent / Worship Leader /
Preacher / Trainer
meanntytee@yahoo.com

Veia Lim-Viñas
Event Host and Singer
veiallim@gmail.com

Tina Santiago Rodriguez
Writer / Editor / Speaker / Host
trulyrichandblessed@gmail.com

Erika Pauline Mendoza
Executive Assistant
epaulmendoza@gmail.com

Ruby Albino
Marketing Director
r_jean07@yahoo.com

Anthony Rodriguez
Project Manager
anthony.r@svrtv.com

Joy Sosoban-Roa
Writer / Editor
jsosoban@gmail.com

Edwin Marcelo
Events Technical Head /
Meta-Coach / NLP Practitioner
imboodoo@yahoo.com

Kristine Anne Mutuc
Marketing Manager
kristinemutuc@shepherdsvoice.com.ph

MEET YOUR DIDACHE WRITERS

Mirella Santiago
Author / Editor
lellams88@gmail.com

Gina Verdolaga
Author
mgjver@yahoo.com

Josiel Erica
Web Content Manager / Writer / Trainer
osy.erica@gmail.com

Orange V. Garcia
Nation Builder / Author
og@orangegarcia.com

Alvin Fabella
Manages an IT Company/ Speaker/Writer
alvinfabella@yahoo.com

Marc Lopez
Author / Speaker
lamblightschool@yahoo.com

Judith M. Concepcion
Freelance Writer / Translator
svp_jmc@yahoo.com

Beth Melchor
Author / Educator / Missionary
epmelchor6@gmail.com

Eleanore Teo
Marketing Manager
elyo.lee@gmail.com

Bella Estrella
Writer/Catechist
blestrella@gmail.com

MEET YOUR DIDACHE WRITERS

Ariel B. Driz
Corporate Consultant /
Businessman
adriz77@yahoo.com

Mari Sison-Garcia
Servant Leader,
Bukas Loob sa Diyos
Covenant Community
mari_sison_garcia@yahoo.com

Cristy Galang
Licensed Psychologist /
Registered Counselor
cristy_cc@yahoo.com

Rolly España
Businessman / Lay Leader
rollyespana@homeliving.com.ph

Dr. Henry L. Yu, RGC
Physician /
Registered Guidance Counselor
henrio_md@yahoo.com

Cynthia Ulanday-Santiago
Citizen Journalist
cusantiago@gmail.com

Donna España
Real Estate Broker /
Lay Leader
donna.espana@yahoo.com

Grace Relucio-Princesa
Former Phil. Ambassador to the
United Arab Emirates
grprincesa@yahoo.com

Danny A. Tariman
IT Consultant
dtariman.loj@gmail.com

Marisa G. Aguas
Consultant
jojangaguas@yahoo.com

MEET YOUR DIDACHE WRITERS

Sol Saura
Wife / Mom / HR Manager
sol_saura@yahoo.com

Kitty Dulay Ferreria
Org. Dev. Consultant / Coach
kittydulay@yahoo.com

Ronna Singson Ledesma
Dentist / Audiologist
ronna_ledesma@yahoo.com.ph

Rod Velez
IT and Operations Manager
rod.velez@live.com

Cecilia Lim
Head of Compensation and Benefits
cez_lim@yahoo.com

Jun Asis
eLearning Professional
mabuting.balita@gmail.com

Jane Gonzales-Rauch
Freelance Writer
mgr516@gmail.com

Teresa Gumap-as Dumadag
Management, HR and Training
Consultant / Career Coach and
Counselor / Speaker / Author
teresa@fulllifecube.com

Geraldine G. Catral
Teacher
catral.geegee@beaconschool.ph

Ems Sy Chan
Early Childhood Educator / Missionary
Writer / Proofreader / Copyeditor /
Translator / Blogger / Sojourner
leeannesy7@yahoo.com

MEET YOUR
DIDACHE WRITERS

Rene Espinosa
Lighting Design Consultant
drekki@gmail.com

Rissa Espinosa
Wife / Mom / CFA Parent-Coach
rissa_d_espinosa@yahoo.com

Banjoy Santillan
Light of Jesus Counselor
santillanbanjoy@yahoo.com

Edwin Soriano
Life Coach / Speaker / Author
edwin@winningcoaching.net

Monty Mendigoria
Pilgrimage Tour Leader
montymendigoria@yahoo.com

Marie C. Franco, PIE
Independent Management
Consultant
mariefranco_pie@yahoo.com

Mary Mae M. Ignacio
IT Consultant
maemi04@aim.com

Erwin Roceles
Business Analyst
erwin_roceles@yahoo.com

Lala Dela Cruz
Teacher / Entrepreneur
bella.delacruz@gmail.com

Eugene A. Cailao
Session Singer / Vocal Coach
eugenecailao@gmail.com

MEET YOUR
DIDACHE WRITERS

Ma. Luisa dela Cruz
Christian Author /Entrepreneur
theessence_byluisa@yahoo.com

Mary Jo Ann C. Fauni
Mom / Feast Servant/
e-Educator / Service
Excellence Trainer
joann_fauni@yahoo.com.ph

Marie G. Ferrer
Wife / Mother
smgferrer@gmail.com

Sem. Kein Harvey P. Chito
Author / Seminarian
kein.chito@gmail.com

Gracious B. Romero
Communications Professional
graciousromero@gmail.com

Jan Ada Gerangaya
Financial Controller
jan.gerangaya@gmail.com

Rye Belen
Customer Support Supervisor
rye.belen@gmail.com

Ithan Jessemar Dollente
Chemical Engineer
tanji6@gmail.com

Shari Anas
Online Teacher and Writer
sharianas26@gmail.com

Sarrah Jane Cea
Teacher / Writer
sjbcea@gmail.com